Illinois Central College
Learning Resource Center

A GLOSSARY FOR COLLEGE ENGLISH

MARTIN STEVENS
Ohio State University

CHARLES H. KEGEL
Idaho State University

McGraw-Hill Book Company
NEW YORK / ST. LOUIS / SAN FRANCISCO
TORONTO / LONDON / SYDNEY

A GLOSSARY FOR COLLEGE ENGLISH

PREFACE

A Glossary for College English is designed to provide the college student with concise, practical definitions of grammatical, linguistic, and literary terms as well as readable, up-to-date discussions about acceptable practices in written English. For convenience and ease of reference, we have divided the book into four parts, each alphabetically organized and each focusing on a major area of concern for the college student: (1) "Common Usage Problems," (2) "Conventions of Editorial English," (3) "Linguistic, Stylistic, and Grammatical Terms," and (4) "Literary Terms." Preceding each of the four parts is a brief introduction explaining the range and scope of the material that follows.

Designed for use both in the classroom and for individual reference, this book is the most comprehensive single glossary currently available to students of language, composition, and literature. We have tried to make each entry self-sufficient, although we have also provided cross references for the user who wishes to find related material elsewhere in the book. For greater flexibility, the general index at the end of the text classifies entries individually and by subject matter. Thus it has been our hope to produce a glossary which is at once compact, flexible, and easy to use—a glossary that the student can use with profit throughout his undergraduate career.

It would be difficult to express our vast indebtedness to the many lexicographers, linguists, and literary scholars who have contributed both directly and indirectly to this book. Without their exacting scholarship the book could not have been produced. We wish also to thank those many colleagues, past and present, who have offered encouragement and advice. For careful and perceptive editorial reading, detailed criticism, and manuscript preparation, we wish to express particular thanks to Lawrence Rice and Barbara Tydeman of Idaho State University. Finally, we wish to thank our wives, Anne and Carol, for their editorial assistance as well as their patience and understanding while we wrote this book.

MARTIN STEVENS
CHARLES H. KEGEL

CONTENTS

COMMON USAGE PROBLEMS

The question "What is good English" has no simple answer. Effective expression varies with the particular purpose of the writer or speaker, with the demands of the reader or listener, and with the situation in which the language is used. At its best, every kind of language perfectly well fits the circumstance for which it is designed. Consequently, to judge one variety of English by the requirements of another is folly. The language of the classroom or business office is not "better" English than that of the workshop; it is different English. Both are good English if they satisfy the demands of their contexts.

"Good" English, therefore, is a matter of usage. When our language communicates clearly, forthrightly, and appealingly— when it communicates without calling attention to itself by violating the expected patterns of its social contexts, it is good English. It follows that each variety of English must be judged by its own standards. One must not condemn informal conversation because it fails to take on the formal conventions of the public lecture. Nor must one judge a personal letter by criteria that apply to the formal essay.

Expositional writing, as practiced in most English classrooms, in journal articles, and in books, is one variety of English. The standards for this type of expository writing are set largely by editors whose job it is to see a manuscript into print. They determine which of two spellings, or word choices, or punctuation practices should stand. Teachers very often emulate editors. They, too, must make choices when they "correct" papers, and these choices are no doubt influenced by the practice of editors. English classes, in fact, often study models of expository writing collected in anthologies from books and magazines—reflections once more of the English as "corrected" by editors. This is not to say that editors make rules. Rather, they use their own wide reading experience to judge what elements may distract a reader's attention from the writing they edit. Who then makes the rules?

Ever since the eighteenth century, the belief that grammarians make rules has been a very popular one and, in some measure, an accurate one. Grammarians in this context are writers of stylebooks. And they have, indeed, tried to make rules, often in an endeavor to provide the language with more logic and propriety than they thought it possessed. It is to such writers of stylebooks that we owe, for example, the condemnation of the double negative on the grounds that "two negatives make an affirmative." In logic, two negatives do make an affirmative—but not in writing. The command "Don't say nothing" may be inelegant, may be roundly disapproved, may attract undue attention, but it does not ever—even in the most pietistic circles—mean "Say something." Stylebook writers nevertheless invoked logic, and they managed by virtue of their precept to remove the double negative in most of its forms from the vocabulary of the expository writer.

Often they were less successful. Eighteenth-century stylebook writers, for example, wanted as well to prohibit the use of notice as a verb. They advised judiciously the use of take notice (because, they argued, we should have a different form for the noun and the verb). But even in the eighteenth century notice was used as a verb, and today it is firmly established in our language. Here, as in so many other instances, the stylebook writers failed to stem the tide of usage. When enough expository writers came to use notice as a verb, they inevitably warded off the editor's blue pencil.

Grammarians did, in fact, make some of our rules; but general usage is responsible for their enforcement. Today, when millions of words are printed daily in our newspapers, magazines, and books—when even more words travel the airwaves and click onto teletype machines—the grammarians' rules which conflict with popular habits of expression are losing ground to the force of usage. Purists may deplore the fact that finalize sometimes appears in print, but if a President can use it in a press conference (Eisenhower and Kennedy did), it will, sooner or later, go the way of notice.

In the usage guide of this book, preferences are recorded where two or more choices are available to the writer. These preferences are based on the English found characteristically in the informational articles of mass-circulating magazines like Newsweek, Harper's, and Saturday Review as well as in nonfiction books addressed to the general reader. This English, in its accepted form, we label editorial English. We shall refer to the impromptu spoken language as colloquial English, which is subject to the dialect traits of the different geographical and social environments in which it is found. The labels dialectal or colloquial, as used in this book, are therefore meant not to disparage but to describe usages. Any person's speech is colloquial, and each person must of needs speak in a dialect. The terms formal and informal *are used throughout this guide to describe levels of editorial English. The language of a learned journal may thus be regarded as* formal editorial English, *particularly if it maintains established usages even in the face of change dictated by popular preference.* Informal editorial English *is more casual; it is typically the English of the sports column or the town-gossip column of the daily newspaper.* The style of this book is formal editorial English.

As a usage guide, this book is considerably more selective than a standard desk dictionary. Ideally, of course, dictionaries aim to record the usages in all varieties and on all levels of English. However, a dictionary—whether it be unabridged or abridged—has not the space to indicate the fine discriminations of usages that writers often seek. A writer may consequently look without avail in a general dictionary for the stylistic guidelines he needs. He may, for example, need help in deciding between the use of lit *and* lighted *as past participles. Not even Funk and Wagnall's* Standard College Dictionary, *the desk dictionary which contains the most copious usage notes for editorial English, will give him this information. It is the purpose of the following guide to present such information quickly, concisely, and accurately.*

In setting down preferred usages, we have drawn on the research undertaken by a number of linguistic studies. Foremost among them is Professor Margaret Bryant's Current American Usage, *an extensive survey of studies on present-day editorial English in America. We have also consulted Hans Kurath's* A Word Geography of the Eastern United States, *Kurath and Raven I. McDavid's* The Pronunciation of English in the Atlantic States, *Webster's* Third New International Dictionary *(referred to as* Webster III), *and a variety of articles in professional journals including* American Speech, College English, The English Journal, *and* Word Study.

A, An

The choice between the two indefinite articles (*a* or *an*) depends entirely on the initial sound of the word which follows the article. Actually, the best guide to written usage is to pronounce the intended passage; whichever indefinite article sounds smoother is the appropriate form. One who does not trust his voice, however, should observe the following patterns of usage, remembering that the initial sound of a word does not always correspond with its initial letter. The form *a* occurs before all words beginning with a consonant sound (*a* box, *a* zebra, *a* union [*y* sound]). The form *an* occurs before all words beginning with a vowel sound (*an* orphan, *an* example, *an* honor [*o* sound]). American usage is divided for words beginning with an *h* sound but which are not accented on the first syllable (*a* or *an* historical event, *a* or *an* heretical idea), though *a* is preferred in editorial English.

About, Around, Round

In the sense of "approximately," *about* and *around* occur interchangeably in informal English (The book is *about* [or *around*] 600 pages long). In editorial English, however, the preferred form is *about* (He came *about* [not *around*] a half hour late). As a preposition, *round* is often substituted for *around* (I saw him run *around* [or *round*] the block), especially in spoken English, though the preferred usage in editorial English is *around*.

Above

In addition to its use as an adverb (the apartment *above*) and as a preposition (*above* the ground), *above* occurs frequently in editorial English as both an adjective (the *above* paragraph, the *above* photograph) and a noun (The *above* are recipes which require fresh peaches). It is generally a good practice to avoid using *above* when referring to something on a previous page.

Accept, Except

Because the initial syllables of *accept* and *except* are unstressed, the two words sound alike. As a result they are often confused in writing. *Accept* is a verb meaning "to receive" (We shall *accept* late donations), while *except* is most commonly a preposition meaning "with exclusion of" (This store is open every day *except* Sunday) and sometimes a verb meaning "to exclude" (We shall *except* anyone who doesn't pay dues).

A.D.

An abbreviation for Latin *anno domini* meaning "in the year of our Lord." *A.D.* is used to designate any year after the birth of Christ. It most commonly precedes the year cited (*A.D.* 1066). Unless there is a real chance that ambiguity might otherwise result, the abbreviation is generally omitted except in formal documents with legal or historical significance.

Ad

A common shortening of *advertisement* used on all but the most formal levels of expression. Since *ad* is a shortening and not an abbreviation, it should not be followed by a period.

Adopt, Adapt

Though often confused, *adopt* and *adapt* have quite different meanings. *Adopt* generally means "to take as one's own" while *adapt* means "to make suitable." The two verbs can also be differentiated by their customary usage: *adopt* must take a direct object (*adopt* a *motion*, a *child*); *adapt* is generally followed by *to, for,* or a form of the reflexive pronoun (*myself,* etc.).

They *adopted* the customs of their new environment.

They *adapted to* the demands of a new way of life.

Adviser, Advisor

Adviser is the preferred spelling in editorial English, but *advisor* occurs as an alternate form.

Affect, Effect

Effect is most frequently used as a noun, and *affect* almost always as a verb.

The *effect* of the war was widespread starvation.

Teen-agers are *affected* by the curfew.

The most frequent meanings of the two words are the following:

Effect, as a noun: "result," "logical consequent."

Effect, as a verb: "to bring about" (The faculty *effected* a change in the curriculum).

Affect, as a verb: "to influence" (He was *affected* by the strike) or "to put on" (He *affected* a British accent).

Agenda

Even in the most formal editorial English, *agenda* is used as a collective noun in the singular (An *agenda* was prepared). In Latin *agenda* is a plural noun, and it was so used until recently in editorial English as well; hence, one will still encounter plural constructions like *agenda were* in written English. A new plural form, *agendas,* now appears occasionally in informal English, but it should be avoided on the more formal levels of usage.

Aggravate, Irritate

In editorial English *aggravate* is rarely used in the sense of *irritate;* rather it is used to mean "intensify" or "make more severe" (His feelings of insecurity were *aggravated* by his failure). *Aggravate* in the sense of *irritate* is used widely even by the most educated speakers on all but the most formal levels of expression (The neighbors were *aggravated* by Erik's pranks).

Agreement

See p. 110.

Ain't

In editorial English, *ain't* is used only to reflect a colloquial or folksy tone. Except as a stylistic device to affect dialectal English, it is rigorously avoided in expository writing. *Ain't* stands as a contraction for *am not, is not, are not, has not,* and *have not.* Its usage in the place of *am not,* particularly in questions involving the first person construction *am not I,* is widespread in all dialects of American English.

All, All of

Despite the fact that some style manuals consider *all of* redundant, the *of* is necessary in certain contexts. Before *whom* or a proper name, *all of* is required on all levels of editorial English (*all of* whom, *all of* Milton's works). The *of* is generally avoided in editorial English when there is an option in usage (*all* [*of*] the men, *all* [*of*] the secretaries). *All of* should not be used when it is part of an *of*-phrase (The best of *all* [not *all of*] our military Presidents was Theodore Roosevelt). In the sense of "fully" or "as much as," *all of* is informal editorial English.

All ready, Already

The adverb *already* is often misspelled *all ready.* Written as one word, *already* means "by this time" or "before this time"; *all ready* may mean either "all are ready" or "completely ready," depending on the context.

They had *already* left the hotel (meaning "before this time").
They were *all ready* to leave the hotel (meaning "all were ready").
Their baggage was *all ready* to be moved (meaning "completely ready").

All right, Alright

All right is the standard spelling in editorial English. *Alright* is an alternate spelling which occurs quite frequently in informal writing (it is called "reputable" by *Webster III*). *Alright* was probably influenced by the spellings *already* and *altogether.*

All the (with comparative)

Expressions like *all the harder, all the happier, all the more* occur regularly in editorial English. The construction *all the* with a comparative adjective is of long standing in English. It developed from the same Old English instrumental form which gave rise to such constructions as *the more, the merrier* and *the longer, the better.*

All the farther (further), As far as

The standard form in editorial English is *as far as* (The county line is *as far as* [not *all the farther that*] prohibition can be enforced). *All the farther* and *all the further* are dialect variants in the Midland and Southern regions of the United States.

All together, Altogether

The adverb *altogether,* meaning "entirely" or "all told," is often misspelled *all together* (The accident was *altogether* [not *all together*] the other driver's fault).

Allusion, Illusion

Because they sound alike, these two words are often confused. *Allusion* means "reference" (He began his paper with an *allusion* to Ovid). *Illusion* means "misconception" or "misapprehension" (The notion that we live in the best of all possible worlds is an *illusion*).

Almost, Most

Most as a substitute for *almost* is not found in editorial English. In colloquial English, *most* is frequently used in place of *almost,* especially before *all, anybody, anyone, anything, everybody, everyone, everything, always, surely,* and *certainly.* This usage is dialectal and should be avoided in expository writing.

Alright

See **All Right, Alright,** p. 6.

Although, Though

These two words are interchangeable in editorial English in all sentence positions. However, *though* occurs much more frequently than *although,* which some linguists believe will eventually disappear from the language. The spellings *altho* and *tho,* despite their approval by certain crusaders for spelling reform (e.g., *The Chicago Daily Tribune*), are unacceptable in editorial English.

Altogether

See **All together, Altogether,** p. 7.

Alumnus, i, a, ae

This noun has retained its Latin masculine and feminine, singular and plural inflections. The following list indicates the established usages:

alumn-**us**	masculine singular
alumn-**i** (pronounced *eye*)	masculine or generic plural
alumn-**a**	feminine singular
alumn-**ae** (pronounced *ee*)	feminine plural

Among, Between

In editorial English, *between* occurs regularly to refer to two (The Channel lies *between* England and France). Many handbooks prefer *among* over *between* when the reference is to more than two (The choice for captain was *among* three seniors). However, even in editorial English, *between* regularly refers to more than two when it expresses: (1) a relationship of one thing to several in the same category (a treaty *between* [not *among*] three nations; a number *between* one and ten); (2) intervals between repeated events (*between* classes); (3) a collective action of members in one group (*between* us students).

Amount, Number

In editorial English, *amount* is used to refer to quantities which are uncountable, while *number* is used with countable quantities (a large *amount* of coffee, of help, of interest; a large *number* of friends, of dimes, of houses).

A.M., P.M.

A.M. is the abbreviation for Latin *ante meridiem* ("before noon"), and *P.M.* is the abbreviation for *post meridiem* ("after noon"). The abbreviation for noon is *M.* (from *meridiem,* "noon"). *Meridiem* is sometimes erroneously rendered *meridian* in English, a usage that should be avoided in editorial English. The abbreviations *A.M.* and *P.M.* are used in editorial English only after numerals, not word numbers, referring to hours of the day (8 *A.M.* or 8:00 *A.M.* [not *eight A.M.*]). *A.M.* and *P.M.* are not used as words in editorial English (She stopped in for coffee this morning [not *A.M.*]). Either capitals or lower-case letters may be used for the abbreviations.

An

See **A, An,** p. 3.

And (But, Or, Nor)

And, as well as other coordinating conjunctions, is frequently used at the beginning of sentences in even the most formal editorial English. In fact, this usage has been noted as a mark of sophistication in writing. The objection to the use of coordinating conjunctions at the beginning of sentences is therefore not only unrealistic but also misleading.

And etc.

This usage is redundant since the meaning of *and* is contained in *etc.* (see p. 23). Delete the *and.*

And/or

Though *and/or* frequently appears on all levels of editorial English, its most common occurrence is in business and legal writing. Some style manuals object to the use of *and/or* because of its legalistic connotations. However, when three alternatives are being expressed, *and/or* may be the most precise connective available to the writer (He is hoping to take a course in Chaucer *and/or* Shakespeare [alternatives: (1)

in Chaucer, (2) in Shakespeare, (3) in both Chaucer and Shakespeare]).

Ante-, Anti-

These prefixes are often confused. *Ante-*, as in *antecedent,* means "before"; *anti-*, as in *anticommunist,* means "against." The prefix *anti-* occurs much more frequently than *ante-*. (See also **Prefix,** p. 169.)

Antennae, Antennas

Zoologists still use the Latin form *antennae* for the plural when referring to the sense organs on the heads of insects. *Antennas,* however, has become an accepted plural for television or radio equipment.

Anyhow, Anyway

Though these two words, in the sense of "in any case" or "at any rate," appear as synonyms on all levels of editorial English, *anyhow* is the more formal usage (The reviews of Albee's latest play were scathing; yet it appears to be a box-office success *anyhow* [less formal: *anyway*]). *Anyway* is written as one word only with the meaning "at any rate" or "in any case." With the meaning "whatever way," it is written as two words (*Any way* one looks at it, the essay is a failure).

Any more

In the sense of "nowadays," the expression is dialectal when it is used in an affirmative context (The bus stops at the courthouse *any more*). This usage is not found in editorial English, where *any more* is used most frequently in a negative context (The bus doesn't stop at the courthouse *any more*). The spelling *anymore* is an acceptable variant.

Anyplace

Anyplace as a synonym for *anywhere* occurs on all but the most formal levels of editorial English, where *anywhere* is preferred (Grits are served with breakfast almost *anywhere* [less formal: *anyplace*] in the South). This usage notation applies as well to *everyplace, no place, someplace,* for which formal English requires *everywhere, nowhere,* and *somewhere,* respectively.

Anyway

See **Anyhow, Anyway,** p. 9.

Anywhere, Anywheres

In editorial English the standard usage is *anywhere* (Travelers' checks can be cashed *anywhere* in the United States). *Anywheres* is a dialectal variant used by the little educated. It should be avoided in writing.

A-prefix (A-singing, A-laughing)

The use of an *a-prefix* before present participles is dialectal and should

be avoided in editorial English. It is used facetiously in the expression "time's a-wasting."

Apt, Liable, Likely

These words are differentiated in formal editorial English as follows: *apt* means "naturally endowed or inclined" (to be *apt* at numbers); *liable* means "responsible" or "susceptible" (*liable* for damages, *liable* to colds); *likely,* as an adverb, means "probably" (*likely* to do something). In informal editorial English *apt* now appears frequently as an adverb in the sense of "likely" (He is *apt* [formal: *likely*] to arrive late). *Liable* as a synonym for *likely* (It is *liable* to rain any minute) is often disapproved by style manuals. This usage should be avoided in editorial English.

Archaic, Current, Obsolete

See p. 114.

Around

See **About, Around, Round,** p. 4.

As (conjunction)

In formal editorial English there is a decided preference for the causal conjunctions *because* or *since* over *as* (*Because* [not *as*] there was mild turbulence, we were strapped in our seats throughout the flight). The reason for avoiding causal *as* is illustrated in the foregoing sentence, in which *as* would be ambiguous: it could mean "because," "while," or "when." Because of the risk of imprecision, causal *as* should be avoided in editorial English.

As . . . as, So . . . as

In the most formal editorial English, *so . . . as* is still the preferred form when the comparison expressed is negative (The effect of the frost on the orange groves was *not so* devastating *as* was at first believed). The correlative conjunction *as . . . as,* however, occurs frequently even in negative comparisons on all levels of editorial English. In affirmative contexts, *as . . . as* is the standard usage (*as* bright *as, as* soon *as*). *As long as* requires special consideration. When used to express physical comparisons, *as long as* is the standard form in editorial English (The sedan is almost *as* [not *so*] *long as* the microbus). *As long as* is similarly preferred over *so long as* on all levels of usage when the meaning is "if" or "while" (I shall help him *as long as* he doesn't resent my doing so).

As far as

See **All the farther (further), As far as,** p. 6.

As if, As though

In the most formal editorial English, *as if* and *as though* are followed by subjunctive forms (He talked *as if* he *were* not coming until next week). The use of the indicative, however, is frequent on all levels of expression. (See also **As, Like,** below.)

As, Like

The word *like,* usually a preposition, often functions as a conjunction when it substitutes for *as* or *as if* in introducing a clause (He looked *like* [for *as if*] he saw a ghost; That bread is baked *like* [for *as*] mother used to bake it). So used, *like* sounds particularly appropriate when the clause which follows it is elliptical (He takes to skiing *like* a duck [takes] to water; Winstons taste good *like* a cigarette should [taste]). This use of *like* as a conjunction dates back to 1579, and it has since gained ascendancy on all levels of usage.

As though

See **As if, As though,** p. 11.

As to

Though some style manuals object to the usage of *as to* in the sense of "concerning" or "about," it occurs commonly in editorial English (The freshman Senator was the wrong man to consult *as to* the reclamation legislation). In formal editorial English, this usage is avoided because it sounds stilted or because it may be redundant. The latter is generally the case when *as to* is followed by *when, where, whether,* or *why* (Professor Diddle expressed some doubt *as to whether* [better: *whether*] he could cover all the course material). In such contexts, *as to* can be deleted without affecting the meaning of the sentence.

(A)wake, (A)waken

These verbs have the following principal parts in editorial English:

PRESENT	awake	wake	awaken	waken
PAST	awoke	woke	awakened	wakened
	awaked	waked		
PAST PARTICIPLE	awaked	waked	awakened	wakened

The forms in *o* are not used as past participles in editorial English (I had *wakened* [or *awakened,* but not *(a)woke* or *(a)woken*] before sunrise). The most frequently used of the four variants is the form *wake.* The least frequent is *waken,* which is also used exclusively as a transitive verb (They came to *waken* me after I failed to answer the phone). In the passive voice, forms of the verb *awaken* or *waken* tend to be preferred (We were *awakened* by the sonic boom).

Away
See **Way, Away,** p. 57.

Awful, Awfully
The adjectival usage of *awful* in the general sense of "bad" is avoided in editorial English. *Awful* should be used to mean "awe-inspiring" or "exalted." *Awfully,* used as an intensifier, appears frequently in informal editorial English (It was an *awfully* difficult problem). Formal editorial English tends to substitute such intensifiers as *very* or *exceedingly* for *awfully* in this context. The use of *awful* in place of *awfully* (He is an *awful* good friend) is colloquial and should be avoided in written English.

Bad, Badly
Almost all the confusion between these two words occurs when they are used with the verb *feel.* Originally, a careful distinction was observed between the adjective *bad* and the adverb *badly;* however, for many years both uneducated and cultivated users of the language have allowed *badly* to function as an adjective in complement position following *feel* (Clarice felt *bad* [or *badly*] about having failed history). With other verbs, however, editorial English observes the distinction between the adjectival and adverbial forms.

> ADJECTIVE: Hannah smelled *bad* after three months without a bath.
>
> ADVERB: Hannah smelled *badly* after her nose operation.

B.C.
An abbreviation meaning "before Christ." *B.C.* is used to identify dates belonging to the pre-Christian era. It always follows the year cited (426 *B.C.*).

Be (subjunctive)
See **Mood,** p. 153.

Because of, Due to, Owing to
A few persons still object to the use of *due to* as a prepositional substitute for *because of* or *owing to.* Nevertheless, the three constructions occur regularly and synonymously in editorial English (*Due to* [or *Because of* or *Owing to*] the rapid population increase after World War II, our colleges and universities are bursting with students).

Being as, Being as how
The dialect variants *being as* and *being as how* as substitutes for *since* or *because* are avoided in editorial English.

Beside, Besides

Beside is a preposition meaning "by the side of" or "next to" (The priest walked slowly *beside* the coffin). *Besides* functions in three different ways, but always with the meaning "also," "in addition to," or "except."

PREPOSITION:	Nobody *besides* me knew the way home.
ADVERB:	I caught a salmon and several trout *besides*.
CONJUNCTIVE ADVERB:	I can't afford to go skiing again today; *besides,* I have to study for an examination.

Between

See **Among, Between,** p. 7.

Between you and me

Some persons have been so fear-stricken by the prejudice against *you and me* in subject position (*You and me* should go to the dance) that they substitute *between you and I* for the perfectly correct *between you and me*. Prepositions are regularly followed by objective pronouns (*me*), not nominative pronouns (*I*).

Bit, Bitten

Bit and *bitten* are the forms for the past tense and past participle, respectively, of the verb *bite*. In Southern dialect speech *bit* occurs as a participle (I have *bit* off more than I can chew), but this usage is avoided in editorial English.

Blame for, Blame on

Both constructions occur regularly in editorial English. Where *blame* functions as a noun, both *for* and *on* may follow it (I *blame* my failure *on* the teacher; I *blame* the teacher *for* my failure; I place the *blame* *for* my failure *on* the teacher).

Blew, Blown, Blowed

Blew and *blown* are the only acceptable written forms for the past tense and past participle, respectively, of the verb *blow*. The dialect variant *blowed* occurs only in the speech of the illiterate or little educated.

Blond, Blonde

In editorial English *blond* is the more frequent spelling (see *Webster III*). Formerly *blonde* was used only as the feminine form.

Born, Borne

Born occurs only with reference to birth (*born* in Canada, a newly *born* child, a *born* comedian). *Borne,* on the other hand, has the meaning "endured" or "carried."

The soldier had *borne* hunger and defeat.

He had *borne* the weight of three men on his back.

My mother had *borne* three children before she had reached my age.

Bought, Boughten

Bought is the only acceptable written form for the past tense and past participle of *buy*. *Boughten,* however, does occur as an attributive adjective (*boughten* bread, as contrasted with homemade bread) in some dialect speech.

Broke, Broken

Editorial English observes the principal parts of the verb (*break, broke, broken*). The use of *broke* as a past participle (Th'ey have *broke* the record) is dialectal. As an adjective *broke* has become an acceptable synonym for *bankrupt* or *without money* (Despite his sizable inheritance, Rothchild was *broke* within three years).

Brought, Brung, Brang

Brought is the only acceptable form for the past tense and past participle of the verb *bring*. Both *brung* and *brang* occur only in the speech of the illiterate.

Burst, Bust

Originally a variant of the verb *burst,* meaning "to break open by internal pressure," *bust* has gained increasing currency as a verb roughly synonymous with *break*. Except in specific contexts (e.g., *busted* to a private, *bust* a wild horse, trust-*busting* lawyers, economic boom and *bust*), the usage is generally avoided in editorial English. Other idiomatic uses (*bust* him in the nose, going on a *bust* [noun], a real *bust* [noun] as a date) are considered substandard.

But, But that, But what

But is most commonly used as a coordinating conjunction connecting sentence parts of equal grammatical weight.

WORD TO WORD:	Janice swam swiftly *but* awkwardly.
PHRASE TO PHRASE:	Sam didn't enter by the door *but* by the window.
CLAUSE TO CLAUSE:	I like to ski, *but* she likes to skate.
SENTENCE TO SENTENCE:	Carol ate seven trout! *But* I ate only one.

Frequently *but* functions as a preposition with the meaning "except" (We saw nothing *but* two hen pheasants).

But that and *but what* are constructions which are generally avoided in formal editorial English (With those clouds above there can't be much doubt that [not *but that*] it will rain), though they do appear in informal writing.

Buy (noun)

Like many other verbs, *buy* has gained currency as a noun. As a synonym for *bargain* (an excellent *buy*), the noun form is widely accepted in informal English. It should, however, be avoided in formal editorial English, in which *purchase* is a suitable synonym.

Can, May, Could, Might

Can regularly appears as a substitute for *may* on all levels of usage except formal editorial English, where the distinction between ability (*can*) and permission (*may*) is maintained. For negative expressions, particularly those involving questions and answers, *can't* has won acceptance over the awkward *mayn't* on every level of usage (*Can't* your secretary leave work early? She *can't*).

Could and *might*, originally past tense forms of *can* and *may*, are now used to express a lesser degree of possibility. Note how the following three statements of intent progress from the positive to the possible to the doubtfully possible:

I *will* take a vacation this year.

I *may* [or *can*] take a vacation this year.

I *might* [or *could*] take a vacation this year.

Cannot (Can't) help but

The construction *cannot help but* plus the infinitive form of the verb occurs regularly on all levels of written and spoken English (She *cannot help but realize* her errors). In formal editorial English, however, *cannot help* plus a gerund is the preferred construction (She *cannot help realizing* her errors).

Censure, Censor, Censer

These homonyms are sometimes confused. *Censure*, which occurs as both a noun and a verb, always carries the sense of "blame" or "condemnation" (The *censure* of public opinion is feared by politicians; The U.S. Senate rarely *censures* one of its members). *Censor* also occurs as both noun and verb and refers to the act of "examining something for possible objections" (The group of citizens tried to *censor* the history books; The Hays Office *censors* Hollywood movies). A *censer* is a container in which incense is burned.

Center around

Some stylebooks object to this phrase because it is logically inconsistent; one can *center on* a point or a topic, but one cannot *center around* it (The discussion *centered on* [not *around*] the projected newspaper strike).

Charges

The expression *on charges of* is often followed by a singular in editorial English (The young woman sought a divorce *on charges of* mental cruelty).

Cite, Site

Because they are pronounced alike, these two words are often confused in writing. *Cite* is a verb meaning "refer to" (He wished to *cite* evidence for his contention). *Site* is a noun meaning "location" (The committee picked a *site* for the new school).

Combine (noun)

For many years, *combine* (with accent on the first syllable) has been accepted as a noun referring to multiple-operation farm machinery. Only recently, however, has editorial English accepted *combine* as a noun referring to an alliance of persons, organizations, or nations in the pursuit of some purpose, which is often illegal or contrary to the common interest (The supporters of federally subsidized medical care for the aged fought a strong *combine* of doctors, dentists, and druggists).

Come, Came

Editorial English employs *come, came, come* as the verb's principal parts. *Come* used in the past tense (He *come* home yesterday) and *came* used as a past participle (He *had came* home often) are dialectal variants which should be avoided in writing.

Comparative, Absolute

Occasionally the comparative degree is used without actually expressing the idea of comparison (the *better* life, the *younger* generation). This usage, known technically as an *absolute comparison,* is widespread in colloquial as well as editorial English. Some phrases, in fact, no longer can be restated in the positive degree: we say *higher education* (never *high*), *elder statesman* (never *old*). The absolute comparative is frequently used by advertisers as a way of enhancing products (in *better* stores everywhere, *higher*-priced merchandise).

Compare, Contrast

These words are not synonymous. To *compare* is to look for similarities; to *contrast,* for differences. Hence to compare Chicago and Seattle is to note their likenesses, but to contrast them is to note their differences.

Comparison, Illogical
See p. 120.

Considerable, Considerably
In formal editorial English, *considerable* is the standard form before nouns (He showed *considerable* insight). The use of *considerable* in place of *considerably* as a verb modifier is colloquial and should be avoided in editorial English (The change in the weather helped *considerably* [not *considerable*] in bringing more tourists). *Considerably* is also colloquial when it is used before an adjective as an intensifier in the sense of "very" (He was *considerably* modest).

Consul
See **Council, Counsel, Consul,** p. 18.

Contact
As a verb meaning "to get in touch with" or "to meet," *contact* is used infrequently in formal editorial English but widely in informal and colloquial English. Purists, however, still regard this usage with disfavor. As a noun, *contact* has reference to "a useful acquaintance" (He has many *contacts* in show business). This usage appears in all but the most formal English.

Contemptible, Contemptuous
These two words are sometimes confused. *Contemptible* means "despicable" (I regard anyone who beats children and animals as *contemptible*), while *contemptuous* means "scornful" (I am *contemptuous* toward anyone who beats children and animals).

Continual, Continuous
These two adjectives are so nearly synonymous in some contexts that they are often confused. Careful writers, however, use *continual* to refer to something which is repeated frequently (Mrs. Larson was a *continual* customer at the Safeway Market) and *continuous* to refer to something which is uninterrupted (The *continuous* freeway stretches from San Francisco to Los Angeles). The same distinction applies to the adverbs *continually* and *continuously*.

Contractions
See p. 125.

Contrast
See **Compare, Contrast,** p. 16.

Could
See **Can, May, Could, Might,** p. 15.

Could of, Might of, Should of, Would of
These substandard constructions should be avoided in editorial English. They result from the fact that in rapid speech *have* is often pronounced like *of*.

Council, Counsel, Consul
These homonyms often confuse inexperienced writers. *Council* and *consul* are nouns; the first refers to an advisory group (Sacramento Business *Council*) while the second refers to a governmental official representing the interests of his country in a foreign land (The American *consul* explained Italian customs to the tourists from Texas). *Counsel* can be used as both noun or verb. As a noun it means "advice" (I went to my priest for *counsel*) or "a person who gives legal advice" (Perry Mason is the *counsel* for the defense). As a verb it means "to give advice" (A father should *counsel* his son about evil in the big city). The idiom *counsel with* is gaining colloquial frequency, but it is avoided in editorial English.

Couple (of)
In editorial English *couple* refers to two related persons or things (a handsome *couple*). The word appears colloquially to refer to any unspecified small number, particularly when the speaker wishes to minimize (I stopped briefly for a *couple of* drinks). It also appears colloquially without *of* (Could you loan me a *couple* dollars). This usage should be avoided in editorial English.

Course Names
See p. 80.

Credible, Credulous
These two adjectives are often confused. *Credible* means "believable" (Three of the suspects furnished *credible* alibis). *Credulous* means "tending to believe easily" (Confidence men thrive on *credulous* persons). Conversely, *incredible* means "unbelievable" and *incredulous* means "not tending to believe easily," hence "skeptical."

Curriculum, Curricula
The Latin form of the plural, *curricula,* and the anglicized plural, *curriculums,* appear with about equal frequency in editorial English. The use of *curricula* as a singular and *curriculas* as a plural is substandard and should be avoided.

Dangling Modifier

See p. 126.

Dare

Several questions arise over the use of *dare*. In the present tense, third person singular, both *dare* and *dares* occur in editorial English, though the more formal usage is still *dare* with a negative (This country *dare* not risk global war over the incident). The standard form for the past tense is *dared;* the older form *durst* is now considered archaic. *Dare* may be followed by an infinitive with or without *to* (He *dared* [*to*] come back). There is no standard American contraction for *dare* and *not: daren't* is encountered primarily in British English, and *dasn't* or *daresn't* are American dialectal forms.

Data

Historically *data* is the Latin plural of *datum*. However, in present-day usage *data* occurs both as a singular and a plural (*Those data need* to be checked; The *data* on the case *is* now being processed). Formal editorial English tends still to prefer the plural usage, but neither formal nor informal editorial English will condone a mixed usage (*A* little *data are* now available). Most linguists predict that *data* will eventually replace *datum* altogether. At such time, it will probably develop the standard plural ending of *-s* (as the word *opera*, with a similar linguistic history, has already done).

Date

In colloquial and informal editorial English, *date* occurs both as a noun meaning "escort" or "social engagement" (My *date* should arrive in ten minutes; Cindy made a *date* with her boyfriend) and as a verb meaning "to make social engagements" (My daughter is not allowed to *date* on school nights). These usages appear rarely in formal editorial English.

Definitely

In colloquial and informal editorial English, *definitely* is often used as an intensifier with the meaning of "certainly" or "quite" (I was *definitely* exhausted). Formal editorial English generally replaces this usage with words like *quite, rather,* or *certainly.*

Desert, Dessert

These spellings are often confused. *Desert* is an arid region; *dessert* is the last course in a meal.

Did, Done

In editorial English the only acceptable form for the past tense is *did*

(He *did* the task yesterday) and for the past participle, *done* (He had *done* it a week ago). The use of *did* as a past participle or *done* as a past tense is dialectal and must be avoided in editorial English.

Different from, than, to

In formal editorial English the preferred form is *different from* (The climate of northern California is *different from* that of Florida). The use of *different than*, however, is widespread in informal editorial English as well as in colloquial English. *Different to* occurs mostly in British English, though occasionally it may also be found in informal editorial American English. The preferred adverbial construction in formal editorial English is similarly the form with *from* (He parts his hair *differently from* the way he used to). It is noteworthy that the preference for *different from* often forces the writer into wordiness. It would be more economical to say, "He parts his hair *differently than* he used to." But as is true of so many other usages, convention, not economy, dictates stylistic preference.

Disinterested, Uninterested

In formal editorial English these words are still differentiated as follows: *disinterested* means "unbiased" (a *disinterested* arbitrator) and *uninterested* means "without interest" (an *uninterested* student). In informal editorial English *disinterested* is very often used as an exact synonym for *uninterested*. Despite the prohibitions by style manuals, this usage occurs so frequently that *Webster III* lists "uninterested" as one of the standard meanings for the word *disinterested*.

Dived, Dove

Though *dived* is still the preferred past tense in editorial English, it is losing currency in spoken English on all levels of usage. Dialect studies show a strong preference for *dove* in the Northeastern part of the country and for *dived* in the Southeast.

Doctor (verb)

The verb *doctor* appears in formal editorial English when it is used transitively in the sense of "to treat medically" (He has been *doctoring* my family for years). In informal editorial English and in colloquial English, *doctor* as a verb is also used to mean "repair" or "mend" (After receiving a rejection, he *doctored* the article and sent it off again), and sometimes to mean "tamper with" or "falsify" (To *doctor* a passport is a capital crime in Slabovia). The intransitive use of *doctor,* meaning "to practice medicine," is also reserved for the less formal levels of expression (He has been *doctoring* for nearly fifty years).

Doesn't, Don't
The only acceptable form with the third person singular in editorial English is *doesn't* (He *doesn't* like football). In certain dialect areas, particularly in the South and the South Midlands, even cultivated speakers will use *don't* in third person singular constructions. Such usage, however, does not transfer into written English anywhere in the United States.

Done
See **Did, Done,** p. 19.

Double Comparative, Superlative
See p. 131.

Double Genitive, Possessive
See p. 131.

Double Negative
See p. 131.

Double Superlative
See **Double Comparative, Superlative,** p. 131.

Dove
See **Dived, Dove,** p. 20.

Drank, Drunk
In editorial English *drank* is the standard form in the past tense (He *drank* his medicine without protest) and *drunk* the standard form for the past participle (He *had drunk* it before I arrived). In certain dialect areas, *drank* occurs as an alternate usage for the past participle. This usage, however, is not acceptable in writing.

Dreamed, Dreamt
In editorial English *dreamed* is the preferred usage both as a past tense form and as a past participle. *Dreamt,* though it is acceptable as an alternate form in editorial English, occurs most often in speech.

Drowned, Drownded
The only acceptable form in editorial English is *drowned. Drownded* occurs as a dialectal variant, particularly in the speech of the uneducated.

Due to
See **Because of, Due to, Owing to,** p. 12.

Each and every
This usage appears frequently as an emphatic form in editorial English.

Some style manuals object to it because it is considered redundant, and it is therefore avoided by many writers in formal editorial English.

Each other, One another

These two usages are interchangeable, and they are acceptable on all levels of editorial English. The old rule that *each other* should be used with reference to two while *one another* should be used to refer to more than two is simply not observed by many of the most educated speakers and writers of American English.

Earmark (verb)

Originally a noun referring to identification marks on cattle, *earmark* has in recent years won acceptance on all but the most formal levels of editorial English as a verb meaning "specially designated or marked" (The legislature *earmarked* liquor tax proceeds for use in the state mental hospitals).

Effect

See **Affect, Effect,** p. 5.

E.g.

Abbreviation for Latin *exempli gratia,* meaning "for example." Its principal use is to introduce parenthetical examples (Many leading educators [*e.g.,* James B. Conant, Arthur Bestor, Jacques Barzun, James D. Koerner] have criticized the training of American teachers).

Either, Neither

The stylebook rule that *either* and *neither* can refer only to the choice of two alternatives is still widely observed in formal editorial English. Occasionally, however, even the most fastidious writers are likely to use *either* or *neither* in a context involving more than two (My German professor recommended that we read something by [*either*] Brecht, Grass, Böll, or Uwe Johnson). For subject-verb agreement involving *either* and *neither,* see **Agreement,** p. 110.

Enthuse

The verb *enthuse,* a back formation of the noun *enthusiasm,* is frowned upon by many style manuals. However, it is gradually gaining acceptance on all levels of editorial English. Those who prefer to avoid *enthuse* may use "to become enthusiastic" or "to arouse enthusiasm" as substitutes.

Equally, Equally as

In editorial English *equally* has much greater frequency than *equally as.* Handbooks generally observe that the *as* in *equally as* is superfluous (*equally as good* has the same meaning as *equally good*). However, *equally as* does occasionally appear in editorial English, especially in newspapers. Often *equally as* gives emphasis to a comparison (*Equally as* brilliant, but less friendly, is the youngest son in the family).

Etc.

An abbreviation for the Latin *et cetera,* meaning "and so forth." *Etc.* should always be followed by a period and preceded with a comma. In formal editorial English, *etc.* should be avoided wherever possible. A partial enumeration can be introduced by *such as* or *for example* rather than concluded with an *etc.* Nevertheless, *etc.* does occasionally appear, though usually in a footnote or in a partial enumeration enclosed in parentheses, where space is at a premium.

Every

Every in such phrases as *every now and then* and *every so often* is informal English. In formal editorial English *every* is used most frequently as a determiner before nouns (*every* time, *every* person), adjectives (*every* yellow canary), and, though less often, adverbs (*every* moderately priced house).

Except

See **Accept, Except,** p. 4.

Expect, Suspect

The substitution of *expect* for *suspect* in the sense of "suppose" should be avoided in editorial English (I *suspect* [not *expect*] that he will not say a word about his former marriage).

Fact, The fact that

In many contexts *the fact that* is redundant for *that* (The butler admitted *that* [not *the fact that*] he held the murder weapon in his hand).

Famed, Famous

The adjective *famed* as a synonym for *famous* is a feature of advertising and sports jargon (The Fontainebleau is a *famed* hostelry). The preferred form in editorial English is *famous*.

Farther, Further

In editorial English, usage of *farther* and *further* is divided. Conservative editors and handbooks still prefer to use *farther* in reference to distance (They traveled *farther* and *farther* into the interior) and *further* with the meaning of "more" or "in addition to" (He read *further* into Eastern philosophy). In present-day editorial English *farther* and *further* occur interchangeably when the meaning is "more"

(We want to see *further* [or *farther*] proof), but *farther* still appears more often than *further* when the reference is to distance (They rode *farther* [less often: *further*] in their Model A than we did in our Cadillac). Some linguists believe that *farther* and *farthest* will eventually be dropped altogether from the language. Used as a verb, *further* is already the standard choice (He *furthered* his career by accepting the position).

Fellow

In formal editorial English *fellow* has the general meaning of "associate." Colloquially and informally, it is often used to designate any male person (Those were the *fellows* I saw in the convertible) or a boyfriend (She said that David was her *fellow*).

Fewer, Less

Many style manuals observe that *fewer* can have only countable referents (*fewer* numbers, *fewer* parts) while *less* can have only uncountable referents (*less* courage, *less* snow). These observations are only partly accurate. *Fewer* is consistently used in editorial English to refer to countable items. However, *less* is not any longer reserved for uncountable referents. Advertisers, for example, speak of 38 percent *less* cavities, and *less than* followed by a number occurs even in formal editorial English (There are now *less than* seventy strong verbs in our language).

Fiancé, Fiancée

The spelling of these words is often confused. *Fiancé* is masculine and *fiancée* is feminine. In informal editorial English the accent mark is sometimes omitted.

Fine

As an adjective, *fine* occurs frequently in editorial English with a vague and generally favorable connotation (a *fine* concert, a *fine* person). Precision usually demands a more specific descriptive word (a *well-balanced* concert, a *helpful* person). As an adverb, *fine* is generally avoided in formal editorial English where *well* is likely to be used in its place (The dress fits *well* [not *fine*]).

Fish

The plural can be *fish* or *fishes* according to the context. The form *fish* is used when the reference is to fish in general (all the *fish* in the ocean) or to a catch (He caught six *fish* in an hour). *Fishes* is used especially with reference to different species (The Shedd Aquarium in Chicago is noted for its large number of freshwater *fishes*).

Fit, Fitted

Both words are standard in the past tense (The gentleman *fit* [or *fitted*] the description perfectly), though educated speakers tend to prefer *fit*. For the past participle, *fitted* is the preferred form (The receptionist said that she *had fitted* an appointment in for the lunch hour). When *fit* is used in reference to tailoring or to preparing oneself for a task, *fitted* is the required past tense and past participial form (Abercrombie was *fitted* for a suit; His extensive training in French *had fitted* him for diplomatic service).

Fix

Many style manuals, using British English as their model, insist that *fix* must not be used in formal discourse with the meaning of "repair." The fact is, however, that *fix* is so used on all levels of editorial English. Though this usage is well established in the United States, one may nevertheless object to it on grounds of slovenly diction. *Fix* simply has too many meanings to be precise. One can *fix* a clock, a ticket, a friend, a meal, a game, a scheme, a limit, an eye, a position—the list could be expanded manyfold. In the interest of clarity, one should substitute a precise verb for *fix* wherever possible. Certain expressions involving *fix*, moreover, are colloquial or informal and should be avoided in formal editorial English: *to be in a fix* (a bad situation), *to fix a person* (get even with him), *to be well-fixed* (well-provided), *to be fixed up with a person* (have an engagement). *Fix* also occurs in underworld jargon as a term for a dose of narcotics, in sports jargon for a dishonest contest, and in navigation or aviation for a position determined by the taking of bearings. As a dialect word, the verb *fix* sometimes occurs as a synonym for *prepare* (to *fix* to do something). This usage should be avoided in editorial English.

Folk, Folks

Both forms are used as plurals in editorial English. *Folks* is a colloquial and informal usage which generally refers to relatives, though in some dialect areas it applies specifically to the members of one's immediate family. *Folk* occurs on all levels of editorial English to refer to an ethnic group, a people, or a race (Many rural *folk* still live without electricity).

Former, First; Latter, Last

In editorial English *former* and *latter* are usually limited to references involving two antecedents (Truman and Eisenhower were in office during the Korean War. It began in the administration of the *former*, and it ended in that of the *latter*). *First* and *last* should be used to refer to the first and last mentioned in an enumeration of more than two parts (Columbus, Cincinnati, and Cleveland are the largest cities in Ohio; the *first* is the capital, the *last* a thriving industrial town on the shores of Lake Erie).

Fragment

A term widely used by handbooks to refer to unsuccessful incomplete sentences. Conservative commentators on the language consider any declarative sentence without a subject and/or verb, a fragment on the premise that a true sentence needs both of these constituents. A few, realizing the effectiveness of certain subjectless or verbless sentences, discern between successful and unsuccessful fragments. The success of a sentence which lacks a subject, a verb, or both, can only be decided in context. To say that the word *yesterday* could never be punctuated as a sentence would be unrealistic. "Yesterday" is a perfectly good sentence when it comes as an answer to such a question as "When did you arrive?" Sentences made up of single words or of phrases occur remarkably often as answers to questions, as transitions, and as stylistic variations for emphasis. Teachers and editors must rely on their experience as readers to decide when such word groups are used successfully.

Freshman, Freshmen, Frosh

When used as a modifier (the *freshman* dance), *freshman* is always singular. The plural form for the noun is *freshmen*. The words *freshman* and *freshmen* are capitalized only when they refer to the name of an event, organization, or activity (the *Freshman* Mixer, *Freshman* Registration Day). The term *frosh* is campus and sports jargon.

Funny

Because the word *funny* has several denotative and connotative meanings, it is usually replaced by a more precise word in formal editorial English. *Funny* is often used in the sense of "strange" or "curious" in informal editorial English (I had a *funny* sensation when I stepped ashore). Other synonyms for *funny* are *amusing, comical, diverting, droll, humorous, laughable, ludicrous,* and *ridiculous.*

Further

See **Farther, Further,** p. 23.

Get, Got (Gotten)

The verb *get* incurs a great many usage problems of which the following are among the most prominent:

(1) Both *got* and *gotten* occur as past participles in editorial English in the sense of "acquired," "received," or "become," though *got*

is more frequent (I *had got* [or *gotten*] my reservation already). In British English *got* is the only form of the past participle.

(2) *Got* in the sense of "possess" or "have" is informal in *have got* or *has got* (and such contracted forms as *I've got, she's got*). *Gotten* is not used in this sense. The omission of *have* or *has* in the construction *have got* or *has got* is substandard (He *got* rhythm).

(3) *Have got to* in the sense of "must" is a standard alternate for *have to* (John *has* [*got*] *to* bring his report card home). *Have got to* is likely to occur more often in speaking, but it is completely acceptable in editorial English.

(4) *Get to* or *got to* with an infinitive in the sense of "be able to" is standard on all levels of editorial English (The civil rights leaders *got to* see the President).

(5) *Get* or *got* with an *-ing* form of the verb in the sense of "begin" is standard in editorial English (to *get* this country *moving* again, *get going*), though it occurs more often in informal than in formal English.

(6) *Get* or *got* as passive auxiliaries (to *get* married, to *get* invited) is standard on all levels of editorial English, though some fastidious writers avoid it on the most formal levels of expression.

(7) *Get* or *got* in combination with such adverbs as *ahead, along, by, over, out* is colloquial. In formal editorial English a more precise synonym is usually available in place of such phrases (*to succeed* for *get ahead, to cooperate* for *get along*, etc.).

Go

This verb (principal parts: *go, went, gone*) occurs with great frequency in the language, and it has developed many uses and meanings. *Webster III* lists twenty-one definitions of *go* as an intransitive verb, and nine as a transitive verb. In addition, *go* has developed numerous idiomatic uses, many of which appear in editorial English (*to go in for, to go back on, to go insane, go after, go against, go far, go for, go one better, go places, go steady, go through a fortune, go to pieces, go without, go without saying, on the go, no go*).

Modern missile jargon has established fresh uses of *go* as both an adjective (The *go* condition will continue through the fourth orbit) and a noun (The astronaut received a *go* from Central Control Headquarters). Though too recent for inclusion in *Webster III*, these uses have begun to appear in editorial English.

Good, Good and, A good many

Good, good and, and *a good many* occur colloquially as intensifiers (It hasn't rained in a *good* long time; Carol was *good and* angry; Anne has *a good many* virtues). These usages, however, appear rarely in editorial English.

Good, Well

The adjective *good* is sometimes substituted for the adverb *well* in colloquial and informal editorial English, particularly with reference to the workings of mechanical or other inanimate things (The old car works *well* [colloquial: *good*] except in the winter). Formal editorial English maintains the distinction (A *good* car ought to run *well* in the winter). *Well* is the standard usage when the reference is to health (Though weary from overwork, Nora feels *well*).

Got, Gotten

See **Get, Got (Gotten)**, p. 26.

Grew, Grown, Growed

Grew and *grown* are the only acceptable written forms for the past tense and past participle, respectively, of the verb *grow*. The dialect variant *growed* occurs only in the speech of the illiterate or little educated.

Grounds

The expression *on the grounds of* is often followed by a singular in editorial English (The defense based its case *on the grounds of* insanity). *On the grounds that* is regarded by some stylebooks as jargon, especially when it is used as a synonym for *because* (He refused to take the examination *because* [not *on the grounds that*] he was unprepared).

Had better, Had best

These constructions often substitute for *should* or *ought* in contexts implying advice or indirect command (You *had better* file your income tax return before April 15). Both occur in editorial English, though *had best* only rarely. The related contraction *'d better* and *better* without an auxiliary are colloquial.

Had rather

This construction often substitutes in editorial English for *would rather* in contexts dealing with preference (Everyone knew that I *had rather* [or *would rather*] vacation in Europe than in South America). The related contraction *'d rather* is colloquial, while the verb *druther* and the noun *druthers* are dialectal variants; these forms should be avoided in editorial English.

Half

In editorial English the expression *a half* is preferred over the colloquial *half a* or *a half a* (The new shopping center grossed more than *a half* [not *half a* or *a half a*] million dollars in its opening weekend).

When it refers to a countable plural noun, *half* takes a plural verb (Of the eighteen new representatives to the Colorado legislature, *half are* lawyers). When it refers to an uncountable noun, each part of which can be considered a single entity, *half* regularly takes a singular verb (*Half* of the water in Palisades Reservoir *is* earmarked for irrigation).

Hanged, Hung

Hung appears regularly as both the past and past participial forms of the verb *hang* in all contexts except that of an execution, in which *hanged* is preferred in editorial English (The horse thieves were *hanged* at dawn; The stockings were *hung* by the chimney with care).

Have got

See **Get, Got (Gotten),** p. 26.

Heaved, Hove

Except when used in a nautical context, *hove* has been replaced in editorial English by *heaved* in both the past and past participial forms of the verb *heave* (He *heaved* the sacks of potatoes onto the truck; The ship *hove* to just outside the three-mile limit). *Webster III* identifies *hoved* and *hoven* as dialectal forms, which should be avoided in editorial English.

Height

Inexperienced writers sometimes corrupt *height* to *heighth,* by analogy with *width, breadth,* and *length. Webster III* calls *heighth* a dialectal variant; it should be avoided in editorial English (I didn't know the exact *height* [not *heighth*] of the building).

He or she, His or her

He or she and *his or her* are stiff and affected constructions occurring most commonly in pretentious formal writing and in legal documents. The more frequent practice in editorial English is to use the pronouns *he* and *his* when the referent could be a person of either sex (A careful speaker always avoids offending *his* [not *his or her*] audience). Occasionally, when the group of persons referred to is commonly composed of women, the pronominal reference is *she* or *her* (A good secretary leaves *her* [not *his or her*] office only after *she* [not *he or she*] has cleared *her* [not *his or her*] desk).

No problem is encountered when such sentences are cast in the plural, for the third person plural pronouns *they* and *their* apply to both sexes (Careful speakers always avoid offending *their* audiences;

Good secretaries leave *their* offices only after *they* have cleared their desks).

His, Him (with gerund)
See **Gerund,** p. 137.

Home
After the verbs *go* and *get, home* occurs regularly in editorial English without being preceded by a preposition (The meeting was adjourned early so that everyone could *get home* before dark; Jim *went home* earlier than the others). After forms of the verb *to be,* the preposition *at* is normally retained in editorial English (Dr. Rice will be *at home* all morning). The use of *to home* as a substitute for *at home* is dialectal and should be avoided in writing.

Hoofs, Hooves
Both forms occur in editorial English as the plural of *hoof,* though *hoofs* is the more common.

Hove
See **Heaved, Hove,** p. 29.

Human, Humane
These two words are sometimes confused. *Human* means "pertaining to or characteristic of man" (Every once in a while Charles actually shows some *human* kindness), and *humane* means "characterized by kindness" or "benevolent" (Many persons object to medical experimentation upon animals because it is not *humane*).

Hung
See **Hanged, Hung,** p. 29.

I.e.
Abbreviation for Latin *id est,* meaning "that is." Its principal use is to introduce parenthetical clarifications (Many leading ichthyologists [*i.e.,* zoologists who specialize in the study of fish life] have joined Rachel Carson in her condemnation of insecticides).

If, Whether
According to the traditional prescription in handbooks, *if* should be used to express conditions (*If* we can manage it, we shall take a trip to England next year), and *whether,* often with its correlative *or,* should be used in statements of doubt (We don't know *whether* we can take a trip to England next year). In actual usage, however, *whether* and *if* appear with nearly equal frequency in editorial English to introduce

noun clauses that express doubt. In fact, after the verbs *ask, doubt, know, see,* and *wonder, if* occurs more frequently than *whether* (We asked *if* [or *whether*] reservations were available at the Hilton Hotel). In formal editorial English, *whether* is still the preferred form, especially when correlative *or* follows it (The old man could not recall *whether* he had visited there before *or* [or *or whether*] he had simply read about the place). *Whether* always occurs in editorial English when the correlative construction *or not* precedes the noun clause (A skillful politician determines *whether or not* [not *if or not*] his constituents want him to support increased foreign aid).

Illusion
See **Allusion, Illusion,** p. 7.

Imperial, Imperious
These two words are sometimes confused. *Imperial* means "pertaining to an emperor" or, more generally, "majestic" (India was once an *imperial* colony), while *imperious* means "haughty" or "domineering" (In the medieval drama, Herod was played as a boisterous and *imperious* villain).

Imply, Infer
These two words are often confused. *Imply* means "to suggest by word or manner" (By his sarcastic tone and his strained facial expression, the lecturer *implied* that he was condescending to his audience). *Infer* means "to draw a conclusion about the unknown on the basis of known facts" (After observing their recent space achievements, one might *infer* that the Russians will be the first to reach the moon).

In back of
Despite its redundancy, this construction has won acceptance in colloquial and informal editorial English, though *behind* is preferred in formal writing (An even higher group of mountains loomed *in back of* [formal: *behind*] the coastal range).

Infer
See **Imply, Infer,** p. 31.

Ingenious, Ingenuous
These two adjectives are often confused. *Ingenious* usually means "inventive" or "clever" (Even the police admitted that the plan for the holdup was *ingenious*), while *ingenuous* means "straightforward" or "naive" (Li'l Abner is a product of the soil; though totally unsophisticated he is an *ingenuous* spokesman for intellectual honesty).

In, Into, In to

In some contexts the prepositions *in* and *into* are interchangeable (Scared by the lightning, the young girl went *in* [or *into*] the house). Note, however, that *in* and *into* may differentiate meaning in other contexts (The girl ran *in* the house [*in* designating the place of running]; The girl ran *into* the house [*into* designating the place toward which she ran]).

When either *in* and/or *to* is related to a verb, two separate words are used (The girl came *in to* avoid the lightning). In the previous example *in* is an adverb modifying *came*, and *to* is part of the infinitive *to avoid*. In the spoken language single and double word usages are differentiated by stress and juncture patterns.

In (with) regard to

This construction, though considered jargon by some stylebooks, occurs regularly in editorial English (The government's action *in* [or *with*] *regard to* the gold flow has been decisive). *In* (*with*) *regards to* is a corruption formed by analogy with *as regards* and is avoided in editorial English.

Inside of

Inside of occurs frequently in colloquial and informal editorial English where the reference is either to time (I hope to finish this book *inside of* a month) or place (She broke into tears as soon as she was *inside of* her own room). In formal editorial English *within* is preferred.

In the case of

See **Jargon**, p. 148.

Into

See **In, Into, In to**, p. 32.

Invite (noun)

The use of *invite* as a noun substituting for *invitation* is identified by *Webster III* as dialectal. The usage should be avoided in editorial English (The President received an *invitation* [not *invite*] from the Soviet Embassy).

Irregardless

Because of its double negation (*ir-* and *-less*) the word *irregardless* is avoided in editorial English. *Webster III* identifies it as a substandard form (We will go *regardless* [not *irregardless*] of the cost).

Irritate

See **Aggravate, Irritate**, p. 5.

Is when

See **When, Is when,** p. 58.

Is where

See **Where, Is where,** p. 58.

It

The neuter third person singular pronoun has developed a wide variety of uses, both functional and substantive, in modern English. The most prominent of them, and those most likely to occur in editorial English, are the first three of the following:

(1) *Anticipatory it.* In certain sentence types, *it* precedes and governs the verb while the real subject, usually a noun phrase or clause, is placed after the verb (*It* is certainly justifiable to seek a better job). Usually, the *it* can be eliminated by moving the real subject (in the previous example: *to seek a better job*) to initial position in the sentence, yet the result is often undesirable because the sentence rhythm is unnatural. (See also **Expletive,** p. 133.)

(2) *Impersonal it.* It frequently occurs as the subject of an impersonal verb expressing a condition or action which is dissociated from a causal agent. This use of *it* is common in statements and questions about the weather (*It* is getting cold tonight), the time (*It* will soon be midnight), physical or mental condition (Will *it* hurt me?), and distance (*It* is another hundred miles to New Orleans). Impersonal *it* also occurs in certain formula patterns such as *it can be said that, it should be noted that, it appears obvious that.*

(3) *Indefinite it.* It is used widely with reference to a general situation or condition. This use of *it* is most common in statements about a matter which has been considered or is about to be considered (The committee voted *it* down), a general state of circumstances (*It* hasn't gone well for me this year), an action which should be done (Marty planned to do *it* tomorrow), a solution or discovery (I've found *it* at last).

(4) *Emphatic it.* Though generally avoided in editorial English, *it* occurs colloquially in certain emphatic situations, particularly with reference to something that is without equal. The connotation may be either favorable (San Francisco is *it*) or unfavorable (Sally really thinks she is *it*).

Its, It's

Its is a possessive pronoun and has no apostrophe (The nation cannot avoid *its* [not *it's*] responsibilities to the poor). *It's* is a contraction of the words *it* and *is,* the apostrophe indicating the omission of a letter (*It's* never cold in Omaha).

It's me, It's I, It is I

Grammarians have long made an issue over the use of an objective pronoun after a form of the verb *to be* (*It is me* [instead of *It is I*]; *It was him* who screamed [instead of *It was he* who screamed]; etc.), arguing that an objective pronoun cannot appear in a position calling for a predicate nominative. The evidence of usage clearly indicates a predominance of *it's me* over *it's I* in the speech of both the educated and the uneducated. Except in dialogue, however, editorial English prefers the "correct" nominative form (Without doubt *it was I* who needed psychiatric help).

Just

As an adverb, *just* has several uses in editorial English. It may mean "exactly, precisely" (I cannot describe *just* what happiness Carol enjoys); "barely" (The snow measured *just* under ten feet deep); "in immediate proximity" (Oakland is *just* east of San Francisco); "only, merely, simply" (I *just* speak when I am called upon). In this last usage, however, *only* occurs far more frequently than *just* in editorial English. The use of *just* as an intensifier (I *just* love that hat) is colloquial and is avoided in writing.

Just usually appears immediately before the element it modifies, but with the meaning "only" it often is placed elsewhere. The discussion of the position of *only* in a sentence applies as well to the synonymous use of *just* (see **Only,** p. 42).

Kind of, Sort of

The use of *kind of* or *sort of* as an adverbial substitute for *somewhat* or *rather* is a common colloquialism which sometimes occurs in informal editorial English (The rain *sort of* [*kind of*] diminished in the late afternoon). In formal writing *kind of* and *sort of* are followed only by nouns (J. F. Kennedy was the *kind of* [*sort of*] President the people could trust). The constructions *kind of a* and *sort of a* are redundant and are avoided in editorial English.

Kneeled, Knelt

Both occur regularly in editorial English as past and past participial forms of the verb *kneel* (Stricken with awe, they *knelt* [or *kneeled*] and faced the heavens).

Knew, Known, Knowed

Knew and *known* are the only acceptable written forms for the past tense and past participle, respectively, of the verb *know*. The dialect variant *knowed* occurs only in the speech of the illiterate or little educated.

Know-how

This compound has become firmly established in informal editorial English, particularly that of the commercial world. It rarely appears in formal writing (The *know-how* [formal: *technical competence*] of Japanese shipbuilders has resulted in a thriving industry).

Last, Latest

In editorial English *last* occurs with the meanings "final" or "most recent" and *latest,* only with the meaning "most recent" (Bergman said that his *latest* movie will not be his *last* experiment with symbolism on the screen).

Latter, Last

See **Former, First; Latter, Last,** p. 25.

Lay, Lie

These two verbs are often confused in colloquial usage; however, editorial English preserves the distinction between them. *Lay* (principal parts: *lay, laid, laid*) is a transitive verb meaning "to put something down" (Carol *laid* her cigarettes on the dashboard). *Lie* (principal parts: *lie, lay, lain*) is an intransitive verb meaning "to rest in a reclining position" (I *lay* down for an hour yesterday after lunch).

Learn, Teach

In spoken English, particularly among the uneducated in the eastern half of the United States, *learn* is often substituted for *teach.* This substandard usage is avoided in editorial English (Ray *taught* [not *learned*] me how to ride a horse). *Teached* as a substitute for *taught* is also substandard and occurs in written English only when the writer wishes to represent illiterate dialogue.

Leave, Let

These two verbs are often confused. Despite the warning in some stylebooks that *leave* should not be used with the meaning "permit" or "allow," *Webster III* lists them as synonyms meaning "to refrain from preventing." A good rule of thumb is to use *leave* in the sense of "depart" (We have to *leave* at eight o'clock) or of "remain in position" (*Leave* [not *let*] the key in the lock; Don't *leave* [not *let*] Sarah home alone) and to use *let* in the sense of "permit" or "allow" (*Let* [not *leave*] us pray; The United States will never *let* [not *leave*] China overcome Southeast Asia). In editorial English *allow* or *permit* connotes a stronger sense of permission than does *let.*

Lend, Loan

Lend and *loan* are now acceptable synonyms when used as verbs (The

First National Bank will *lend* [or *loan*] money at 5 percent interest), though formal editorial English prefers *lend*. Only *loan* is used as a noun (I obtained a small *loan*).

Less

See **Fewer, Less,** p. 24.

Let's

A contraction of *let us, let's* occurs frequently in informal editorial English (*Let's* [formal: *Let us*] examine the economic potential of Brazilian forest products). The colloquial *let's us* (*Let's us* go hunting) is obviously redundant and is avoided in editorial English.

Let us not, Let's not, Let's don't

In editorial English the preferred usage is *let us not,* particularly in exhortations (*Let us not* underestimate the power of public opinion). *Let's not* appears occasionally in written English, while *let's don't* (or its opposite *don't let's*) are restricted to colloquial usage.

Liable

See **Apt, Liable, Likely,** p. 10.

Lie

See **Lay, Lie,** p. 35.

Lighted, Lit

Both forms occur interchangeably in editorial English as the past tense and past participle of the verb *to light* (The fire *lighted* [or *lit*] the entire village). *Up* often follows *lighted* or *lit* colloquially, but since the *up* is redundant, the construction is avoided in editorial English (We had *lit* [not *lit up*] our cigarettes in the wind).

Like

See **As, Like,** p. 11.

Like for

Followed by an infinitive with its subject, *like for* has been firmly established in speech for centuries. However, the *for* is redundant, and the construction is avoided in editorial English (The priest would *like* [not *like for*] you to visit him tomorrow).

Likely

See **Apt, Liable, Likely,** p. 10.

Like to, Almost

The use of dialectal *like to* for *nearly* or *almost* should be avoided in editorial English (I *almost* [not *like to*] froze before the bus arrived).

Lit

See **Lighted, Lit,** p. 36.

Loan

See **Lend, Loan,** p. 35.

Locate

Locate, long a colloquial substitute for *settle,* has begun to win acceptance in editorial English (General Motors announced plans today to *locate* a new assembly plant in California). But when the reference is to people, *settle* is still preferred in formal editorial English (Lyndon Johnson's grandparents *located* [formal: *settled*] in Texas during the last century).

Lot, Lot of, Lots of

Used as nouns with the meaning "a great many," these words are colloquial, though they are occasionally found in informal editorial English (A *lot of* people were gathering in front of the bank; The President shook *lots of* hands in Pittsburgh). *Lot* also occurs colloquially as an adverb meaning "much" or "a great deal"; again, however, the usage is avoided in formal editorial English (Glendon Swarthout's latest book is *a lot* [formal: *much* or *a great deal*] more interesting than the last one).

Luxuriant, Luxurious

These two adjectives are often confused. *Luxuriant* means "lushly abundant" or "ornate" (After the profuse spring showers, the valley lay *luxuriant* in its budding foliage), and *luxurious* means "characterized by luxury" or "sumptuous" (Even by the standards of the very wealthy, his penthouse is *luxurious*).

Mad

Some traditionalists still insist that *mad* be used only in its original meaning of "insane." Its occurrence, however, as a synonym for *angry* has become so common, both with educated and uneducated Americans, that this usage is acceptable even in the most formal written English.

Mad about

The colloquial expression *mad about* does not occur in editorial English, where *fond of* or another synonymous expression will appear (Marty and Anne have always been *fond of* [not *mad about*] children).

Marvelous

Experienced writers generally reserve the word *marvelous* for a truly unusual situation rather than waste its impact by using it to show simple approval (That certainly was a tasty [not *marvelous*] bowl of soup; the sight of the geyser Old Faithful erupting is truly *marvelous*).

May
See **Can, May, Could, Might,** p. 15.

May be, Maybe
May be and *maybe* are sometimes confused by inexperienced writers. The former is a compound verb (Sally *may be* arriving late); the latter is a synonym for *perhaps* (*Maybe* I should go to the doctor with you).

Might
See **Can, May, Could, Might,** p. 15.

Might could
This is a dialectal expression which is avoided in editorial English, where *could probably* would likely occur (Anne *could probably* [not *might could*] get a job in the library).

Might of
See **Could of, Might of, Should of, Would of,** p. 18.

Mighty
The use of *mighty* as an intensifier in the sense of "very" is colloquial and should be avoided in editorial English (Carol served a *very* [not *mighty*] fine meal).

Moral, Morale
These two words are often confused. *Moral,* an adjective or a noun, should not be substituted for *morale,* which can function only as a noun. *Morale* means "spirit" and *moral* refers to "right conduct" (Employee *morale* has never been higher; The *moral* code requires occasional acts of charity; This story has a *moral*).

More than one
In editorial English the expression *more than one* plus a noun regularly takes a singular form of the verb even though the sense of the expression is plural (*More than one nation is* involved in the exploitation of Africa). However, when the noun intervenes between *more* and *than*, both it and the verb are plural (*More nations than one are* involved in the exploitation of Africa).

Most
See **Almost, Most,** p. 7.

Must

Must has recently found limited acceptance even in formal editorial English as a noun (Tax relief legislation is considered a *must* by many leaders in the present Congress). As an adjective, however, its use is restricted to informal editorial English (Three items of *must* [formal: *urgently needed*] legislation remain before the lawmakers).

Neither

See **Either, Neither,** p. 22.

Nice

This word is overused by inexperienced writers as a modifier showing mild approval (It was a *nice* party). Experienced writers try to achieve specificity (It was a riotous party with plenty of food and drinks).

No account, No good

Both these constructions occur in speech with the meaning "worthless" or "useless." So used, *no account* rarely appears in informal editorial English, and neither expression is found in formal editorial English. When *no good* does appear, it is likely to refer to a less specific situation, while *worthless* refers to a particular thing (The movie at the Crest Theater is *worthless;* in fact, movies in general are *no good*).

In other contexts *no good* appears on all levels of editorial English, particularly where it functions as a noun (*No good* will come of his drinking and smoking) or as an adjective with the meaning roughly equivalent to "without value" (The used cars on that lot are *no good*).

No such

See **Such, No such,** p. 52.

Not (placement of)

The logical placement of *not* before the element it modifies is often violated in informal editorial English (All men are *not* created equal). Quite obviously, *not* in the previous example refers to *all men* rather than to *created,* yet it is not placed before *all,* where it logically belongs. Very seldom can the illogical placement of *not* cause ambiguity, for the context generally dictates the intended meaning. Nobody, for example, would argue that the minister in the following sentence was an unbeliever: The minister did *not* believe it possible that we missed services. Nevertheless, formal editorial English prefers the logical placement of the negative (*Not* all men are created equal; The minister believed it *im*possible that we missed services).

Notable, Noticeable

These two words are sometimes confused. *Notable* means "remarkable" or "worthy of note" (The step-up of the war in the Far East has been, perhaps, the most *notable* event of the past year), while *noticeable* means "perceptible" (John bears a *noticeable* resemblance to his father).

Not as, Not so

The distinction between *as* and *so*—the former used in affirmative, the latter in negative comparisons—is still generally observed in formal editorial English. In informal editorial English, however, *not as* occurs regularly as a substitute for *not so* (The present governor is *not as* [formal: *not so*] colorful as his predecessor). See also **As . . . as, So . . . as,** p. 10.

Not (or another negative) but

The use of *not* or another negative followed by *but* occurs regularly in spoken English and occasionally in informal editorial English (I saw *nothing but* a single light in the distance; *Nobody but* the suspect knew the combination to the strongbox). Formal editorial English substitutes *only* in these sentences, even though the emphatic negative construction might be more effective. Formal writing does, however, condone *none but* (*None but* the strong can survive the Arctic winter) and *nothing but* (France could do *nothing but* defend her territory against the aggressors). See also **Cannot help but,** p. 15.

Not only . . . but also

These correlative conjunctions are always followed in editorial English by sentence elements of similar grammatical standing (He paid *not only* his rent *but also* his taxes; Carol *not only* telephoned her Senator *but also* wired the President). Inexperienced writers, however, often shift constructions, particularly when *but* and *also* are separated by intervening words (Larry was an excellent shot *not only* with a rifle *but* could handle a shotgun excellently *also* [corrected: *but* with a shotgun *also*]). Some stylebooks insist that *but* must always be followed by *also* in this construction; however, *also* is frequently omitted even in formal editorial English (He *not only* kept house, *but* he cooked, washed the dishes, and even mended his own clothes). See also **Shifted Construction,** p. 181.

Notorious

In editorial English *notorious* means "widely but unfavorably known" (Al Capone was *notorious* for his absolute control of the Chicago underworld). The noun *notoriety* carries the same unfavorable connotation.

Not so

See **Not as, Not so,** above.

No use

With the meaning "useless," *no use* occurs frequently in informal editorial English, but rarely in formal editorial English, where *of no use* or *useless* takes its place (Some people think it is *no use* [formal: *of no use* or *useless*] negotiating with the Russians). The idiom *have no use for* appears on all levels of written English (I will *have no use for* my horses in New York) when the meaning refers to "utility." However, the same construction is informal when the meaning is "dislike" (Emil *has no use for* Irishmen).

Nowhere near

This expression appears occasionally in informal editorial English (The national debt is *nowhere near* the limit of our deficit potential. It is normally avoided in formal writing and replaced by a different wording (The national debt *does not approach* our deficit potential).

Nowheres

Nowheres is a dialectal variant for *nowhere* and is avoided in editorial English.

Number

See **Amount, Number,** p. 8.

O, Oh

O appears more in formal than in informal editorial English; it is a sign of direct address and is not followed by a comma (*O* Lord, I ask thy blessing). *Oh* is an exclamation, quite often mild, and is usually followed by a comma (*Oh,* I don't care whether I go or not). When used in an emphatic situation, it is often followed by an exclamation point (*Oh!* Anne's dress is on fire).

Off of

This construction has wide colloquial usage, though it is avoided as redundant in editorial English (The weathered paint was peeling *off* [not *off of*] the house).

Of which

See **Whose, Of which,** p. 59.

Oh

See **O, Oh,** above.

OK, O.K., Okay

These terms are accepted colloquialisms for "all right" or "correct." They appear occasionally in informal writing, where the spelling *okay* predominates, but are never used in formal editorial English. They may be used as verbs (The clerk will *okay* your application); as nouns (The boss gave his *okay*); as adjectives (The car is *okay*); or as interjections (*Okay,* call me a liar).

One
See **You, One,** p. 60.

One another
See **Each other, One another,** p. 22.

One in (of, out of) three (four, etc.)
Most writers of editorial English use a singular form of the verb after the constructions *one in three, one of four, one out of five* (A survey of seven thousand doctors indicated that *one out of three has* quit smoking during the past five years). Since these constructions most frequently report a sample statistic from a large number of observations, a plural form of the verb could be justified and, indeed, does occasionally occur (The Bureau of the Census reports that *one of* every *five* Americans *move* to another state each year). When the numbers are absolute, however, the singular verb form always occurs in editorial English (*One of five* prisoners who escaped this afternoon *is* still at large).

One of those who (which, that)
Ordinarily one expects to find a plural verb after the construction *one of those who* (Jim Backes is *one of those who were* given a leave of absence). Occasionally, however, writers of editorial English regard *one,* rather than *those,* as the antecedent of *who,* in which case a singular form of the verb follows (Dwight D. Eisenhower is *one of those* men *who,* despite his age, *understands* the pulse of the people). The latter usage is most likely to occur when a singular reference to the subject (*his* referring to *Eisenhower* in the previous example) intervenes between *who* and the verb in the dependent clause. The same observations apply to the constructions *one of those which* and *one of those that.*

Only
The "correct" position of *only* in a sentence has been the subject of much concern to rigid grammarians. Logic dictates that a limiting adverb should be placed immediately before the element it modifies; however, usage has established its placement in other positions of the sentence as well. Consider the following sentences:

Sam is *only* working four days per week.

Sam is working *only* four days per week.

Both versions have the same meaning, that Sam's work is restricted to four days per week. No other meaning makes sense, yet *only* precedes the verb *working* in the first version. Both these patterns occur regularly in editorial English.

In emphatic situations, *only* appears after the word it modifies (God *only* can determine the day of judgment). Yet this construction is generally avoided in written English because of the possibility of ambiguity: God can do one thing and nothing else, that is, determine the day of judgment. The same sentence in spoken English is unambiguous because *God only* receives the stress. When *only* does appear after the noun in written English, it often comes at the end of the sentence, where there can be no question concerning the word modified (Courses numbered 600 or above may be taken by graduate students *only*).

In informal editorial English *only* occurs as a connective substituting for *but* (I wanted to go to the show, *only* I didn't have the money for a ticket). This usage is avoided in formal editorial English.

On, Onto, On to

As prepositions *on* and *onto* are used interchangeably in editorial English (Carefully inching his way, the climber pulled himself *onto* [or *on*] the narrow ledge). *Onto* usually appears as one word; however, when *on* is used as an adverb, *on* and *to* appear as two words (He turned the light *on to* see his way [*on* related to *turned, to* related to *see*]; Pamela held *on to* her virtue [*on* related to *held*]). In the spoken language the single and double word usages are differentiated by stress and juncture patterns.

On, Upon

These two prepositions have generally the same meaning and are in almost all instances interchangeable. Nevertheless, in editorial English the simpler *on* occurs far more frequently than does *upon*.

Oral, Verbal

These two words are occasionally confused. *Oral* refers to spoken communication; *verbal* has the more general meaning of written or spoken communication. For *verbal* in its grammatical sense, see p. 197.

Ought not

As a substitute for *should not, ought not* (and other negative forms: *oughtn't, hadn't ought*) has wide colloquial distribution. Except in dialogue, however, it is avoided in editorial English.

Outside, Outside of

In editorial English, *outside* and *outside of* are generally avoided when their meaning is "except" (*Outside of* French, he passed all his courses). Both, however, occur frequently in colloquial English. As prepositions denoting place, the two forms are interchangeable on all levels of usage (He lives *outside* [or *outside of*] the city limits).

Owing to
See **Because of, Due to, Owing to,** p. 12.

Ox, Oxen
Ox is one of the few words remaining in the language which still form their plurals with the suffix *-en*. *Oxes* occurs only in dialectal speech.

Pair, Pairs
Although both forms occur as plurals in editorial English, the more formal usage is *pairs*. After a number, *pair* tends to occur more frequently than *pairs* (Erik broke two *pair* of skis this winter). Without a number, *pairs* is the usual form (The drawer contained matching *pairs* of socks).

Percent
Percent is so overwhelmingly favored over *per cent* on all levels of editorial English that *Webster III* lists only the compound word. As a substitute for *percentage* or *proportion, percent* occurs only in informal writing (Only a small *percent* [formal: *percentage*] of the employees will be promoted). The percent sign (%) is used only after numerals (14%, fourteen *percent*).

Phenomenon, Phenomena
The Greek form of the plural, *phenomena,* remains the more common usage in formal editorial English, though *Webster III* lists *phenomenons* as an acceptable variant of the plural. The use of *phenomena* as a singular and *phenomenas* as a plural is substandard and should be avoided.

Pleaded, Pled
Both forms occur regularly in editorial English as the past tense or past participle of the verb *plead* (The lawyer *pleaded* [or *pled*] the case before the Supreme Court).

Plenty (adjective, adverb)
In informal editorial English *plenty* occasionally occurs as an intensifier substituting for *very* (Nights in the mountains are *plenty* cold; The game was *plenty* exciting). This usage, however, is avoided in formal editorial English. *Plenty* also appears as an adjective in colloquial usage, but editorial English requires the construction *plenty of* (College students today seem to have *plenty of* [not *plenty*] spending money).

P.M.
See **A.M., P.M.,** p. 8.

Possessive Form of Inanimate Nouns
See **Apostrophe,** p. 65.

Possessive Form with Gerund
See p. 169.

Practicable, Practical
These two words are often confused. *Practicable* should be applied to untested but feasible schemes, theories, or plans (The United Nations seeks a *practicable* plan to ease world tensions). *Practical* should be used in all other contexts.

Precipitate, Precipitous
These two words are often confused. *Precipitate* can be used as a verb in the sense of "hasten" (Russia *precipitated* the quarrel with the arrest of the American officer) and as an adjective in the sense of "hasty" or "rash" (The union's strike vote was a *precipitate* action since it came before the management had been able to discuss the grievances). *Precipitous* is an adjective only; it refers to *precipice* and means "steep."

Prepositions at End of Sentences
See p. 171.

Pretty
For more than two centuries *pretty* has occurred as an intensifier with the meaning "considerably" or "moderately" (*pretty* evenly divided, *pretty* good day, *pretty* late in the evening). Despite the objection in some stylebooks, the usage appears frequently in informal editorial English. The adverb *prettily* (She danced *prettily*) and the noun *pretty* (Come here, my little *pretty*) are labeled dialectal by *Webster III*.

Price (verb)
Price occurs regularly as a verb on all levels of editorial English with the meaning "to fix or set the value of" (Sears Roebuck *prices* its products to meet competition) and in informal editorial English with the meaning "to ask the price of" (I *priced* both the Ford and Chevrolet before making a decision).

Principal Parts
This section on "Common Usage Problems" contains separate entries on many troublesome verbs, all in their appropriate alphabetical position. An additional list appears on p. 172.

Principal, Principle

These homonyms are often confused. *Principal* occurs both as an adjective meaning "chief" or "most important" (His *principal* virtue is tolerance) and as a noun meaning "head person" or "sum of money drawing interest" (a school *principal;* a $5,000 *principal* at the bank). *Principle* occurs only as a noun with the meaning "fundamental truth or doctrine" (The United Nations serves the *principle* of human brotherhood).

Proved, Proven

Both forms occur in editorial English as the past participle of *prove* (General Motors has *proved* [or *proven*] that a giant corporation can operate efficiently), though *proved* is generally favored. As an adjective, however, *proven* appears with much greater frequency (a *proven* product, of *proven* ability).

Provided (that), Providing (that)

With the meaning "on the condition that," both *provided* and *providing* occur regularly as connectives in editorial English (The stock market should experience another record year, *provided* [or *providing*] consumer spending continues at present levels). The use of *that* after *provided* or *providing* is optional.

Quite a (an)

This construction occurs on all levels of editorial English as an indefinite quantifier (*Quite a* few people attended the civil rights rally). It also appears in contexts in informal editorial English with the meaning "very" (My professor is *quite an* interesting person) or as an expression of approval (My son is *quite a* skier).

Raise, Rise

These two words are often confused by inexperienced writers. *Rise* is an intransitive verb (principal parts: *rise, rose, risen*) used most often with the meaning "to stand or get up" (I *rose* this morning at dawn). *Raise* is a transitive verb (principal parts: *raise, raised, raised*) with the usual meaning "lift" or "elevate" (*Raise* your hand when you have a question). *Raise* occurs regularly in editorial English with the meaning "rear" or "bring up" (I didn't *raise* my boy to be a soldier) and as both a noun and verb with regard to "increase," usually in wages (General Motors *raised* all its salaried employees; The manager gave all employees a *raise*).

Rang, Rung

Both *rang* and *rung* occur as the past tense form of the verb *ring,* but *rang* is the usual form in editorial English (John Ball *rang* the bell). *Rung* is the standard form for the past participle (He has *rung* the bell).

Rarely ever

This redundant construction occurs colloquially, but it is avoided in editorial English (Though he had lived many years in San Francisco, he *rarely* [not *rarely ever*] dined at Fisherman's Wharf).

Real

This word is often used as a colloquial substitute for the adverbial intensifier *very* (The movie was *real* good). This usage probably developed because, as adjectives, the two words share the same meaning; both mean "true" or "actual" and may often be interchanged (Thou art the *very* [or *real*] God).

Reason is because, Reason is that

The redundant construction *reason is because* occurs frequently in informal editorial English and occasionally in formal editorial English, particularly when other words intervene between *reason* and *is because* (The *reason* that men are not wearing hats, according to the results of a recent questionnaire, *is because* they spend more time indoors). Nevertheless, *reason is that* remains the preferred construction on all levels of editorial English (The *reason* General Lee lost the war *is that* he could not maintain his supply lines). Some stylebooks advise against the use of either construction in favor of a briefer revision (General Lee lost the war *because* he could not maintain his supply lines).

Reference of Pronouns

See p. 176.

Respectfully, Respectively

These two adverbs are occasionally confused. *Respectfully* means "with respect" (I *respectfully* submitted my plan to the manager). *Respectively* means "in the order listed" and is used to refer in sequence to sets of enumerated items in a sentence (The first and second prizes were awarded to Idaho State and Harvard, *respectively*).

Right

Right occurs as an adverb with the meaning "very" or "extremely" in colloquial usage, particularly in the South. Generally, however, it is avoided in editorial English (He knew *very* [not *right*] well that I supported the United Nations).

Rise

See **Raise, Rise,** p. 46.

Round

See **About, Around, Round,** p. 4.

Run

Run occurs frequently in informal editorial English as a transitive verb meaning "operate" (Jim *runs* a drill press) or "manage" (Jim *runs* the Personnel Department). In formal editorial English, however, the preferred usage is *operate* or *manage*.

Rung

See **Rang, Rung,** p. 46.

Said (adjective)

Used as an adjective with the meaning "aforementioned," *said* occurs in legal writing (The judge decreed that *said* property be confiscated by the state). Otherwise, the term appears rarely in editorial English, and then only when the author wishes to approximate a legalistic style.

Seldom ever

This redundant construction occurs colloquially, but is avoided in editorial English (During his final years, Winston Churchill *seldom* [not *seldom ever*] visited the Houses of Parliament).

Set, Sit

In editorial English *set* is principally used as a transitive verb with the meaning "to put something in position" (Hannah *set* the cake on the platter), though it has developed many colloquial usages as an intransitive verb (The hen *set* for two weeks; Oyster stew doesn't *set* well with Marty). *Sit* occurs principally as an intransitive verb with the meaning "to take a seat" (Let us *sit* upon the ground). In some dialects *set* replaces *sit* in the present and *sat* in the past tense, but these variants should be avoided in editorial English (I think I'll *sit* [not *set*] in the same chair I *sat* [not *set*] in yesterday).

Shall, Will

Some traditional grammarians have sought to impose a complex distinction between *shall* and *will* to indicate the notions of simple futurity and determined futurity. Standard usage does not support the distinction. *Shall* and *will* are both used in editorial English to express future and conditional action in *all* persons, *will* being the much more common form. *Shall* is used principally to express obligation (The defendant *shall* pay $200 damages) or emphasis (I *shall* return) and to ask questions in first-person constructions involving permission or consent (*Shall* I leave the room now? *Shall* we dance?).

Shape

In colloquial usage, *shape* occurs frequently with the meaning "condition" (A quarterback must be in good *shape* all the time). This usage is avoided in editorial English.

Shifted Construction

See p. 181.

Should of

See **Could of, Might of, Should of, Would of,** p. 18.

Showed, Shown

Both these forms occur colloquially as the past participle of *show,* but *shown* is overwhelmingly preferred in editorial English (The movie was *shown* in both local theaters).

Show up

With the meaning "arrive" or "expose," *show up* occurs frequently in colloquial English. In editorial English, however, these usages are avoided (I hope the police will *arrive* [not *show up*] in time to *expose* [not *show up*] the crooked gambler).

Shrank, Shrunk, Shrunken

Webster III lists both *shrank* and *shrunk* as standard forms for the past tense of *shrink;* however, *shrank* is the preferred form in editorial English (The dress *shrank* two sizes in the wash). Similarly, *shrunk* and *shrunken* are acceptable past participles, though *shrunk* is preferred (The dress had *shrunk* two sizes). *Shrunken* occurs more frequently after *is* (The dress *is shrunken*) and before a noun (The *shrunken* body contained no life). *Shrinked* is a dialectal variant and should be avoided in editorial English.

[Sic]

From the Latin meaning "thus" or "so." [*Sic*] appears only in formal and scholarly writing, always in brackets, and only for the purpose of indicating that a mistake within quoted material appeared in the original quotation. In the following sentence, the name *Eisenhower* is misspelled, and the wrong year is given for the invasion of France: The student wrote, "Dwight D. Eisenhour [*sic*] directed the invasion of France early in 1946 [*sic*]." [*Sic*] should not be used simply to indicate an archaic or variant spelling occurring within a quoted text.

Sit

See **Set, Sit,** p. 48.

Site

See **Cite, Site,** p. 16.

Slow, Slowly

Both words derive from adverbial forms in Old English, but today *slowly* is far more common in editorial English than *slow* (We drove *slowly* [not *slow*] to the cemetery). *Slow* occurs colloquially as an adverb, particularly in imperative sentences (Go *slow*) and in slogans and signs (Drive *Slow*—Children Playing), but never when it immediately precedes the verb (The injured player *slowly* [never *slow*] limped off the field).

So . . . as

See **As . . . as, So . . . as,** p. 10.

Some

As an indefinite pronoun (see p. 144) *some* is treated as a plural when used with a countable plural noun (*Some* of the applicants for the position *were* able to arrange for *their* interviews). It is treated as a singular when used with uncountable nouns (*Some* of the liquid *was* left in the bottle). The colloquial use of adjectival *some* to express either approval or disapproval (That was *some* weekend we had) is avoided in editorial English.

Some time, Sometime, Sometimes

These three expressions are often confused. *Some time* refers to "duration" (We walked for *some time* in the park); *sometime* refers to an "uncertain or unspecified time" (I want to visit Alaska *sometime*); *sometimes* means "occasionally" (Arthur gets me angry *sometimes*, but usually I like him).

Sort of

See **Kind of, Sort of,** p. 34.

So, So that

Adverbial *so* occurs regularly in editorial English when it (1) intensifies an idea from a preceding clause or sentence (During the last two years of the war it appeared that the South was doomed; only the tactical abilities of its military leaders had held it together *so* long); or when it (2) serves as an intensive before verbs, adverbs, or adjectives (One wonders whether reform is possible, teacher training practices having been *so* distorted for *so* long by *so* many colleges). The colloquial use of *so* meaning "very" (I'm *so* happy; Sally is *so* pretty) is avoided in formal editorial English.

As a conjunction, *so* appears colloquially in place of *so that* to introduce clauses of purpose (We built a huge fire *so* we could keep warm), but editorial English prefers *so that*. Similarly, the colloquial use of *so* with clauses of result (The temperature dropped thirty degrees, *so* we built a large fire) is avoided in editorial English in favor of *so that* or a reconstruction of the sentence with *since* or *because* introducing the first clause (*Because* the temperature dropped thirty degrees, we built a large fire). The unrestricted use of *so* as a coordinating conjunction (*So* this girl asked me to buy her a drink; *so* I did) and as an introductory word to certain questions or statements (*So* what? *So* you think you'll go? *So* he is rich) are avoided in editorial English.

Specie, Species

These two words are often confused. *Specie* is a little-used collective noun meaning "money in coin" (He paid $38.36 in *specie*). *Species* means "kind" or "type" and has the same form in both the singular and plural (Contrary to opinion, Darwin in *The Origin of Species* did not define man as a *species* descended from the ape).

Sped, Speeded

Both occur as past participial and past tense forms in spoken English; however, in editorial English *sped* is preferred (The police car *sped* to the scene of the robbery).

Spelled, Spelt

Both occur colloquially as past and past participial forms of the verb *spell*. In editorial English, however, *spelled* is the preferred form (Erik *spelled* all twenty-five words correctly).

Spilled, Spilt

Both occur in editorial English as past and past participial forms of the verb *spill*, though *spilled* is more common (Mark had *spilled* his soup again). *Spilt,* when it does appear, is most commonly used in adjectival position (The *spilt* soup stained the tablecloth).

Split Infinitive

See p. 182.

Stationary, Stationery

These two homonyms are often confused. *Stationary* is an adjective meaning "in one place" (The weather bureau reported a *stationary* front), while *stationery* is a noun referring to writing paper and envelopes (Cuspid's *stationery* is embossed with a golden flower).

Stomp

Webster III lists *stomp* as a variant form of *stamp,* yet many observers have noted a difference in meaning between the two verbs. *Stomp* is used most often with reference to the act of crushing something with a forcible movement of the foot (The horse *stomped* the fallen rider).

Such (pronoun)

Such appears occasionally as a pronoun in editorial English when the reference to a person or thing is clearly indicated in the surrounding context (Mr. Smednor is our minister, and, as *such,* he should conduct himself properly). The colloquial use of *such as* with the meaning "those who" or "those which" (*Such as* are ready may leave the ship) is avoided in editorial English.

Such, No such

The use of *such* as an intensifier is found regularly in editorial English (The effect of *such* a long war was a large national debt). Many writers, however, prefer to follow such constructions as the foregoing with an *as-* or *that*-clause or phrase. The words *as the foregoing* in the previous sentence exemplify that practice. *No such* serves a similarly acceptable function in the negative (Though mathematicians use the word regularly, there is *no such* thing as infinity). *No such a* does not occur in editorial English.

Sure, Surely

Editorial English maintains the distinction between the adjective *sure* (a *sure* thing, *sure* path) and the adverb *surely* (Jim *surely* will graduate next June). The adverbial use of *sure* occurs colloquially as an intensive affirmative answer to questions (Will Jim graduate? *Sure,* next June). Similarly, *sure* appears colloquially as a mild intensifier (That dinner was *sure* good) as well as in idioms like *as sure as shooting* and *sure enough,* both of which are generally restricted to spoken English.

Suspect

See **Expect, Suspect,** p. 23.

Suspicion (verb)

One occasionally hears *suspicion* used as a verb in dialectal speech, but it never occurs in editorial English except in dialogue. The standard verb is *suspect* (I *suspect* [not *suspicion*] that the murderer is in this room).

Syllabuses, Syllabi

Like many other words with Greek or Latin plurals, *syllabus* has developed an anglicized plural. Either form is acceptable in editorial English.

Take sick

This expression is used colloquially in New England and, though less frequently, in the South. Editorial English employs *become ill* or *become sick*.

Teach

See **Learn, Teach,** p. 35.

Terrific

In colloquial English, *terrific* is often used to indicate simple approval (That hot dog was *terrific*). Editorial English replaces this usage with a specific adjective (e.g., *delightful, refreshing, nourishing*).

Than

See **Then, Than,** p. 54.

That there, This here

These constructions, along with *these here, those there,* and *them there,* are dialectal. They are redundant expressions and should be avoided in editorial English (*This* [not *This here*] dog is good on coons; *that* [not *that there*] one is good on birds).

That, This

Despite considerable academic resistance, *this* and *that* have won a place in editorial English to refer to a preceding clause or sentence without being accompanied by either a specific antecedent, a summarizing noun, or a noun phrase, as in the following sentences:

She never looked a person straight in the eye, and *this* always bothered me.

The dry summers of the Ukraine have caused three successive wheat failures, but *that* is Russia's problem.

Since many persons still object to this usage, it is probably wise to employ a summarizing noun wherever possible with *this* or *that,* just as has been done in the first clause of this sentence. Similarly, the two sample sentences above would probably be improved by the insertion of *mannerism* after *this* and *difficulty* after *that.*

Accompaniment by a summarizing noun or noun phrase is particularly important when *this* or *that* is used for transition between two paragraphs. Otherwise the force of the transition is lost upon the reader, who is likely to respond only vaguely to the single transitional word.

That, This (adverbs)

For five centuries *that* and *this* have been used as adverbs meaning "to that (or this) degree" (No woman is worth *that* much; No university can be *this* great without a dedicated faculty). The usage is accepted in editorial English.

That, Which, Who

See **Relative Pronoun,** p. 177.

Then, Than

These two words are sometimes confused in written English because they have a similar pronunciation. *Then* is an adverb referring to time (The children opened their presents, and *then* bedlam reigned); *than* is a conjunction used with comparisons or contrasts (Erik was a better skier *than* Garth).

There is, There are

These two expressions serve to delay the appearance of the subject in a sentence (see **Anticipatory Subject,** p. 113). When the real subject is singular, *there is* is regularly used (*There is* a good movie at the Orpheum). When it is plural, *there are* is used (*There are* three cars in the driveway). However, when the real subject is compound, the first member being singular, *there is* appears much more frequently than the more logical *there are* (*There is* a restaurant and a gas station in the next town). When the first member of the compound subject is plural, *there are* is the appropriate form (*There are* two restaurants and a gas station in the next town).

There or *there is* (*are*) can often be eliminated with no loss of meaning to the sentence; in fact, the sentence is usually improved by their elimination.

There are too many businessmen who use jargon. Improved: Too many businessmen use jargon.

There is a new book by C. P. Snow at the library. Improved: A new book by C. P. Snow is at the library.

They

In colloquial English *they* has long been used as an indefinite pronoun (*They* raise a lot of cattle in Wyoming). This usage occurs frequently in informal and occasionally in formal editorial English. Many style manuals object to the use of indefinite *they* and suggest the substitution of a more specific word.

> *They* make fine watches in Switzerland. Improved: The Swiss make fine watches.

This
See **That, This,** p. 53.

This here
See **That there, This here,** p. 53.

Those, These, Them
In both written and spoken English, the standard forms of the demonstrative are *these* and *those* (*These* skates are mine, *those* are yours). *Them* is used as a demonstrative by uneducated speakers (*Them* apples were good), but it is avoided in editorial English.

Though
See **Although, Though,** p. 7.

Threw, Thrown, Throwed
Threw and *thrown* are the only acceptable written forms for the past tense and the past participle, respectively, of the verb *throw*. The dialect variant *throwed* occurs only in the speech of the illiterate or little educated.

Till, Until
These two words have the same meaning and are both acceptable in editorial English. *Until* appears more often at the beginning of a sentence (*Until* he had graduated, he did not choose a career), while *till* is more common within a sentence (He did not choose a career *till* he had graduated). *Until* tends to be preferred in formal editorial English.

Too
In the sense of "also," *too* is usually set off by commas when it appears at the beginning or within a sentence (I, *too,* have been to the Ludlow Fair). More often than not, particularly in informal writing, the comma is omitted when *too* ends the sentence (I have been there *too*).

Toward, Towards
Either form is acceptable in editorial English. *Toward* appears more commonly in the United States; *towards* is preferred in England.

Try to, Try and
The colloquial substitution of *try and* for *try to* (*Try and* catch some

fish for dinner) appears occasionally in informal writing, particularly in dialogue, but it is rarely found in editorial English, in which *try to* is preferred (*Try to* catch some fish).

TV

See **Video, TV,** below.

Type, Type of

In recent years *type* plus a noun (new *type* aircraft, quiet *type* neighborhood) has gained in frequency, though *type of* plus noun (new *type of* aircraft, quiet *type of* neighborhood) is still preferred in formal editorial English. The use of hyphenated adjectives with *type* in business English (*electric-type* toothbrush, *automatic-type* elevator) is frowned upon by style manuals because -*type* is redundant.

Uninterested

See **Disinterested, Uninterested,** p. 20.

Unique

Some persons argue that *unique* is an absolute adjective, one that is incapable of being compared because it means "unequaled" or "without another like it." However, like many other absolute adjectives (a more *perfect* union, the most *complete* index, the *straight*est line), *unique* has lost some of its original force, and it is now regularly used with the meaning "unusual." As a result, the construction *unique* preceded by a qualifying word (*more, most, nearly, almost,* etc.) appears frequently in editorial English.

Until

See **Till, Until,** p. 55.

Verbal

See **Oral, Verbal,** p. 43.

Very

Some grammarians argue that the intensifier *very* can modify only a quality (*very sad, very bright*); therefore, it cannot modify a past participle, which involves an action (*very disturbed, very pleased*). One might return the argument on etymological grounds: *very* developed from the meaning "true" (Thou are the *very* God), and an action has just as much right to be true as a quality. Disregarding pedantry, however, the construction *very* plus a past participle appears frequently in editorial English.

Video, TV

Both forms have gained wide currency in editorial English (a *video* tape, the *TV* industry). Formal editorial English, however, usually avoids *TV* in favor of the unabbreviated word (the *television* industry).

Wait for, Wait on

The substitution of *wait on* in place of *wait for* (Don't *wait on* me later than ten o'clock) is a dialectal feature which is avoided in editorial English. *Wait on* is a standard construction with reference to "service" (Marty found a clerk to *wait on* his wife).

Want

The verb form is rarely used today in its original meaning "to lack" (Milton *wanted* a sense of humor). The accepted pattern is *want* plus an infinitive (I *want* you *to go* home). The dialectal variants *want for* plus an infinitive (I *want for* you *to go* home) and *want that* plus *should* (I *want that* you *should* go home) are avoided in editorial English. *Want* with the meaning "should" or "ought" (You *want* to visit Old Faithful while you're in Yellowstone Park) is a colloquial construction, though it sometimes occurs in informal writing.

Want in, Want out, Want off

These elliptical constructions are dialectal features in Eastern and North Central United States (China *wants* [to get] *in* the United Nations; I *want* [to get] *out* of the game by ten o'clock; You will *want* [to get] *off* the bus at 45th Street). They are avoided in formal editorial English.

Way, Away

Way in place of *away* is well established in American speech (The problem was *way* too tough; She swam *way* out from shore; The stock market went *way* up in November). The usage occurs occasionally in informal, though not in formal, editorial English.

Way, Ways

Used as an adverb to indicate distance, *ways* is an informal or dialectal substitute for *way,* which is the preferred from in editorial English (He works a long *way* [not *ways*] from his home).

Well

See **Good, Well,** p. 28.

Were (subjunctive)

See **Mood,** p. 153.

What all, Who all

These two constructions have wide colloquial dispersion, but they are particularly prevalent in the South. *All* added to *what* or *who* serves as an intensifier (He was charged with murder, rape, larceny, and I don't know *what all;* I have no idea *who all* will be at the party). Both idioms are avoided in formal editorial English.

What with

This idiom has long standing in the English language with the meanings "as a result of, in view of, in consequence of" (*What with* the dry summer we've had, the corn crop will not set a record). The idiom appears in informal editorial English, primarily with dialogue.

When, Is when

Though frowned upon by some style manuals, the construction *is when* occurs frequently in editorial English, particularly when an adverbial element is placed between *is* and *when* (It *is* only *when* we are deprived of freedom that we really know its value) and when the context could allow the substitution of *occurs* for *is* (The most heartrending scene in the entire opera *is* [or *occurs*] *when* Desdemona pleads for her life). In definitions *is when* is avoided on all levels of editorial English (A legal holiday *is when* the banks are closed). Such sentences must be rewritten entirely.

Where, Is where

Though disapproved by some style manuals, the construction *is where* occurs frequently in editorial English, particularly when an adverbial element is placed between *is* and *where* (It *is* only *where* people are free to vote that government is really democratic). In definitions *is where* is avoided on all levels of editorial English (A successful hunt *is where* everybody gets an elk). Such sentences must be rewritten entirely.

Where, That

Colloquial usage often substitutes *where* for *that* (I heard on the news *where* a storm is expected here tomorrow). This usage should be avoided in editorial English.

Whether

See **If, Whether,** p. 30.

While (conjunction)

In addition to its regular usage meaning "although" or "during the time when," *while* has gained wide acceptance in editorial English as a substitute for *whereas,* a connective expressing mild difference (Oregon winters are rainy, *while* the summers are very dry). In some sentence contexts the use of *while* can be ambiguous. In the following sentence, for example, one cannot be immediately certain whether it means "during the time when" or "although," one of which should be substituted for *while* in the interest of clarity (*While* he was a practicing physician, he favored socialized medicine).

Who all
See **What all, Who all,** p. 57.

Whose, Of which
The possessive pronoun *whose* is used regularly in editorial English with animate and inanimate nouns (Peaceful coexistence is the alternative *whose* consequences are less frightening). Some style manuals prefer *of which* to *whose* when the reference is to an inanimate noun; however, the usage *of which* often results in awkwardness. The sentence cited, for example, would have to read: Peaceful coexistence is the alternative, the consequences *of which* are less frightening.

Who, Whom
These two words cause a good deal of confusion for many writers. Technically, *who* is the subject form of the pronoun, *whom* the object form. *Whom,* therefore, should be used in the position of a direct object (He fired *whom?*), an indirect object (You gave *whom* the book?), or as the object of a preposition (You gave the book to *whom?*). However, when the interrogative pronoun appears, as it frequently does, at the beginning of a sentence, a position most often occupied by a subject word, *who* has won acceptance on all levels but formal editorial English (*Who* [formal: *whom*] did he fire? *Who* [formal: *To whom*] did you give the book to [formal: *to* shifted to initial position]?).

Some writers and speakers who are unsure of the distinction between the two words often substitute *whom* where *who* is the appropriate form in a mistaken effort to be "correct." This faulty substitution most often occurs when other words intervene between the interrogative or relative pronoun and its verb (*Who* [not *whom*] do you think would make a good chairman? The instructor gave passing grades to those students *who* [not *whom*] he believed were working to the limits of their ability). In the first of these two sentences the verb *would make* governs the pronoun *who;* in the second the verb *were working* governs it.

Whoever and *whomever* follow the same usage patterns as *who* and *whom*.

Will
See **Shall, Will,** p. 48.

-wise

See **Adverb**, p. 108.

Without, Unless

Without is frequently substituted for *unless* in the dialectal speech of a few Southern and Midland areas. The usage should be avoided in editorial English (I can't fail *unless* [not *without*] he fails).

Word Order

See p. 201.

Would of

See **Could of, Might of, Should of, Would of,** p. 18.

Xmas, Christmas

At one time X and Xt were used as common and perfectly acceptable abbreviations for Christ. This usage survives only in *Xmas*, which has been generally relegated to commercial and extremely informal situations. Formal editorial English requires *Christmas*.

You, One

Informal editorial English, both written and spoken, employs *you* as an indefinite pronoun, particularly to express a principle or to speak of people in general (Whether or not *you* like the system, *you* have to live with it). This usage is gaining favor even in editorial English, though *one* is still preferred (Great tragedy makes *one* [or *you*] forget petty vexations). *You* should never be used as an indefinite pronoun when the context does not clearly distinguish it from the personal pronoun. The result might otherwise be insulting (A further question is obvious: how can *one* [not *you*] handle an alcoholic wife?). In speech third person singular pronouns (*he, his, him, she, her*) regularly refer to *one* in order to avoid stilted repetition. Sometimes the *one* is eliminated altogether by the substitution of another impersonal construction (*One* [or *A person*] must be tactful if *he* [rather than *one*] wishes to achieve *his* [rather than *one's*] goals). In formal editorial English, however, the alternative expression *one . . . one* appears much more often.

Though mathematicians might argue the logic of plural *ones*, the usage is fully acceptable as an indefinite pronoun (The only women that bother me are the young *ones*).

2

CONVENTIONS
OF
EDITORIAL
ENGLISH

Good written English requires the mastery of certain conventions of expression. The following glossary of terms is a guide to accepted practices in abbreviation, capitalization, format, and punctuation. The norms in every instance have been the conventions widely followed by publishers of editorial English. We have included alternate practices wherever they are in accepted usage.

Abbreviations

Abbreviations appear more commonly in informal English than in editorial English. The following discussions deal with the conventions governing their use:

(1) *Technical abbreviations*

Technical writing such as industrial and scientific reports often makes use of abbreviations which are so commonly used in the particular field that they have almost become part of its jargon. Since each field, and often each corporation, tends to manufacture its own set of abbreviations, the writer learns them only by cultivating a familiarity with the literature of the particular field. Similarly, the footnotes and bibliographies of research papers make use of many abbreviations (e.g., ibid., *op cit.,* pp., chap., vol.). The use of these abbreviations varies somewhat from field to field and from one style sheet to another. Students writing research papers will usually be told by their professors which style sheet to follow; persons writing for publication should determine the form used by the journal in which they intend to publish their work. This glossary describes a common form for footnoting under the entry **Footnote Form,** p. 84.

(2) *Common abbreviations*

Some words are far more often abbreviated than not. Among them are the following:

Ph.D., M.A., B.A., B.S., and abbreviations of other academic degrees;
B.C. and A.D., used with specific dates (see pp. 4, 12);
Mr., Mrs., Dr., Jr., used with proper names;
H_2O, NaOH, $MgSO_4$, and the formulas of other chemical elements;
e.g. (for *exempli gratia,* for example), i.e. (for *id est,* that is), cf. (for *confer,* compare), etc. (for *et cetera,* and so on), and other common abbreviations from the Latin;
yd., ft., gal., qt., bbl., km., and other units of measure when accompanied by a number;

St., Ave., Blvd., Rd., used after an address.

In editorial English some titles (e.g., President, Senator, Governor, Reverend) appear as full words when they are followed by only the surname, yet they are often abbreviated when they are followed by initials or given names.

Reverend Kolburger (or) Rev. James R. Kolburger
Senator Smith (or) Sen. Margaret Chase Smith

(3) *Uncommon abbreviations*

Most American dictionaries have two separate sets of abbreviations. One lists the technical abbreviations used in the work; the other lists common abbreviations in current American English. It is a good rule of thumb generally to avoid uncommon abbreviations on all levels of usage. In those rare instances which require their use for the sake of naked economy, you should employ the full word or title the first time you use it, then abbreviate it in subsequent uses. If there are many such uncommon abbreviations used, supply the reader with a list of them.

(4) *Pronounceable abbreviations*

Some abbreviations, particularly of organizations, can be easily pronounced as written (NATO, UNESCO, AMVETS). Such abbreviations tend to be used so frequently as words that the periods are omitted. In fact, most persons even forget what the initials stand for.

(5) *Periods with abbreviations*

Most abbreviations are followed by a period in editorial English, with the following exceptions:

(*a*) Abbreviations of compound names of international organizations (UN, METO); government agencies (TVA, USIA, CIA); well-known unions, clubs, fraternal orders (AFL, CIO, KKK, LOOM) appear without periods.

(*b*) A few publishers and business firms, mainly British, omit the period after Dr, Mrs, Mr, and other abbreviations which end with the last letter of the abbreviated word.

(*c*) In popular and informal usage the period is omitted after the shortened forms of some words (*exam* for *examination, math* for *mathematics, home ec* for *home economics, gas* for *gasoline*). Such words, however, occur rarely in editorial English.

(*d*) Symbols for chemical elements are not followed by periods (H_2O, U 235).

(*e*) While the period is required after initials in lowercase letters (t.b., i.e., e.g.), usage in informal English is divided when uppercase letters are used (I.Q. or IQ, A.D. or AD).

(*f*) The abbreviation TV has become so common as both noun and adjective that it always appears without a period.

Apostrophe (')

The *apostrophe* is used in the following situations:

(1) To indicate possession in nouns and indefinite pronouns (the girl's coat, the girls' coats, somebody's coat). The apostrophe is also used with time modifiers (a month's vacation, a year's study). The apostrophe is usually omitted, however, in adjective-noun combinations which are names of places or organizations (Mens Lounge, Veterans Administration, Mississippi Nurses Association). Editorial practice differs in forming the possessive of proper nouns ending in *s* (Davis' [or Davis's] best paintings were done in 1958). The unbracketed form is becoming the more common.

Many stylebooks observe that the possessive of inanimate nouns should be expressed by means of the *of*-phrase rather than *'s* (the color *of the house*, the size *of the firm*, the nature *of love*). While this observation holds true for many types of inanimate nouns, it is by no means applicable to all. Certain inanimate nouns regularly take the possessive form *'s* (a *dollar's* worth, the *bank's* error, the *nation's* youngest Senator, *Ford's* new models, his *heart's* content). Though there seems to be no systematic pattern to the use of the form *'s,* it frequently occurs with inanimate nouns that name a product or an organization (*Westinghouse's* stockholders, *Lifebuoy's* fragrance), a country (*France's* nuclear force), a personified abstraction (*evening's* glow, *beauty's* perfection), and a unit of time (a hard *day's* work, a *year's* time).

(2) To form contractions (I'll, ain't, don't, isn't) and to indicate omitted sounds of informal dialogue (A couple o' fellows were makin' trouble).

(3) To form the plurals of letters, numbers, symbols, and words used as words rather than for their meaning (four *D's*, three *g's*, two *five's*, five *86's*, several *+'s*, no *if's* or *but's*). This practice is beginning to decline, however, particularly in scientific writing.

Asterisk (*)

A mark sometimes used in place of footnote numerals to refer the reader to a source identification or an explanatory footnote. Once widely used, the *asterisk* is now used only in less formal papers which make only a very few source identifications. Another use of the asterisk occurs in linguistics, where it serves to identify hypothetical or reconstructed words. Thus, the asterisk would be required in the citation of any word from Indo-European, a language of which no records remain and which is known to us only through reconstructions made by comparative linguists.

Bibliography

A list of books, pamphlets, and articles from magazines and newspapers used in connection with a formal research or reference paper. In the process of doing such a paper, the student actually compiles two separate bibliographies, each of which is discussed below.

(1) *Bibliography cards* are made during the initial stage of research, and they constitute a working bibliography. Each time the researcher locates a source which might be of some value to his particular project, he lists the important information concerning it on a 3- by 5- or 4- by 6-inch card according to the following regular patterns:

824
M614m ————————————→ Library call number

Meynell, Esther ————————→ Author's name, inverted
Portrait of William Morris ——→ Full title of book
London, 1947 ———————→ Publication facts
                                        Place
                                        Date

[pp 162-82 contain discussion of Morris']——→ Annotation to yourself
socialist work]   in brackets

Sample Bibliography Card — Book

Goshko, John M.————————→ Author's name
"Doctors, Drugs, and the AMA"——→ Title of article
The Progressive, XXVIII————→ Publication facts
(December 1964), 31-35   Name of journal
                                            Volume number
                                            Date
                                            Pages of article

[Goshko is an editor for the ——→ Annotation to yourself
Washington Post]   in brackets

Sample Bibliography Card — Magazine Article

"Nixon Seeks Party Unity" —————→ **Author's name if by-line is given**

→ **Headline title**

New York Times, December 20, 1964, —→ **Publication facts**
sec. III, p. 4, col. 3

- Name of newspaper
- Date
- Section
- Page
- Column

[discusses recent meeting with Governor Romney] —→ **Annotation to yourself in brackets**

Sample Bibliography Card — Newspaper Article

"Goldsmith, Oliver" —————→ **Title**

Encyclopedia Britannica, —————→ **Publication facts**
14th ed., X, 494-98

- Name of reference
- Edition
- Volume number
- Pages

Sample Bibliography Card — Reference Source

The researcher should as a rule of thumb include any additional information which might be important. The following list includes commonly occurring items of information which should be cited on bibliography cards:

(*a*) *Edited works:* When the work of a particular author is edited by another, an additional line should be inserted under the title of the book.

ed. Samuel B. Larsen

When an editor has collected the works of many others, as in an anthology of seventeenth-century poetry, the editor's name appears above the title of the book.

Larsen, Samuel B., ed.

(*b*) *Translated works:* The translator's name should be identified in a line under the title of the book.

trans. Joseph M. Tanner

(*c*) *Important introductions:* If an important person has written the introduction to a book, his name should appear on a separate line under the title of the book.

introd. by G. B. Shaw

(*d*) *Institutional or organizational authorship:* Some books and many pamphlets are issued without author identification. The name of the institution or organization should appear on the line above the title.

National Safety Council

(*e*) *Multiple authorship:* When a book has more than one author, only the first name appears inverted.

Jones, Charles G. and William Ellison

If a book has more than three authors, only the principal one need be listed; *et al.* or *and others* is used after the name.

Baugh, Albert C. et al.

(*f*) *Multiple volumes:* This information should be inserted immediately before the place of publication (26 vols.).

(2) The *final bibliography* generally appears on a separate page at the end of the finished paper, and it contains a list of those references which have actually been cited. For each item listed on the bibliography page there should be at least one footnote or textual reference somewhere in the paper. Except with very long studies such as doctoral dissertations, where the references are often separated into special categories, all bibliographic items are arranged alphabetically according to the last name of the author, or, if the source is anonymous, according to the first significant word (disregarding *a, an, the*) of the title.

There are various forms which may be employed on the bibliography page; however, one of the most common is that recommended by the Modern Language Association. The following items are recorded in the MLA form:

Goshko, John M. "Doctors, Drugs, and the AMA," *The Progressive,* XXVIII (December 1964), 31–35.

Meynell, Esther. *Portrait of William Morris.* London, 1947.

Morris, William. *The Collected Works of William Morris.* ed. May Morris. 24 vols. London, 1910–1915.

"Nixon Seeks Party Unity," New York *Times,* December 20, 1964. Sec. III, p. 4, col. 3.

Strange, G. Robert, and Walter E. Houghton, eds. *Victorian Poetry and Poetics.* Boston, 1959.

Brackets [ ]

Brackets are seldom found except in legal documents and in scholarly writing, where they have three standard uses:

(1) To set off parenthetical material inserted within other parenthetical material.

> The two plaintiffs (Meredith Samuels [née Willard] and William Cooper) filed suit for damages resulting from the aforesaid accident.

(2) To make corrections or to supply additional information within a quotation.

> "Mansfield's parents had emigrated to New Zeeland [*sic*] early in 1893 [actually in December, 1892] to start a new life."
> "Shelley's elegiac tribute [*Adonais*] was written four months after Keats died [in February, 1821] of consumption."

(3) To designate phonetic transcription.

Business Letters

While the exact form for business letters often differs from one organization to another, the following conventions are generally observed.

(1) *The envelope*

(*a*) *The address* on almost all typewritten correspondence appears in blocked form with open punctuation.

> Albert E. Taylor, Manager
> Intermountain Freight Lines
> 3755 South Bowman Avenue
> Denver, Colorado 61394

Closed punctuation (a comma at the end of each line except the last, which is followed by a period) is no longer common. Nor, except for hand-addressed envelopes, does one often find indented form (each successive line indented to the right). Letters written to an organization are sometimes directed to the attention of a particular person within the organization by placing the words

> ATTENTION: Albert E. Taylor

to the left and slightly below the main address.

(*b*) *The return address* appears on the upper left hand corner of the envelope in the same form used for the address. When letterhead envelopes are used, the sender's name is usually typed above the printed letterhead.

(c) Sample Envelopes:

```
Lawrence Rice
926 Center Street
Chico, California 39261


                              Albert E. Taylor, Manager
                              Intermountain Freight Lines
                              3755 South Bowman Avenue
                              Denver, Colorado 61394

```

```
Lawrence Rice
926 Center Street
Chico, California 39261


                              Intermountain Freight Lines
                              3755 South Bowman Avenue
                              Denver, Colorado 61394
         ATTENTION: Albert Taylor

```

(2) The letter

(a) The heading, since most business correspondence is written on letterhead stationery, is usually printed. Only the date needs to be added, and it is ordinarily placed against the right margin or centered underneath the printed name and address. If plain stationery is used, the writer's address and the date appear at the right margin, usually in blocked form and open punctuation.

> 626 East Park Lane
> Denver, Colorado
> December 8, 1966

(b) The inside address always appears at the left margin. Personal identifications (Dr., Professor, Mr., Mrs., Miss, Messrs.) precede the name of the addressee, but they are usually omitted if the name is followed by a title or position (Sales Manager, Treasurer, Dean, Chairman, Executive Secretary, etc.). Blocked form with open punc-

tuation is most commonly used, and zip code numbers should be omitted on the inside address.

Dr. Allan Linder		Allan Linder, Chairman
Department of Zoology		Department of Zoology
Idaho State University	(or)	Idaho State University
Pocatello, Idaho		Pocatello, Idaho

(*c*) *The salutation* also appears at the left margin and is separated from the inside address by one line of space. In business correspondence a colon regularly follows the name of the specific addressee (Dear Dr. Linder:). When the writer does not know the name of a specific person to whom the letter should be addressed, *Dear Sir:* or *Dear Madam:* (when the writer is certain that the addressee is a woman) should be used.

(*d*) *The body* of business letters is most commonly single-spaced. Paragraphs are separated by an extra line of space, and they often appear in block form (i.e., without indentation). A clear, accurate, and direct style characterizes effective business correspondence.

(*e*) *The complimentary close* usually appears at the right margin. It is separated from the body of the letter by a line of space and is always followed by a comma. This list contains those most commonly used:

Cordially yours,	Yours respectfully,
Respectfully yours,	Yours sincerely,
Sincerely yours,	Yours truly,
Very truly yours,	Yours very truly,

(*f*) *The signature* in ink or ball-point pen appears in the four-line space between the complimentary close and the typewritten name of the writer.

(*g*) *The initials,* usually in lowercase letters, of the person sending the letter and the typist, usually in lowercase letters and separated by a colon, appear against the left margin below the signature identification.

(*h*) *Enclosures* should be indicated below the initials at the left margin. When carbon copies of the letter are sent to other persons, the abbreviation *cc* should appear at left margin, followed by a colon and the name of the person(s) to whom copies are sent.

(*i*) *Sample business letter* employing blocked form and open punctuation:

2218 Cooper Lane
Cedar City, Minnesota
April 24, 1966

Charles G. Fermor, Director
Idaho Fish and Game Department
Suite 16, Capitol Building
Boise, Idaho

Dear Mr. Fermor:

The Director of Student Placement here at the University of
Minnesota has informed me of the position which your department
wishes to fill. Because experience and academic training prepare
me for wildlife management work, I wish to become an applicant.

I am presently a senior in the School of Forestry and will graduate
with a major in Wildlife Conservation on June 7, after which date
I will be immediately available for employment. As requested in
your advertisement of the position, I have asked that my academic
transcript be sent to you immediately.

I am twenty-five years old, am a veteran of three years in the
U.S. Navy, am married, and have two children. During the last
two summers I have worked for the Minnesota Department of
Conservation, Game Management Division. Mr. James Mentor, the
director of that division, is writing you concerning my work
in the field; and Professor Nevin Chambers, Department of Wildlife
Conservation, University of Minnesota, has agreed to write
concerning my work as a student.

Final examinations will take place between May 24 and June 2.
Otherwise I will be available for examination and interview
at your convenience. Meanwhile, I shall be pleased to furnish
any additional information you may request.

Respectfully yours,

John P. Merriam

John P. Merriam

jpm:fp

Capitalization

The following discussions deal with the use of capital letters in editorial English:

(1) *Sentence capitals.* The first word in a sentence should be
capitalized. Likewise, the first word of a direct quotation is capitalized,
but only if it is the first word of a complete sentence.

The instructor said, "These themes are the best of the semester."
"These themes," said the instructor, "are the best of the semester."
The instructor said that our themes were "the best of the semester."

A complete sentence inserted parenthetically within another sentence is usually not capitalized when its purpose is to add additional information about something in the main sentence which surrounds it.

Thomas Carlyle's collected letters (a scholarly edition is being prepared) provide a panoramic view of Victorian intellectual currents.

A parenthetically inserted sentence, however, is often capitalized when its purpose is to exemplify something stated in the main sentence which surrounds or introduces it.

Some persons have been so fear-stricken by the prejudice against *you and me* in subject position (You and me should go to the dance) that they substitute *between you and I* for the perfectly correct *between you and me.*

(2) *Proper nouns and adjectives.* These forms, even when abbreviated, are regularly capitalized.

Though Jim had been raised in the East, he found the scenery around Cal Tech much to his liking.

The Castro beard has become the symbol of Cuban independence.

The police have closed Riverside Drive until the Payette River has subsided.

(3) *Pronoun I.* *I* is always capitalized regardless of its position in the sentence.

(4) *Titles of articles, books, poems, essays, plays, etc.* Regular practice is to capitalize the first word; the last word, and all other words within the title except articles, conjunctions, and prepositions with fewer than five letters.

Of Human Bondage	*I Will Fight No More Forever*
Lord of the Flies	*The Egg and I*
A World Without End	*Rime of the Ancient Mariner*

(5) *Lines of verse.* Until recent years the first word in a line of verse was regularly capitalized. Some modern poets do not follow this practice.

(6) *References to Deity.* Nouns referring to a deity (e.g., *God, Savior, Lord, Holy Spirit, Bodhisattva, Allah, Aesir*) are regularly

capitalized. Pronouns referring to a deity are usually, though not always, capitalized.

> The women gave thanks to God for His (or *his*) munificence.

(7) *Names and titles of individuals.* Used with reference to the highest office in the Federal government, the word *President* is always capitalized. Similarly, the titles of other important persons (e.g., *Secretary of the Treasury, Chief Justice, Senator*) are capitalized. The titles of other responsible positions should be capitalized only when the reference to a particular person is obvious.

> The *Secretary of State* called a news conference after his talk with the President.

> It is unlikely that another governor could gain the widespread support that Governor Romney has attracted.

Mother, father, brother, aunt, uncle, and other names of family relationship are often capitalized in informal letters, though not in editorial English.

> Wordsworth's mother died while he was very young.

In direct address, however, names of personal relationships are capitalized (Please come here, Dad).

(8) *Stylistic capitals.* Some professional writers employ capitals for emphasis, particularly when they use personification.

> We speak of the Volume of Nature,—and truly a Volume
> it is,—whose Author and Writer is God. To read it! Dost
> thou, does man, so much as well know the Alphabet there-
> of? (Thomas Carlyle, *Sartor Resartus.*)

Conversely, some modern novelists, particularly when they are attempting to describe the chaotic stream of consciousness (see p. 231), deliberately violate some or all of the regular conventions governing capitalization.

Colon (:)

A mark of punctuation which directs attention to that which follows it. Current editorial practice establishes its use in the following situations:

(1) To precede a series of enumerated items. The *colon* at the end of the second sentence above illustrates this usage. Each of the six items which follow it refers back to the introductory sentence.

(2) To precede a series which has been introduced by a complete statement. The introductory statement usually contains the words *following* or *as follows*.

> The following students should board the Greyhound bus in front of the Student Union at noon Friday: Helen Schatz,

Austin Patty, Clarence Sloat, Sam Baskett, William Baker, Eugene Dawson, Maxine Gauthier.

(3) To introduce lengthy examples or quotations in editorial English.

On September 17, 1787, Benjamin Franklin summarized his attitude toward the Constitution which his small audience had prepared: "I doubt whether any other Convention we can obtain, may be able to make a better Constitution. For when you assemble a number of men to have the advantage of their joint wisdom, you inevitably assemble with those men, all their prejudices, their passions, their errors of opinion, their local interests, and their selfish views. From such an Assembly can a perfect production be expected?"

(4) To precede an independent clause which has been directly introduced by another independent clause.

There is one maxim that many fraternity boys do not know: a girl in the bush is worth two on the quad.

(5) To separate hours and minutes (My train leaves at 4:55 p.m.).

(6) To follow the salutation of a business or formal letter (Dear Senator Church: Dear Sir:). The salutation of an informal letter is usually followed by a comma or dash.

Comma (,)

The *comma* is the most used as well as the most versatile mark of punctuation. Many of its routine or arbitrary uses, which generally offer little difficulty to the writer, are listed under *routine uses* below. Its other uses, all of which separate major sentence elements, are discussed individually.

(1) *Routine uses*

(a) *Dates:* To separate the year from the rest of a date (May 21, 1965). Usage is divided when the day does not appear, but it is becoming more common to omit the comma (May 1965). If the entire date appears within a sentence, the year is followed by a comma.

November 22, 1963, is the date on which President Kennedy was assassinated.

When the year stands alone or when it is used as an adjective, no comma is used.

The 1964 Winter Olympic Games were dominated by Russia.
I cannot think of 1937 without getting nostalgic.

(b) *Places:* To separate successively larger geographical identifications.

Boise, Idaho	Vancouver, British Columbia, Canada
Paris, France	Salt Lake City, Utah, United States
First Ward, Chicago	Dixon County, Tennessee

When the location consists of two elements and appears within a sentence, the last element is followed by a comma.

I attended a meeting in Omaha, Nebraska, last winter.

Paris, France, has many art galleries.

When the location has only one element, no comma is used.

I attended a meeting in Nebraska last winter.

France has many art galleries.

(*c*) *Numerals:* To separate all numbers except those used for purposes of identification (street numbers, years, telephone numbers, code and serial numbers) into groups of three, starting from the right (4,594,448,783).

(*d*) *Inverted names:* To separate the surname from the given name when they have been inverted (Hamilton, Alexander).

(*e*) *Titles and degrees:* To separate a name from a title or degree which follows it.

Jacques Barzun, Ph.D.	James Allworthy, Esq.
Chester Nimitz, USN Ret.	Robert Smylie, LL.D.
Franklin Roosevelt, Jr.	Martin Nurmi, Sr.

(*f*) *Letters:* To follow the salutation (personal letters only) and the complimentary close.

Dear Jim,　Dear Sally,　Yours truly,　Respectfully yours,

(2) *Between clauses*

(*a*) To separate two independent clauses joined by a coordinating conjunction (and, but, or, nor, for) or by a short connective (still, yet, so, then).

I didn't know a single answer, *and* Sally didn't help me.

The car may have been old, *but* Jim wanted to buy it.

The lawyer presented the evidence carefully, *yet* the jury could not decide on a verdict.

When the clauses are short and have the same subject, the comma is generally omitted before *and, or,* or *nor.*

She put up her hair *and* she went to bed.

(*b*) To separate an introductory adverbial clause from the independent clause which follows it. This very common sentence pattern is usually signaled by the appearance of *when, if, while, since, after, as,* or other common subordinating conjunctions as the first word of the sentence.

After our skis had been waxed thoroughly, we rode the chair lift to the top of the mountain.

If the rain stops before noon, we can go ahead with our plans.

When the adverbial clause is short and has the same subject as the independent clause which follows, the comma is generally omitted.

If you try you will succeed.

(3) *Between a phrase and a clause*

(*a*) To separate a long prepositional phrase from an independent clause which follows it.

With the cooperation of faculty members and the staff of the registrar's office, all students were registered within a single day.

Short prepositional phrases are not separated from the following clause unless a momentary misreading might otherwise result.

In hitting, Mickey Mantle leads the team.

(*b*) To separate a verbal phrase from an independent clause which follows it.

Arguing in his most eloquent style, Senator Dirksen persuaded his colleagues to pass the bill.

To measure the academic potential of the freshman class, the university requires all new students to take entrance examinations.

(4) *Nonrestrictive modifiers*

To set off nonrestrictive (nonessential) modifiers (see **Restrictive and Nonrestrictive Modifiers,** p. 177).

President Johnson, *who wore a grey suit for the ceremony,* appeared to be very tired.

At exactly midnight last night, *when all sensible persons were in bed,* he came into the room singing a bawdy song.

Barbara wanted me to meet her father, *who had just come home from work.*

The italicized modifiers in the above three sentences simply furnish the reader with additional information about President Johnson, last midnight, or Barbara's father. Since they do not limit or restrict an identification which has already been made, they are called nonrestrictive modifiers. Conversely, restrictive modifiers provide information necessary for the identification of the person or thing modified, and they are not set off from the rest of the sentence.

Horses *which have no teeth* are generally very old.

The air *after a spring thunderstorm* is always fresh.

The man *who is sitting on the second barstool from the left* became our dean last year.

Occasionally, depending upon the writer's intended meaning, a modifier could be either restrictive or nonrestrictive.

RESTRICTIVE: Our relatives *who live in Nebraska* are Republicans. [Only the Nebraska relatives are Republicans.]

NONRESTRICTIVE: Our relatives, *who live in Nebraska,* are Republicans. [All our relatives are Nebraskans; all are Republicans.]

RESTRICTIVE: Sorority parties *which do not allow drinking* bore me. [Some sorority parties allow drinking, others do not. The latter are boring.]

NONRESTRICTIVE: Sorority parties, *which do not allow drinking,* bore me. [All sorority parties are boring. Incidentally, none of them allow drinking.]

(5) *Between items in a series*

(*a*) To separate three or more coordinate words.

The government supports the price of *wheat, barley,* and *oats.* [nouns]

An outdoorsman will *hike, fish,* and *explore* during the summer. [verbs]

The *old, worn,* and *battered* car chugged down the highway. [adjectives]

Slowly, quietly, and *gracefully* she walked into the room. [adverbs]

(*b*) To separate three or more coordinate phrases.

The navy operates *on the land, in the air,* and *over the water.* [prepositional phrases]

Jane *will work, will play,* or *will loaf* with equal enjoyment. [verb phrases]

(*c*) To separate three or more short clauses in parallel relationship.

The men shouted, the women screamed, and *the children cried.* [independent clauses]

Defeat is not disgrace *if you have followed the rules, if you have played your best,* and *if you have maintained your dignity.* [dependent clauses]

(*d*) To separate modifiers not connected by *and* when they independently modify the same headword.

He ran *swiftly, gracefully.*

I skied recklessly down the *steep, wooded* slope.

Writers who have difficulty determining whether two modifiers do indeed modify the same noun independently should apply the following test: if an *and* could be inserted between them or if they could be transposed without a distortion of meaning, they modify the noun independently and should be separated by a comma.

He tracked the elk throughout the brisk autumn morning. [No

comma; *brisk* modifies the expression *autumn morning*. The two modifiers could not be transposed, nor could *and* be inserted between them.]

He was glad to get back to the *warm, comfortable* cabin. [Comma belongs; the cabin was both *warm* and *comfortable*. The two modifiers could be interchanged without distortion of meaning.]

(*e*) When two coordinate words or phrases are connected by *and*, they are not separated by a comma.

The man's face was *wrinkled and leathery*.

The boy ran *through the yard and into the street*.

(6) *Sentence modifiers*

To set off a sentence modifier from the remainder of the sentence. A word or phrase is a sentence modifier when it modifies the complete sentence rather than merely one element of it. Sentence modifiers generally fall into one of the following categories:

(*a*) Answers to questions (*yes, no*).

Yes, I will loan you five dollars.

(*b*) Mild interjections (*oh, well, of course*).

Well, we had better get our hats and go home.

(*c*) Transitional words and phrases (*consequently, hence, furthermore, however, indeed, moreover, nevertheless, obviously, on the contrary, conversely*).

Obviously, no student can be employed full time and do his best work in school.

He memorized his lines perfectly; his performance, *nevertheless,* was uninspired.

(*d*) Exemplifying words or phrases (*for example, for instance, that is, on the one hand, in the first place, first, namely, finally*).

The necessity of tolerating an increased noise level, *for example,* is one of the costs of modern civilization.

Finally, we must never forget to keep trying.

(7) *Direct address*

To set off words used in direct address from the remainder of the sentence.

Darling, how would you like to go out for dinner tonight?

You might as well know, *James,* that you are not going to pass this course.

Please try to understand my problem, *Professor Snarf.*

(8) *Parenthetical elements*

(*a*) To set off appositives from the remainder of the sentence.

Jim Dawson, *our great quarterback,* failed three courses.

I dined on ravioli, *my favorite Italian dish.*

(*b*) To set off a parenthetical word or phrase which interrupts the sentence's normal rhythm (*indeed, incidentally, of course, to be sure, oddly enough, to tell the truth*).

Small newspapers, *of course,* cannot afford foreign correspondents.

Her shoes, *incidentally,* were purchased in Chicago.

The boy's father, *oddly enough,* had never attended college.

(*c*) To set off modifiers which follow their headword.

The skater, *tired but undaunted,* sped around the final turn.

The dogs, *nervous and restless,* could hardly wait to begin hunting.

The old house, *ravaged by time,* was to be torn down.

(9) *Absolute phrases*

To set off an absolute phrase (a noun or pronoun plus a participle) from the remainder of the sentence.

The deer having bounded over the ridge, I lowered my rifle.

He dated my girlfriend, *his own being out of town.*

(10) *Omission*

To indicate the place of omission in an elliptical construction.

The Ford required four gallons of gasoline to go ninety miles; the Volkswagen, [required] only three.

A rifle is used for elk; a shotgun, [is used] for pheasants.

(11) *Contrast*

To set off a contrasting coordinate element from the remainder of the sentence.

Carol's clothing was *tasteful,* though not *expensive.*

The car was *small,* yet *comfortable.*

Native genius, not *acquired learning,* makes a great poet.

(12) *Direct quotations*

To set off from a direct quotation that portion of the sentence which identifies the speaker or writer.

"The only thing we have to fear," *Roosevelt said,* "is fear itself."

Hannah wrote, "I will see you at the dance next Saturday."

"Evil men will spend eternity in hell," *the preacher thundered.*

When a question mark or an exclamation point appears at the end of a direct quotation, the comma is omitted.

"Do you want to go pheasant hunting?" he asked.

"Don't you dare try to kiss me!" the sorority girl screamed.

Course Names

The names of specific courses and departments in a college are always capitalized (The Department of Philosophy will offer Western Thought 151 at the same time that the Department of History is offering Introduction to Western Civilization). Academic subjects, however, are not capitalized unless they are the names of languages (The Evening College is offering courses in philosophy, geology, sociology, English, home economics, and German).

Dash (—)

Standard editorial practice establishes the use of the *dash* in the following situations:

(1) To indicate a shift in the thought process. Usually the first clause is unfinished and the sentence changes from a question to a statement or from a statement to a question.

> Why do you refuse to see my side of the—but I'm a fool to ask.
> I've tried, George, to earn your—but why should I carry on this way?

Often the thought itself, rather than the syntax of the sentence, is incongruous.

> Each year Dean Samson picked the instructor who was most popular with his students—then fired him!

(2) To set off a sentence element which summarizes, rephrases, or comments upon the previous ideas in the sentence.

> Champion Spark Plug's steady earnings progress was reversed in 1961 by the loss of its largest customer for original equipment—Ford, which acquired its own source of supply.
> Sun Valley offers a variety of ski slopes, a large skating rink, a heated swimming pool, and an exciting, informal night life—everything a winter sportsman needs.

(3) To set off a parenthetical expression when the writer wishes to retain between the parenthetical material and the rest of the sentence a closer, more intimate, or more emphatic relationship than parentheses would allow.

> Dickens' experience with poverty—he had known the debtor's prison at first hand—created in him an abiding sympathy for the unwashed poor of London's back alleys.
> In spite of his critics—and there were many—Thomas Jefferson has come to be recognized as one of our greatest statesmen.

(4) To set off the identification of a quotation when footnotes are not used.

> Time is but the stream I go a-fishing in. I drink at it, but while I drink I see the sandy bottom and detect how shallow it is. Its thin current slides away, but eternity remains.—Henry David Thoreau, *Walden*

Dates

The preferred form for recording complete dates in editorial English is in the order of month, date, and year.

July 18, 1967   (or)   7/18/67

The governmental pattern, however, is being used with increasing frequency (18 July 1967). Neither numerals nor abbreviations for months should appear in the body of a paper or letter (Columbus' discovery of the New World on *October 12, 1492* [not *10/12/92* or *Oct. 12, 1492*], opened a new era for man). Where abbreviations for months are used, usually on forms and letter headings, *September* is shortened to *Sept.; May, June,* and *July* are written in full; and all the other months are shortened to their first three letters. A.D. and B.C. are used with dates only in extremely formal situations. For the punctuation of dates, see **Comma,** p. 75.

Ditto Marks (")

Ditto marks should be avoided in all writing except lists and tabulations which repeat words in the same vertical position from one line to the next. They should never be used in bibliographies or footnotes.

Division of Words

In order to maintain a reasonably even right margin, writers are often forced to divide words at the end of a line. Good manuscript form requires that words be divided only between syllables (*Cro·a·tian, de·rac·i·nate, pis·ca·tol·o·gy*). Breaks between syllables are shown in all standard dictionaries. Monosyllabic words must never be divided, nor should words be divided if syllables of one or two letters would be isolated in the process (*a·byss, in·sist*).

Ellipsis (...)

A series of three spaced periods primarily used in the following situations:

(1) *With quotations.* The *ellipsis* indicates the omission of unessential material within a quotation.

ORIGINAL: "The interior of Brazil, which my wife and I have had the pleasure of visiting several times, is a bonanza of mineral wealth waiting to be exploited."

SHORTENED: "The interior of Brazil . . . is a bonanza of mineral wealth waiting to be exploited."

The ellipsis should never be used to change the essential meaning of the original quotation, as is done in the following example.

ORIGINAL: "I have always opposed those who attempt to present a distorted picture of inefficiency and dissatisfaction with Britain's nationalized medical program."

SHORTENED: "I have always opposed . . . Britain's nationalized medical program."

(2) *With interrupted or unfinished thought.* When writing dialogue, some authors employ three spaced periods (four when joined to the period ending the sentence) to indicate unfinished sentences or hesitating, slow-moving shifts of thought.

"Try to jump before the truck hits the . . . ." His words were lost in the terrible crash of metal.

Struggling for breath, he whispered, "There's no use trying to . . . I mean . . . just remember that . . . ." His head sank back on the pillow.

Exclamation Point (!)

The *exclamation point* is used to signal the emphatic nature of a word or statement. Appearing primarily in written dialogue, it is used sparingly in editorial English. An exclamation point may follow a word, a phrase, or a complete sentence.

Wow! What a fight. Gee whiz! What a fight. Wow, what a fight! When an exclamatory quotation is followed by the identification of the speaker, the exclamation point precedes the identification.

"Lower the boats!" shouted the captain above the howling gale.

Footnote

A *footnote* is a citation appearing at the bottom of a page or, in some instances, at the end of a paper to indicate the sources used or to amplify a point made in the text of the paper. Footnotes occur primarily in scholarly writing, and they serve the following purposes:

(1) To identify the exact source of direct quotations. Footnotes are omitted only when a quotation is known to all potential readers (e.g., the opening lines of the *Gettysburg Address,* a parable from the *Sermon on the Mount*) or when the text itself makes the identification (e.g., The opening line of *Mending Wall* illustrates Robert Frost's skill with inversion, "Something there is that doesn't love a wall").

(2) To identify the source of all facts, statistical or otherwise, which are unusual, controversial, or not generally known. The writer of a scholarly paper must, of course, decide which facts are to be footnoted. One would not, for example, need to identify a source for the statement that Pearl Harbor was bombed by the Japanese on December 7, 1941, a fact that is well known and is not disputed. One should, however, footnote the not generally known, and perhaps con-

troversial, fact that 55.2 percent of the Nigerian people worship Muhammed.

(3) To identify the source of opinions or judgments taken from published work, regardless of whether the opinion or judgment is quoted directly. That President Eisenhower was a conscious agent of the Communist conspiracy, for example, is not a known fact; it is simply the opinion of Mr. Robert Welsh, the founder of the John Birch Society. Such an opinion should be footnoted.

(4) To allow the writer to furnish relevant information, explanation, or commentary about something in the text of the paper, particularly when the additional material would distract from the smooth flow of ideas in the text. Such footnotes, however, appear sparingly.

Footnote Form

Different universities, textbooks, and publishers require slightly differing footnote forms. Yet the aim of a footnote is always the same: to tell the reader about the source or to give him additional information about a quotation, fact, or opinion appearing in the text. The system which follows corresponds to the widely accepted *MLA Style Sheet*.

(1) *Books and pamphlets.* The first reference to a book or pamphlet should contain the author's name, not inverted; the title, underlined or in italics; the editor or translator, if any; the place of publication and the date in parentheses; the volume, if more than one, in roman numerals; and the page reference. Note that the abbreviations *p.* and *pp.* are used only when the cited work consists of a single volume.

[1] Elton E. Smith, *The Two Voices: A Tennyson Study* (Lincoln, Nebraska, 1964), p. 67.
[2] Edgar Johnson, *Charles Dickens: His Tragedy and Triumph* (New York, 1952), II, 78–79.
[3] Ben Jonson, *The Complete Poetry of Ben Jonson,* ed. William B. Hunter (New York, 1963), p. 241.
[4] *The Epic of Gilgamesh,* trans. N. K. Sandars (Baltimore, 1960), pp. 123–24.

Later footnote references to the same work require only a shortened form. Unless more than one work by a particular author is being cited, subsequent references to the work need contain only his last name followed by the volume and/or page numbers.

[5] Johnson, I, 72.
[6] Smith, p. 114.

If more than one book or article by Elton E. Smith is to be cited, the subsequent footnote should contain his last name and the title, often shortened.

> [7] Smith, *The Two Voices,* p. 34.

(2) *Magazines.* The first reference to a magazine or journal article contains the author's name, not inverted; the title of the article in quotation marks; the name of the magazine, underlined or in italics; the volume in roman numerals; the date in parentheses; and the page reference.

> [8] Noel Annan, "Kipling's Place in the History of Ideas," *Victorian Studies,* III (June, 1960), 334.
> [9] Granville Hicks, "Poet of the Recent Past," *Saturday Review,* XLVIII (April 10, 1965), 32.

Like subsequent references to a book, those to a magazine or journal article are shortened to include only the author's last name and the page number.

> [10] Annan, p. 332.

If more than one book or article by Granville Hicks is to be cited, the subsequent footnote should contain his last name and the title of the article.

> [11] Hicks, "Poet of the Recent Past," p. 31.

(3) *Newspapers.* The first reference to a newspaper article contains the author's name, if known; the headline in quotation marks; the name of the newspaper, underlined or in italics; the date; the section, if paginated separately; the page; and the column.

> [12] "Student Throng Seeks Peace," *Idaho State Journal,* April 18, 1965, p. 1, col. 6.
> [13] "Tornado Deaths Mount," New York *Times,* April 12, 1965, Sec. 1, p. 6, col. 3.

(4) *Standard reference sources.* Citations from reference books which are alphabetically arranged require a minimum of documentation in a footnote. A typical reference to a short encyclopedia article, for example, normally contains only the title of the article in quotation marks; the name of the encyclopedia, underlined or in italics; and the edition (sometimes replaced by the date and volume number).

> [14] "Insomnia," *World Book Encyclopedia,* 1st ed.

If, however, the article is more than a page long, the volume and page numbers may be included as well.

[15] "Indiana," *World Book Encyclopedia*, 1st ed., IX, 154.

(5) *Secondhand material.* Occasionally one needs to footnote material which is not available in its primary source but which is available in a responsible, documented secondary source. Both sources should appear in the footnote.

[16] Thomas Elyot, *Of the Knowledge Which Maketh a Wise Man* (London, 1533), quoted in Joseph Menton, *Humanist Wisdom* (New York, 1947), p. 96.

(6) *Partial footnotes.* Often a part of a reference is given in the text, and that part need not appear again in the footnote. If, for example, the text reads, "Dover Wilson has argued that Shakespeare's ninety-eighth sonnet was written on April 4, 1600," the footnote should begin with the title of Wilson's book.

[17] *An Introduction to the Sonnets of Shakespeare* (New York, 1964), p. 68.

If both the author and the title of the book appear in the text, the footnote should begin with the place of publication.

[18] (New York, 1964), p. 68.

(7) *Special problems.* Every writer of scholarly material occasionally confronts special or unusual footnoting situations, those calling for variations in documentation. Often he has learned from his own reading how they are to be handled; he has perhaps learned that when the citation is to a footnote in another book, he should add *n.* to the page reference.

[19] Wayne Shumaker, *Literature and the Irrational* (Englewood Cliffs, N.J., 1960), p. 89n.

However, when one does not know how to handle the special situation, he should consult *The MLA Style Sheet* or another style manual dealing with research techniques.

(8) *Placement of footnotes.* Footnotes should appear on a typewritten manuscript three spaces under the last line of text. Individual footnotes should be single spaced; an extra line of space separates consecutive footnotes. The first line of a footnote should be indented five spaces, and the number should be slightly elevated. If a lengthy footnote must be continued on the next page, it should appear under a single, continuous line one space below the last line of text.

Hours

The scheduled hour is always written out on formal announcements—for weddings, dedications, inaugurations, etc. Otherwise, usage is divided. Sometimes, particularly when there is a single reference to time, the hour is written (The President will arrive at *four* o'clock in the afternoon). However, editorial English most commonly employs numerals (*4* p.m., *8:30* a.m.). A.m. and p.m. (see p. 8) are often omitted when the context removes any chance of ambiguity (By 7 [or seven] o'clock the sun had dropped below the horizon); they are always omitted when accompanied by the words *morning, noon, afternoon, evening, night, midnight* (at 5:30 [or five-thirty] on a foggy morning, shortly after 10 [or ten] last night).

Hyphen (-)

Standard editorial practice establishes the use of the *hyphen* in the following situations:

(1) *Prefixes*

Prefixes are usually followed by a hyphen when the root word is a proper noun (anti-*American,* pro-*British*); when the prefix ends and the root word begins with the same vowel (sem*i*-independent, r*e*-examination) other than *o* (cooperation or coöperation); when ambiguity might otherwise result (*re-cover* [to cover again], *recover* [to regain]); when *ex*- is used to mean "former" (*ex*-husband, *ex*-champion).

(2) *Compound words*

(*a*) All fractions and compound numbers from 21 to 99 are hyphenated when spelled out (*seventy-four, six hundred twenty-three, three-sixteenths*).

(*b*) Some words indicating marital or blood relationships are regularly hyphenated (*brother-in-law, great-grandfather* [but *half sister, third cousin*]).

(*c*) Two or more words serving as a single modifier are regularly hyphenated (an *up-again-down-again* situation, a *never-to-be-repeated* attraction).

(*d*) Hyphens are often used in particular compounds of a noun plus a noun, an adjective plus a noun, a verb plus a noun, and other combinations; but the practice governing their usage is extremely complex and variable. The writer should consult an up-to-date dictionary.

(3) *Suspended elements*

Suspended prefixes or compounds are regularly followed by a hyphen.

Deliver the ransom money in *five-* and ten-dollar bills.
Each mansion was identified as either *pre-* or post-Civil War.

(4) *Division of words*
Words which are divided at the end of a printed or typewritten line should be hyphenated (see **Division of Words,** p. 82).

Ibid.

An abbreviation of the Latin *ibidem,* meaning "in the same place." It occurs frequently in the footnotes of formal editorial English and is usually not italicized.

Italics

Standard editorial practice establishes the use of *italics* (underlining in typewritten or handwritten manuscripts) in the following situations:

(1) To indicate the titles of books, magazines, pamphlets, newspapers (see also **Titles,** p. 101) and the names of ships.
Norman Mailer's *An American Dream* received favorable reviews in *Saturday Review* and the *London Times.*
Every sailor on the *USS Swordfish* read Mary McCarthy's *The Group.*
(2) To indicate heavy emphasis upon a word or word group. This practice is used sparingly in editorial English because emphasis is usually expressed more effectively by proper word choice.
Some commentators have even argued that we should *withdraw* from the United Nations.
(3) To indicate letters, words, or word groups treated not for their meaning, but as words.
The prefix *re-* is often hyphenated when it precedes a root word beginning with an *e.*
The word *it* is difficult to define when it appears in such expressions as *it should be said* and *it isn't easy.*
(4) To indicate foreign borrowings (see **Loanword,** p. 151) that have not yet achieved wide currency in the language.
Albert Schweitzer believes that service to other human beings is the *raison d'être* of human existence.
(5) It should be noted that most newspapers and some magazines do not use italics at all. Instead, they use quotation marks or capital letters.

Numbers

The following observations concern the use of numbers in written English.

(1) *Types of numerals and word numbers*

CARDINAL			ORDINAL	
numeral		*number*	*numeral*	*number*
Arabic	Roman			
1	I	one	1st	first
2	II	two	2nd	second
3	III	three	3rd	third
4	IV	four	4th	fourth
5	V	five	5th	fifth
6	VI	six	6th	sixth
7	VII	seven	7th	seventh
8	VIII	eight	8th	eighth
9	IX	nine	9th	ninth
10	X	ten	10th	tenth
14	XIV	fourteen	14th	fourteenth
16	XVI	sixteen	16th	sixteer.th
19	XIX	nineteen	19th	nineteenth
20	XX	twenty	20th	twentieth
25	XXV	twenty-five	25th	twenty-fifth
30	XXX	thirty	30th	thirtieth
40	XL	forty	40th	fortieth
45	XLV	forty-five	45th	forty-fifth
50	L	fifty	50th	fiftieth
90	XC	ninety	90th	ninetieth
100	C	hundred	100th	hundredth
500	D	five hundred	500th	five-hundredth
1,000	$\underline{M}$	thousand	1,000th	thousandth
5,000	$\overline{V}$	five thousand	5,000th	five-thousandth
1,000,000	$\overline{M}$	million	1,000,000th	millionth

(2) *Uses of numerals*

Numerals are used in lieu of word numbers according to the following conventions.

(*a*) *Dates* always appear in numerals (May 5, 1932) except in a few formal documents like treaties and invitations to solemn and important events (weddings, dedications, inaugurations, funerals). Ordinal numerals seldom occur as dates in editorial English, and when they do appear, the year is always absent (May 5th). (See also **Dates,** p. 82.)

(*b*) *Hours and minutes* of the day appear as numerals when a.m. or p.m. follows (5:30 a.m , 7 p.m.). In other contexts usage in editorial English is divided (see **Hours,** p. 87).

(*c*) *Exact amounts of money* usually appear in numerals (79¢, $29.50, $37,942.16) except when the exact amount is also a large round number (*a million dollars*). The practice of combining words with numerals for sums rounded by millions and billions, though not thousands, is rapidly gaining acceptance in editorial English (*7 billion dollars, 216 million dollars*).

(*d*) *References* to pages, chapters, lines, cantos, volumes, acts, scenes, and other divisions always appear in numerals (page 548, chapter XII, line 74, volume 3 [or III], act IV, scene iv).

(*e*) *Street numbers* always appear in numerals and are not separated into groups of three by commas (14669 Edgewood Drive).

(*f*) *Fractions* appear as numerals when they follow other numerals (43¾); when they appear in series with other fractions or whole numerals (The child tried to add ³⁄₁₆, 21, and 16⅜); and when they appear in graphs or statistical tables.

(*g*) *Statistics* usually are written as numerals when they appear in the same sentence or paragraph with other numerals (Most of the 723 inmates of the Idaho State Penitentiary come from only 6 states: 219 from Idaho, 116 from Utah, 87 from California, 69 from Washington, 63 from Oregon, 31 from Wyoming). A statistic standing alone in a sentence or paragraph often appears as a word number (Of the many who started the long trek, only forty-three reached California before winter).

(*h*) *Units of measure* in technical and scientific writing are regularly preceded by numerals (The density of water at 4°C. is 1 gram per cc.).

(3) *Uses of word numbers*

Two systems are widely employed in editorial English to determine whether a numeral or a word number should be used. Either is acceptable. First, use words for numbers one through ten, numerals for all others except round numbers in hundreds, thousands, millions, and billions (four, eight, 11, 72, 226, three hundred, ten billion [but see 2c above]). Second, use numerals for all numbers which cannot be written in one or two words (four, eight, eleven, seventy-two, 226, three hundred, ten billion). In addition, words are used for numerals in the following situations:

(*a*) *Hours and minutes* usually appear as words when the time is not followed by the abbreviations a.m. or p.m. (three o'clock, five-thirty in the afternoon, half past six). (See also **Hours,** p. 87.)

(*b*) *Fractions* which appear independent of other numerals are written as words (one-quarter, six twenty-fifths, eighteen thirty-seconds, fifty-seven sixtieths).

(*c*) *Approximate numbers* often appear as words when the writer wishes to indicate the fact that the number is an estimate or approximation (This suit cost me about a hundred dollars [actual cost: $98.50]).

(d) *Numbers at the beginning of a sentence* always appear as words (Seventy-six Democrats and 123 Republicans voted for the bill). Many writers, however, revise such sentences so that they start with another word (The bill received the approval of 76 Democrats and 123 Republicans).

(4) *Plurals of numerals*

Both *'s* and *s* occur in editorial English to form the plural of a numeral (Arnold Palmer shot three 68's [or 68s] during the tournament).

(5) *Punctuation of Numerals*

(a) *Commas:* Except for serial numbers, street addresses, and years, numbers over 999 are broken into groups of three, starting from the right, by commas (18,677,493,600).

(b) *Periods:* A period separates dollars and cents where a dollar sign appears ($12.95, $0.53) and distinguishes a whole number from a decimal (.67, 86.7%, 3.1416).

(c) *Hyphens:* Fractions without hyphens in the numerator or denominator and compound numbers from 21 to 99 are hyphenated (ninety-three, three-eighths, nine-tenths, twenty-two thirty-fifths, eleven twenty-fourths).

(d) *Colons:* Hours and minutes are separated by a colon (8:24 p.m.).

Outline Form

The purpose of an outline is to organize and demonstrate the relationships among coordinate and subordinate elements of a piece of writing. An *outline form* is a system of indentation and enumeration used in making an outline. The following two systems are the most common:

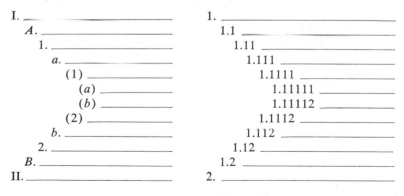

I. _____
  A. _____
    1. _____
      a. _____
        (1) _____
          (a) _____
          (b) _____
        (2) _____
      b. _____
    2. _____
  B. _____
II. _____

1. _____
1.1 _____
1.11 _____
1.111 _____
1.1111 _____
1.11111 _____
1.11112 _____
1.1112 _____
1.112 _____
1.12 _____
1.2 _____
2. _____

Parentheses ( )

Standard editorial practice establishes the use of *parentheses* in the following situations:

(1) *Insertions.* Writers often insert dates, words, phrases, or even short sentences within a sentence in order to clarify or elaborate its meaning. Such insertions usually have no grammatical relationship with the rest of the sentence, and they are used principally to define, to exemplify, or to furnish additional information.

> The New York Stock Exchange sometimes suspends stop-loss transactions (standing orders to sell a stock when it has declined to a specified price) in stocks which are fluctuating widely.
>
> Some nouns form their plurals by changing a vowel within the word (man, men); others add -*s* to the end of the word (gun, gun*s*); still others use a Latin or Greek plural ending (curriculum, curricul*a*).
>
> William Cobbett (1765–1835) was one of the first Englishmen to write at length of American society; his *Year's Residence in the United States* (a scholarly edition has recently been published) presents an excellent account of our emerging democracy.

(2) *Enumerations.* Numbers used in an enumeration are usually enclosed within parentheses.

> Great teachers share two basic qualities: (1) they love learning; (2) they have a facility for communicating their learning to others.

(3) *With other punctuation marks.* Parenthetical insertions do not affect the basic punctuation of a sentence. Except with enumerations, any mark of punctuation belonging at the point of insertion is placed after the final curve, as in the second example under (1). Punctuation marks *within* parenthetical material are retained. The current practice, however, is to drop terminal marks of punctuation (.!?) within parentheses, as in the third example under (1), though question marks and exclamation points are sometimes retained.

Period (.)

Standard editorial practice establishes the use of the period in the following situations:

(1) *Statements.* The most common function of the period is to signal the end of a declarative sentence. The period can also be used at the end of requests or directives which are actually worded as questions.

Will all employees please report their draft status to the payroll office.

(2) *Abbreviations.* Most abbreviations are followed by periods (Fri., Sept., Wm., Sr., Mrs., Dr., e.g., Ltd., rm., bldg., etc.). Periods are omitted, however, in very common abbreviations consisting entirely of capital letters (USA, USSR, UN, TVA, CIA, TV, KKK); in abbreviations for chemical elements (H_2O, H_2SO_4); in acronyms, pronounceable words formed with the initial letters of a series of other words (NATO from North Atlantic Treaty Organization, snafu from situation normal all fouled up); and after shortened colloquial forms (Sally's *econ prof* gave a stiff *exam*).

(3) *Numbers.* A period separates dollars and cents when a dollar sign is used ($29.95, $0.47, 63 cents, 63¢). It is also used to separate or distinguish a whole number from a decimal (3.1416, 0.39, 84.7%).

(4) *Ellipsis.* The ellipsis is a series of three periods (. . .) used to indicate certain omissions and sentence suspensions (see **Ellipsis,** p. 82).

(5) *With other punctuation marks.* When a statement ends with quoted words, the period precedes the quotation mark regardless of whether the quotation constitutes a complete sentence.

> Brutus started his famous funeral oration with the words, "Friends, Romans, countrymen."

Periods are omitted at the end of independent clauses set off by dashes or parentheses from the rest of the sentence.

> Dickens' experience with poverty—he had known the debtor's prison at firsthand—created in him an abiding sympathy for the unwashed poor of London's back alleys.
>
> Thomas Carlyle's letters (they are now being edited for publication) demonstrate clearly his concern with the main currents of Victorian political thought

Question Mark (?)

The *question mark* is used in the following situations:

(1) To mark the end of a direct question.

> Did you watch the baseball game on television?

Note that the question mark does not follow an indirect question.

> He asked whether I had watched the baseball game on television.

(2) To mark the end of a request.

> Will you please let me know how many guests to expect for dinner?

Note, however, that some requests are in the nature of directives or orders. In such instances, particularly when a superior is writing to a subordinate, a period is often used in place of a question mark.

Will all employees please report their draft status to the payroll office.

(3) To mark the end of a quotation which is a question or part of a question. The question mark appears inside the quotation marks when the quoted material itself is a question or when both the entire sentence and the quoted material are questions; it appears outside the quotation marks when the entire sentence, but not the quoted material, is a question.

Professor Snarf asked, "Can you pass this course?"
Did Professor Snarf ask, "Can you pass this course?"
Did Professor Snarf say, "You can pass this course"?

When a speaker is identified after a quoted question, the question mark precedes the identification.

"Can you pass this course?" Professor Snarf asked.

(4) To indicate that a date is subject to question.

The duchy remained at peace with its neighbors until Prince Herman (1392?–1438) came to the throne in 1420.

Quotation Marks (")

Present convention indicates the use of *quotation marks* in the following situations:

(1) *Direct quotations.* To set off the direct words of another writer or speaker (see also **Ellipsis,** p. 82 and **Brackets,** p. 69).

"The true harvest of my daily life is somewhat as intangible and indiscernible," wrote Henry Thoreau, "as the tints of morning or evening."
Thoreau wrote that the real accomplishments of everyday life are as difficult to describe "as the tints of morning or evening."
"I will never vote against my convictions!" the delegate shouted.

Use single (') quotation marks to identify a quotation within a quotation.

"There was," wrote a prominent historian of the Nez Perce War, "a quiet poetry in Chief Joseph's promise that he would 'fight no more forever.' "

In printed copy lengthy quotations are usually indented and set in smaller type. Similarly, lengthy quotations in typewriten manuscripts are indented and single-spaced. In either instance quotation marks are rendered unnecessary.

(2) *Titles.* Titles of short stories, articles, and poems are regularly put in quotation marks when accompanied by the name of the periodical or book in which they appeared (see also **Titles,** p. 101).

I read Carl Taylor's "Medical Care for Developing Countries" in the current issue of *Atlantic*.

The best story in Joyce's *Dubliners* is "The Dead."

Thomas Hardy's "The Mongrel" first appeared in a collection of poems called *Winter Words*.

(3) *Words as words.* Occasionally a word or word group is used not for its meaning, but as a word. In standard editorial English such words are italicized; informal writers usually put such words in quotation marks.

The United States Space Agency employs the word "go" as an adjective.

Occasional use of "conversely" or "on the other hand" will assist you in making smooth transitions between opposites.

(4) *Incongruous usage.* Occasionally a writer of editorial English will employ a word inappropriate to his level of usage, and he will put the word in quotation marks to tell the reader that he knows better. Since this practice savors of affectation, it should be used sparingly, perhaps even avoided, in student writing.

Professor Hunter's explications of medieval ecclesiology distinguished him as the world's leading scholar in the field, yet a new "whodunit" by Gardner always attracted his immediate attention.

(5) *With other punctuation marks.* Current editorial practice places periods and commas within quotation marks whether they belong to the quoted material or not.

After having charged the student with "indiscreet conduct," the professor reported the incident to the dean.

Brutus started his famous oration with the words, "Friends, Romans, countrymen."

Question marks and exclamation points appear inside the quotation marks when the quoted material itself is a question or exclamation.

"Did you fail chemistry?" he asked.

He asked, "Did you fail chemistry?"

"Don't ever try that again!" she screamed.

She screamed, "Don't ever try that again!"

Question marks and exclamation points appear outside the quotation marks when the entire sentence, and not the quoted material, is a question or exclamation.

Did you ever hear a politician say, "I don't want your vote"?

I distinctly remember that the defendant said, "I'm tired"!

Colons and semicolons appear outside quotation marks unless they belong to the quoted material.

The defense attorney said that he would "rest his case"; however, he spoke for an additional half hour.

Seasons

The seasons of the year (*spring, summer, midsummer, fall, autumn, winter, midwinter*) are not capitalized in editorial English.

Semicolon (;)

Standard editorial practice establishes the use of the *semicolon* in the following situations:

(1) *Between independent clauses*

(*a*) To separate independent clauses not joined by a connective.

Federal aid to higher education is not new; the United States Congress has been spending large sums of money on our land-grant colleges and universities for more than a hundred years.

(*b*) To separate independent clauses joined by a conjunctive adverb (except *still* and *then*).

All students have the right to petition for readmission after a second academic dismissal; *however,* the Committee on Standards approves very few such petitions.

(*c*) To separate heavily punctuated independent clauses, even though the clauses are joined by a coordinating conjunction.

The two athletes, both of whom had earned high school letters in football, basketball, and track, thought that they should receive special attention; but the other students, most of whom had come to the university for an education, remained singularly unimpressed.

(2) *Series with other commas*

To separate elements in a series when the elements themselves contain commas.

The three previous homecoming queens were Hannah Snevets, a striking brunet from Cleveland; Carol Legek, a blond from Minneapolis; and Cynthia Lyman, a dimpled redhead from Omaha.

During the past year I have attended professional meetings in Illinois, California, and New York; visited relatives in Utah, Idaho, and Montana; vacationed in Arizona, New Mexico, Texas, and Oklahoma.

Spelling

At first thought it may appear strange that this item should appear in the section of "Conventions of Editorial English." Further reflection, however, suggests that English spelling is in large part a matter of convention, having in many instances little to do with phonetic transcription.

Ideally, every word should be spelled as it is pronounced. Were this the practice in modern English, writers would have little or no difficulty spelling words "correctly." Silent letters would disappear, and any given sound would always be represented by the same letter or combination of letters. Unfortunately, however, written English always tends to be more conservative than spoken English; thus changes in pronunciation are not always followed by corresponding changes in spelling. Many persons, some of them linguists, have urged spelling reform following phonetic principles, yet to do so would require the extension of our alphabet and a lengthy period of education and transition to the new system. Furthermore, all the English writings of the past would have to be modernized into the new alphabet in order to be easily understood by the new generation of phonetic spellers. So great appears the task of accomplishing a major spelling reform that we struggle along instead with an archaic system and an inadequate alphabet.

As a result, very few writers of English can claim to be free of spelling problems. Some rely upon their mastery of the spelling "rules," which are extremely complex and require as well a mastery of countless exceptions. A few persons seem to possess a photographic sense which enables them to spell correctly the words which they have encountered in their reading. Still fewer persons possess such a thorough knowledge of phonetics and of historical change in language that they seldom experience spelling difficulties. Most of us, however, will become good spellers only by wide and perceptive reading, by the study and memorization of troublesome words, and by frequent reference to a standard dictionary.

Recently Dean Thomas Clark Pollock of New York University conducted an exhaustive study of many thousands of student misspellings and found that the majority of them involve three hundred words or word groups. A thorough mastery of this list will eliminate a great many common spelling errors.

THE FIRST 100 MOST FREQUENTLY MISSPELLED

1. accommodate
2. achieve
   achievement
3. acquaint
   acquaintance
4. acquire

5. affect
   affective
6. all right
7. among
8. analyze
   analysis

9. apparent
10. appear
    appearance
11. argument
    arguing
12. began

begin
beginner
beginning
13. belief
believe
14. benefit
beneficial
benefited
15. busy
business
16. category
17. choose
chose
choice
18. comparative
19. conscientious
conscience
20. conscious
21. consistent
consistency
22. control
controlled
controlling
23. controversy
controversial
24. criticism
criticize
25. decision
decided
26. definite
definitely
definition
define
27. describe
description
28. disastrous
29. effect
30. embarrass
31. environment
32. equipped
equipment
33. exaggerate
34. excellent
excellence
35. exist
existence
existent
36. experience
37. explanation
38. fascinate
39. forty
fourth
40. government
governor
41. grammar
grammatically
42. height
43. imagine
imaginary
imagination
44. immediate
immediately
45. incident
incidentally
46. intelligent
intelligence
47. interest
48. interpret
interpretation
49. its
it's
50. led
51. loneliness
lonely
52. lose
losing
53. marriage
54. necessary
unnecessary
55. Negro
Negroes
56. noticeable
noticing
57. occasion
58. occur
occurred
occurring
occurrence
59. origin
original
60. passed
past
61. perform
performance
62. personal
personnel
63. possess
possession
64. practical
65. precede
66. prefer
preferred
67. prejudice
68. prepare
69. prevalent
70. principal
principle
71. privilege
72. probably
73. proceed
procedure
74. professor
profession
75. prominent
76. psychology
psychoanalysis
psychopathic
psychosomatic
77. pursue
78. really
realize

79. receive
    receiving
80. recommend
81. referring
82. repetition
83. rhythm
84. sense
85. separate
    separation
86. shining
87. similar
88. studying
89. success

succeed
succession
90. surprise
91. than
    then
92. their
    there
    they're
93. thorough
94. tries
    tried
95. two
    too

to
96. useful
    useless
    using
97. varies
    various
98. weather
    whether
99. woman
100. write
    writing
    writer

THE SECOND 100 MOST FREQUENTLY MISSPELLED

1. accept
   acceptance
   acceptable
   accepting
2. accident
   accidentally
   accidental
3. across
4. advice
   advise
5. aggressive
6. approach
   approaches
7. article
8. athletic
   athlete
9. attended
   attendant
   attendance
10. author
    authority
    authoritative
11. basis
    basically
12. before
13. Britain
    Britannica

14. careless
    careful
15. carrying
    carried
    carries
    carrier
16. challenge
17. character
    characteristic
    characterized
18. coming
19. conceive
    conceivable
20. condemn
21. consider
    considerably
22. continuous
23. convenience
    convenient
24. curiosity
    curious
25. desire
    desirability
26. dependent
27. difference
    different
28. disappoint

29. disciple
    discipline
30. dominant
    predominant
31. efficient
    efficiency
32. entertain
33. exercise
34. extremely
35. familiar
36. finally
37. foreign
    foreigners
38. friend
    friendliness
39. fulfill
40. fundamental
    fundamentally
41. further
42. happiness
43. hero
    heroine
    heroic
    heroes
44. hindrance
45. humor
    humorist

humorous
46. hypocrisy
    hypocrite
47. independent
    independence
48. influential
    influence
49. involve
50. knowledge
51. laboratory
52. leisure
    leisurely
53. liveliest
    livelihood
    liveliness
    lives
54. maintenance
55. mere
56. ninety
57. operate
58. opinion
59. opportunity

60. oppose
    opponent
61. optimism
62. paid
63. parallel
64. particular
65. permanent
66. permit
67. philosophy
68. physical
69. piece
70. planned
71. pleasant
72. possible
73. propaganda
    propagate
74. quantity
75. quiet
76. relieve
77. religion
78. response
79. ridicule
    ridiculous

80. satire
81. sergeant
82. significance
83. speech
84. sponsor
85. subtle
86. summary
    summed
87. suppose
88. suppress
89. technique
90. temperament
91. therefore
92. together
93. transferred
94. undoubtedly
95. unusual
    unusually
96. villain
97. weird
98. where
99. whose
100. you're

THE THIRD 100 MOST FREQUENTLY MISSPELLED

1. accompanying
   accompanies
   accompanied
   accompaniment
2. accomplish
3. accustom
4. actually
   actuality
   actual
5. adolescence
   adolescent
6. against
7. amateur
8. amount
9. appreciate
   appreciation

10. appropriate
11. arouse
    arousing
12. attack
13. attitude
14. boundary
15. capital
    capitalism
16. certain
    certainly
17. chief
18. clothes
19. completely
20. counselor
    counsel
    council

21. curriculum
22. dealt
23. despair
24. disease
25. divide
26. divine
27. especially
28. excitable
29. expense
30. fallacy
31. fantasy
    fantasies
32. favorite
33. fictitious
34. financier
    financially

35. forward
36. guarantee
    guaranteed
37. guidance
    guiding
38. hear
    here
39. huge
40. ignorance
    ignorant
41. indispensable
42. intellect
43. interrupt
44. irrelevant
45. labor
    laborer
    laboriously
46. laid
47. later
48. length
    lengthening
49. license
50. luxury
51. magnificent
    magnificence
52. mathematics
53. meant
54. medieval
55. moral
    morale
    morally
56. narrative
57. naturally
58. noble
59. obstacle
60. peace
61. perceive
62. persistent
63. pertain
64. phase
65. playwright
66. political
    politician
67. primitive
68. regard
69. relative
70. remember
71. reminisce
72. represent
73. roommate
74. sacrifice
75. safety
76. satisfy
    satisfied
77. scene
78. schedule
79. seize
80. sentence
81. several
82. shepherd
83. simple
    simply
84. sophomore
85. source
86. story
    stories
87. straight
88. strength
89. strict
90. substantial
91. suspense
92. symbol
93. synonymous
94. tendency
95. them
    themselves
96. theory
    theories
97. tremendous
98. vacuum
99. view
100. whole

Titles

In editorial English the following practices are established for handling titles.

   (1) *Capitalization.* The first and last words and every other word within a title except articles, conjunctions, and prepositions with fewer than five letters are capitalized.

   How to Win Friends and Influence People
   Buying Stocks Without Risk
   When the Lights Go Out
   The Miracle of Language

   (2) *Italics.* Titles of books, magazines, newspapers, pamphlets, volumes of poetry or short stories, radio and television series, movies,

operas, and plays appear in *italics* (underlined in manuscript copy).

When Senator Church appeared on *Meet the Press,* he read a short passage from John Kennedy's *Profiles of Courage.*

The lead editorial in the New York *Times* [or *New York Times*] referred to an article in *Saturday Review.*

Gone with the Wind is one of the longest movies ever produced.

Salinger's *Nine Stories* contains some of his best work.

(3) *Quotation marks.* The titles of short poems, articles, and short stories appear in quotation marks when accompanied by the title of the book or periodical in which they appeared. Otherwise, they are often italicized.

The best story in Joyce's *Dubliners* is "The Dead." But: I consider *The Dead* [or "The Dead"] to be Joyce's best story. Hardy's "The Mongrel" appeared in a collection called *Winter Words.* But: Hardy's *The Mongrel* [or "The Mongrel"] is a study of despair.

LINGUISTIC, STYLISTIC, AND GRAMMATICAL TERMS

3

Educated users of language must know the meaning of certain important terms. In the following glossary we have included those terms most widely used in discussions of style, grammar, semantics, and general linguistics. In defining these terms for the general user of the language, we have taken into account the tremendous progress made in the study of language during the past decade, realizing, of course, that some of the definitions will be insufficient for the linguistic specialist in his technical studies. We have not restricted this glossary to any one kind of linguistic concern; instead, we have included terms from traditional, structural, and transformational grammar as well as historical linguistics.

Ablaut

See **Gradation,** p. 138.

Absolute Phrase

An *absolute phrase,* or a *nominative absolute,* as it is sometimes called, contains a present or a past participle and stands as a free functional unit in its sentence (*The job done,* we returned home). Though it modifies no particular word in the independent clause, the absolute phrase *the job done* can be regarded as a contraction of an adverbial clause such as *when the job was done* or *when we finished the job.* With a few common exceptions (e.g., *other things being equal*) the absolute phrase is restricted to formal editorial English. The English absolute construction is a conscious imitation initiated by seventeenth-century stylists of the Latin *ablative absolute.*

Abstract and Concrete Words

A *concrete word* refers to an object or person (*apple, soldier, sun*). *Abstract words* refer to ideas, qualities, conditions, actions (*existentialism, courage, anxiety, work*). To define a concrete word, we can point to its referent. An abstract word, in contrast, can only be defined by means of other words. Excessive or unnecessary use of abstract words (e.g., *educational environs* for *school*) can lead to vagueness and pomposity. In some situations, as when a Fourth of July speaker refers to his audience's *Americanism,* undefined abstractions are used to create emotional responses. Such use of abstractions must be evaluated with great care and should generally be avoided in informative writing or speaking.

Accent

The noun *accent* refers to: (1) the stress (see p. 183) given to prominent syllables in spoken utterance; (2) a regional or social dialect (a Southern *accent,* a Cockney *accent*); (3) any one of several written marks denoting relative stress. The most commonly used accent marks take their names from French: the *acute accent* (') for primary stress; the *circumflex* accent (^) for secondary stress; the *grave* accent (') for tertiary stress; the *breve* accent (˘) for weak stress. In poetic scansion (see **Metrical Foot,** p. 221), the acute accent is used to mark stressed syllables and the breve accent to mark unstressed syllables: "Thăt tíme ŏf yeár thŏu maýst ĭn mé bĕhóld." Many dictionaries use the accent mark in their pronunciation guides to indicate the syllable which customarily receives word stress. Practice, however, varies in the placement of the accent mark; e.g., the Funk and Wagnalls *Standard College Dictionary* puts it after the stressed syllable, while *Webster III* places it before the stressed syllable.

Accidence
A term in linguistics which refers to the study of grammatical inflections. Compare **Syntax,** p. 189.

Accusative Case
The case of the direct object. (See **Case,** p. 117 and **Object,** p. 159.)

Active Voice
See **Voice,** p. 199.

Adjective
According to structural grammar, *adjectives* constitute one of four major form classes (see p. 134), the others being the noun, the verb, and the adverb. Traditional grammar defines the adjective by its function; hence as a word that modifies (or limits) a noun or a pronoun. But since nouns as well as adjectives may modify nouns (the *town* house, the *car* dealer), the functional definition is insufficient. Structural grammar adds to the definition (1) by examining the place of the adjective in an utterance, and (2) by describing its forms.

Adjectives normally occupy the two open slots in the following type of test frames: The _____ house was _____. Words like *white, large, cozy, bewitched* could be used in both slots. However, words like *town, fraternity, cardboard, tree* can only be used in the first slot. Accordingly, the words in the first set, and any others that might fit in the same or in similar test frames, are part of the form class called adjectives. Words in the second set are nouns. The two slots in the sample test frame may also serve to illustrate the usual sentence positions of adjectives in modern English. The first slot is called the *attributive* position, in which the adjective, whether simple or compound, precedes the word it modifies. The second slot is called the *predicative* position, and the adjective which appears in it is traditionally known as the predicate adjective (see p. 169). The only other possible position for an adjective is the *appositional* one in which it is near the noun, though not necessarily before it, and in which the connection is looser (The men, *tired* and *dirty*, trudged back into camp). Appositional adjectives usually consist of more than one word. Adjective phrases, thus, are usually appositional in English (The boy *in the room* screamed loudly).

The form of modern English adjectives is not so clearly marked as that of verbs or nouns. Adjectives are uninflected for number and case; therefore they differ from nouns, which customarily do alter their form to show these grammatical functions. The only inflections still widely attached to adjectives are those which show comparative and superlative degree: the *-er* and *-est* endings (as in *older, oldest*). A number of derivational suffixes also attach to adjectives (though some of them may be used with words from other form classes as well): *-y, -ful, -less, -en, -able, -ible, -ive, -ous, -ish, -al, -ic, -ary, -some* and *-ly.*

Structural grammar does not classify the pronominal adjectives of traditional grammar (*that* book, *my* house) with adjectives. Instead, it labels them *determiners* (see p. 128) along with definite and indefinite articles, and other classes of words traditionally defined as adjectival (*some* men, *five* hours).

One other identifying trait of adjectives is their potential for being modified by a class of words known as *intensifiers* (see p. 146) like *very, quite,* and *rather.* The intensifiers *more* and *most* are particularly important since they assume the same function as the *-er* and *-est* inflections. It is important to note, however, that intensifiers also occur before adverbs.

Adjective Clause

Adjective clauses function like adjectives. They are generally introduced by a relative pronoun and may be restrictive or nonrestrictive.

RESTRICTIVE: I salute the man *who saved my life.*
NONRESTRICTIVE: I salute James Benton, *who saved my life.*

Adjective Phrase

An *adjective phrase* functions like an adjective. It usually takes one of the following forms: a series of adjectives connected with a coordinating conjunction (*tall and handsome* man), a preposition and a noun (man *in the white suit*), an infinitive (work *to be done*), a participial construction (*Entering the house,* I asked for Mark).

Adverb

According to structural linguistics, *adverbs* constitute one of four major form classes (see p. 134), the other three being nouns, verbs, and adjectives. Traditional grammar defines an adverb by its function or its meaning. An adverb may function as a modifier of the following units:

VERB	He advanced *silently*. He drove *away*.
ADJECTIVE	The sky was *deep* purple.
ANOTHER ADVERB	The horse ran *too* slowly.
PHRASE	He ran the mile in *just* under four minutes.
CLAUSE	I knew *exactly* when the plane arrived.
SENTENCE	*Luckily,* we weren't stranded long.

Traditionally, an adverb is associated with three categories of meaning; it may signify *there* (e.g., ahead, everywhere, under), *thus* (e.g., fast, conveniently, aloud), *then* (e.g., late, never, today).

Structural grammar does not fully accept the traditional definition. It classifies adverbs that modify adjectives and other adverbs (*too, very, more, rather,* etc.) as function words which it calls "intensifiers" (see p. 146). Furthermore, it adds to the traditional definition by concentrating on the sentence position and the form of the adverb.

The adverb is the most flexible of all the form classes in the number of positions it can occupy in a sentence. Note the four open slots that *slowly* can fill in the following sentence:

_____ the ship _____ moored _____ along the dock _____.

Adverbs are perhaps most clearly identified by their occurrence in the following sentence position: He threw the rock _____ (viciously, there, out, over, etc.). Only adverbs can appear in this context.

The form of adverbs is not distinctive; that is, one cannot identify a word as an adverb by its form alone. However, a few suffixes and prefixes occur frequently: the suffix *-ly* (appearing most often in *thus* adverbs [happi*ly*, bright*ly*, bitter*ly*]); the prefix *a-* (appearing most often in *there* adverbs [*a*head, *a*long, *a*way]); the suffix *-wise* (clock*wise*, slant*wise*); and the suffix *-ward* or *-wards* (after*ward*, north*ward*, back*wards*). In addition, certain adverbs are combined forms (*everywhere, no place*); and a great many adverbs are undifferentiated from other parts of speech (same as adjectives: *fast, quick, hard;* same as prepositions: *in, down, under, around*).

Adverbs, like adjectives, are uninflected in modern English. A few, however, add *-er* to form the comparative and *-est* to form the superlative. Adverbs that take these endings are those which are identical with adjectives (*fast, quick, hard,* etc.). A few adverbs, moreover, have irregular comparative and superlative forms (*well/better/best, far/farther* [*further*]/*farthest* [*furthest*], *ill/worse/worst*). In all other instances, the comparative and superlative degrees are expressed by the intensifiers *more* and *most.*

Adverbs present writers with only a few stylistic problems:

(1) In colloquial English, there is a tendency to drop the *-ly* ending and thus to confuse adverb and adjective (e.g., drive *slow* for drive *slowly*). In editorial English the *-ly* is required in such constructions.

(2) Some speakers and writers, in an effort to sound "correct," mistakenly use an adverb after a linking verb (see p. 151).

He made an effort to sound *correctly* (for *correct*).

It turned out *badly* (for *bad*).

An adjective is used after a linking verb in editorial English.

(3) The adverbial ending *-wise* with the meaning of "in regard to" is often used in business English (e.g., market*wise*, dollar*wise*, profit*wise*). This usage is associated with Madison Avenue by many style manuals, and it should be avoided in editorial English.

Adverbial Clause

An *adverbial clause* is a dependent clause which functions like an adverb. There are several types of adverbial clauses: (1) those introduced by subordinating conjunctions (*after, since, while,* etc.), (2) those introduced by forms with *-ever* (*whichever, whatever,* etc.), and (3) those that function as interjection or confirmation within a sentence (*The shoes, he said, are too large for him; You don't believe him, do you?*). At the beginning of a sentence, an adverbial clause is usually followed by a comma in editorial English (*While we are waiting, we might as well play a few hands of poker*).

Adverbial Genitive

The *adverbial genitive* is an adverb of time or place with an *-s* ending, and it is used frequently in informal written and spoken English (evening*s*, night*s*, day*s*, etc.). In editorial English, however, prepositional phrases are generally used in preference to adverbial genitives.

He likes to work *at night* (not *nights*).

The *-s* endings in adverbs like *nights, nowadays,* or *upwards* is a remnant of a genitive inflection in Old English. (See also **Way, Ways,** p. 57.)

Adverbial Phrase

An *adverbial phrase* functions like an adverb. It frequently takes the following forms: two adverbs joined with a coordinating conjunction (He moved *slowly and deliberately*); a preposition with a noun (*after lunch, in the morning*); an infinitive of purpose (He came *to buy*); an absolute construction (see **Absolute Phrase,** p. 105); or an adjective and a noun expressing duration, cost, or extent—known technically as an *adverbial accusative* (We drove *500 miles;* He was imprisoned *three years*).

Affix

A general term referring to both prefixes and suffixes in English. (See **Prefix,** p. 169 and **Suffix,** p. 187.)

Affricate

In phonetics the term for a consonant sound consisting of an alveolar (see p. 111) stop and an instant release of air which is marked by friction. The sounds represented by the italicized letters in the following words are *affricates: ch*amp, *j*unk. These sounds are represented by the symbols /č/ and /ǰ/ in the Trager-Smith phonemic alphabet (see p. 165).

Agreement

As a grammatical term, *agreement* describes the concordance of subject and verb (which generally *agree* in number and person) and of pronoun and antecedent (which generally *agree* in number and gender). The colloquial and dialectal *he don't* is said to be out of agreement because it joins a third person singular pronoun with a verb form which in editorial English is generally used with the first person singular, second person singular, or the plural. The following are among the most common agreement problems which writers are likely to encounter:

(1) Compound subjects connected with *and* generally take a plural verb in editorial English. However, when the items enumerated in the subject are thought of as a single group, the verb is singular (Strawberries and cream *is* my favorite dessert). Collective nouns similarly take the singular when their reference is to a group as a whole (Two dollars *is* too much to pay for a movie; Three-fourths of the job *is* done).

(2) Compound subjects connected with *or, nor,* or *but* generally take a singular verb in editorial English. When, however, one noun is singular and the other plural, the verb is governed by the noun which stands closer to it (Neither my roommate nor I *am* going home over Thanksgiving).

(3) Two or more nouns joined with such connectives as *in addi-*

tion to, including, together with, as well as, and *with* generally take a singular verb in editorial English (Governor Clements, as well as many members of the Tennessee legislature, *believes* that capital punishment should be abolished).

(4) The indefinite pronouns *anybody, anyone, each, either, everybody, everyone, neither, nobody, somebody,* and *someone* are construed as singulars when they immediately precede the verbs or reference pronouns they govern (Everyone *is* happy; Somebody *wants his* seat). However, when an indefinite pronoun is separated by intervening phrases or clauses from its verb or reference pronoun, it is sometimes construed as a plural, even in the most formal editorial English (*Everyone* of the many patrons who give financial support to the arts and who contribute so much of their time to the promotion of a superior cultural program in the community *have* signed their names to the petition). Most likely, such constructions slip by editors, and they are not advocated as the preferred usage in stylebooks. Their occurrence, however, indicates that indefinite pronouns are frequently considered plurals. Some constructions, in fact, demand a plural reference (*Everyone* waited with eager anticipation, and when Mr. Mitropolis finally appeared on the stage, *they* greeted him with a thunderous ovation).

(5) The indefinite pronoun *none* is now used more often in the plural than the singular even in editorial English (*None* of the books on the best-seller list *interest* [or *interests*] me). Very formal usage still requires the singular for *none*.

(6) When *what*-clauses are subject of a linking verb which is followed by a plural predicate nominative, the verb is most frequently plural, even in editorial English (*What* interests the police *are* the names of the offenders). For other problems involving agreement, see **One of those who,** p. 42, **There is, There are,** p. 54.

Alveolar

Any sound made by contact of the tongue tip against the ridge behind the upper front teeth is called *alveolar*. In American English, *t, d,* and *n* are alveolar consonants.

Ambiguity

A statement that might be understood in more than one way possesses *ambiguity*. Unintentional ambiguity often results from carelessly placed modifiers (Jim's brother is enjoying a two-week vacation in Mexico, *which he won as first prize in his company's sales contest;* Dad promised *after the Christmas holidays* to take us skiing), from pronouns whose antecedents are not immediately clear (Mary told the sorority president that *her* roommate had been in *her* bed since early evening;

The Buick ran into the Ford, damaging *its* grille), and from the use (usually in a restricted context) of words which themselves have more than one meaning (Maury Wills is a *base stealer*). In most instances ambiguity is the undesirable result of sloppy thought and should be eliminated from expository papers, where the intended aim is to communicate ideas clearly and immediately.

Sometimes, however, ambiguity is intentional. Advertisers are often guilty of deliberate ambiguity, particularly when they are making scientific claims for their products. Their aim, of course, is to stay within the letter of the law and at the same time allow the reader to go away with a mistaken understanding of the product's merits. Another type of intentional ambiguity is found in literature; it is discussed under the heading **Ambiguity** in the section on literary definitions.

Ampersand (&)

The name of the symbol for *and,* known also as *short and.* The symbol itself derives from an abbreviation for Latin *et* (and) in medieval manuscripts. The *ampersand* should be avoided in all but the most informal writing.

Analogy

The term has both a grammatical and a rhetorical meaning. As a grammatical term it refers to the tendency of words to adopt inflectional forms from other words which are used to express similar grammatical functions. When a child, in response to a complaint that he had hung a Christmas decoration too low, said that he "thought of *highering* it," he had formed an inflected form of the word *high* analogous to the word *lowering.* Similarly, the dialect forms *squoze* and *squozen* (for past tense and past participle of *squeeze*) are formed by grammatical analogy with the verb *freeze, froze, frozen.*

As a rhetorical term *analogy* refers to a comparison of two objects or events having at least one quality in common. Logicians differentiate between a *literal* and a *figurative analogy.* In a literal analogy the comparison is drawn between two things in the same general category; in a figurative analogy the comparison is drawn between two things in unlike categories. A writer who argues that it would be unwise to elect a former general as President of the United States because Ulysses S. Grant was one of our worst has employed a literal analogy. Both the hypothetical candidate and Grant were generals in the army. If, on the other hand, the writer had argued that a former general should not be elected because one doesn't hire a former prizefighter to run a bank, he has employed a figurative analogy. A general is not a prizefighter, nor is our nation a bank. As a rhetorical device, analogies are most often used to compare an unfamiliar situation with a familiar one.

Analytic, Synthetic Languages

An *analytic* language is one in which grammatical relationships are expressed primarily by means of function words and fixed word order. A *synthetic* language, in contrast, depends primarily on inflectional prefixes and suffixes to express grammatical relationships. Modern English is an *analytic* language; Old English was a *synthetic* language.

Anglo-Saxon

See **Old English,** p. 160.

Anomalous Verb

The name often used by historians of language to designate those verbs which form their present and past tenses from different roots. In English the verbs *be* (past *was, were*) and *go* (past *went*) are examples of anomalous verbs.

Antecedent

A noun or noun-equivalent to which any of the following types of pronouns refer: personal (*I, you, he,* etc.), reflexive or intensive (*myself, ourselves,* etc.), demonstrative (*this, that, these, those*), and relative (*that, who, which,* etc.). In the following sentences the pronouns and their antecedents are italicized:

> *Mark* is a veritable genius; *he* never studies and yet *he* gets A's.
> The *President* conducted *himself* with dignity and grace.

The failure to recognize the relationship between a pronoun and its antecedent can lead to ambiguous sentences like the following, in which *their* can refer to *youngsters* or to *mother's and father's:*

> Youngsters should treat the club property as well as they do their mother's and father's property in *their* (?) respective homes.

For further discussion, see **Reference of Pronouns,** p. 176.

Anticipatory Subject

It or *there* as subject substitutes are sometimes called *anticipatory subjects* (see also **Expletive,** p. 133). In certain sentence types, *it* or *there* precedes and governs the verb while the real subject (usually a noun phrase or clause) is placed after the verb:

> *It* is illegal for students to park in Zone A.
> *There* were ten new courses in the curriculum.

Antonym

Antonyms are words which have opposite meanings (e.g., *good/bad, grow/shrink, broad/narrow, friend/enemy*).

Apposition, Appositive

These terms are used most often to refer to a noun function in a sentence. An *appositive* is a word or group of words having the same denotative meaning as a noun, pronoun, or noun phrase in the same clause. Appositives usually follow directly after the noun to which they refer. In the following sentences the italicized words stand in apposition with each other:

Dr. Eric Garth, my dentist, is his next-door neighbor.

The Civil Rights Act affects all *Americans* alike—*Northerners, Southerners, Easterners, Westerners.*

The Pierpont Morgan Library in New York, a repository of valuable medieval manuscripts, also holds a large collection of Gilbert and Sullivan documents.

Generally, a comma or another mark of punctuation separates a noun or noun phrase from its appositives. Sometimes, however, the mark of punctuation is omitted as in *my friend Carl* or *William the Conqueror.* This usage is known as *close* apposition. The term *appositive* is also applied to adjectives which follow the nouns they modify (The bridge, *long* and *slender,* sways noticeably on windy days).

Archaic, Current, Obsolete

Archaic refers to words going out of use (*methinks, hight*). *Obsolete* refers to words that have gone entirely out of use (*nithing* meaning "coward," *evagation* meaning "a wandering of one's thought"). *Current* refers to all words now in general use. *Webster III* considers any word obsolete which has not been in use since 1755.

Articles

The words *a, an,* and *the* are articles. They serve as signals that a noun will follow. Structural linguists classify articles together with other function words that can be substituted for them (e.g., *one, that, our*) as *determiners* (see p. 128).

Articulation

A term used in phonetics (see p. 167) to describe the muscular modifications by means of which the speech organs produce sounds. The *p* sound is articulated by the lips. The word *pronunciation* is not a synonym of *articulation* as a term in phonetics. Rather, *pronunciation* has reference to the way sounds are combined to form words.

Aspect

A grammatical concept which defines the span or completedness of an action. The following *aspects* are among the most important in English:

CONTINUING:	He *kept on* ringing the doorbell.
COMPLETED:	He *stopped* seeing her from that moment on.
BEGINNING:	He *started* to drive away.

In Russian, and in some other languages, aspect is expressed by inflectional alterations, much as tense is in English. However, aspect in English is expressed by means of phrasal modifications: the insertion of a verb (*started, stopped*); an adverbial (come *to a screeching halt,* walk *on and on*); or a verb-adverb combination (*kept on*).

Assimilation

In phonemics (see p. 167), the adaptation of one sound to another which immediately precedes or follows it. For example, the last consonants in tap*s* and tab*s* differ in their pronunciation because of the influence of the consonants which precede them: the *s* in *taps* is voiceless because it follows a *p,* which is also voiceless; the *s* in *tabs* is voiced /z/ because it follows a voiced *b.* Speech is marked by a great many such contextual alterations, most of which are not reflected in standard spellings. The study of patterns of assimilations in grammatical inflections is known as *morphophonemics.*

Auxiliary

In traditional grammar, the *auxiliary* is defined as a "helping verb." Structural grammar regards the auxiliary as a function unit which signals the use of or replaces a verb. The following are among the most frequently used auxiliaries: forms of the verb *be, have,* and *do; will, would; shall, should; can, could; may, might; must;* and *ought.* Auxiliaries modify verbs; in the phrase *may have been known,* the auxiliaries *may, have,* and *been* modify *known,* which is the headword of the verb. Auxiliaries may be used to replace verbs in elliptical constructions (see p. 132) (John went [verb] downtown; *did* [auxiliary] you?). Many auxiliaries differ from verbs structurally in their ability to combine with the negative particle *n't.* Moreover, those auxiliaries which are known as *modals* (in the foregoing enumeration the forms *will* through *ought*) do not add the *-s* ending of verbs in the third person singular. It should be noted that *be* and *have* as well as a number of other forms (e.g., *let, got*) may be used as either auxiliaries or verbs (He *has* [auxiliary] moved; He *has* [verb] an appointment).

Awkward

A term sometimes used in the marking of themes to refer to a construction which is inept or clumsy. Writing that inadvertently calls attention to itself because of repetitions, misplacements of words and phrases, or infelicitous rhythmic patternings is usually called *awkward.*

The following are illustrations of awkward sentences:
It made a re*sound*ing *sound.*
That's the dress she came *out in.*
Enlisted men were frightened by the lieutenant *general,* in *particular.*

Back-formation

The making of a new word by the shortening of an existing word. For example, *pup* is a shortened form, hence a *back-formation,* of *puppy* (the anglicized form of French *poupée*); the verb *beg* is a back-formation of *beggar.*

Back Vowel

Those vowels for which the back of the tongue is used to constrict the breath stream. Examples are *moot* /uw/, *moat* /ow/, *caught* /ɔw/.

Balanced Sentence

A sentence containing two or more independent clauses which are similar in grammatical structure. The *balanced sentence* is one of three main rhetorical types (see also **Loose Sentence,** p. 151, and **Periodic Sentence,** p. 163). The following maxims by La Rochefoucauld are in balanced form:

Everyone complains of his memory, and no one complains of his judgment.
We always like those who admire us; we do not always like those whom we admire.

Base

The *base* of a word is also known as its root. It is the part to which prefixes and/or suffixes are attached. While some *bases* are free forms (e.g., *one, list, test*), many cannot stand by themselves (*-cept* in *except*). (See also **Morpheme,** p. 154; and **Bound Form, Free Form,** below.)

Bilabial

A term which refers to those sounds articulated with the two lips. In American English the bilabial phonemes are *p, b,* and *m.*

Blend

See **Portmanteau Word,** p. 168.

Bound Form, Free Form

A *bound form* is a language unit, usually a morpheme, which is never spoken alone (e.g., the *-ation* of *condemnation,* the *-s* of *girls,* the *cran-* of *cranberry*). All other language units are called *free forms* (e.g., *Sally ate* or *Sally* or *ate* or *subtle*). Some free forms are the result of combined bound forms (e.g., *con* plus *fer,* both bound forms, gives *confer,* a free form). Most prefixes and suffixes in English are bound forms.

Case

In modern English, *case* is a grammatical concept that applies only to nouns and pronouns. By means of *case inflections* a noun or a pronoun indicates its relationship to other words in a sentence. Since the English language has constantly been reducing its inflectional distinctions, only a few case inflections remain in the present day. Nouns still have an inflectional signal for the *possessive,* or *genitive, case* (the *'s* of the singular as in *stone's* or of the plural as in *men's*). All other noun functions are handled by what might be called the *common case* form, for modern English nouns do not make any inflectional alterations to differentiate a subject from an object:

> SUBJECT: The *stone* lay in the street.
> OBJECT: He was hit by a *stone.*

Personal pronouns do have three case forms in modern English: the *nominative,* or *subject, case* (*I, he, they,* etc.); the *possessive case* (*mine, his, her,* etc.); and the *objective case* (*him, me, whom,* etc.). As far as the inflectional characteristics of modern English are concerned, one may rightly say that the language no longer differentiates the case of the *direct object* (the *accusative*) and the *indirect object* (the *dative*). Neither does the language retain such other grammatical cases as the following:

(1) *The ablative,* occurring in Latin and other languages. The ablative case expresses a number of grammatical relations, including those of source (an heir *of the Cabots*), separation (to be taken *out of slavery*), cause (to die *for freedom*), instrument (to travel *by ship*), place (to hail *from Chicago*), and several more. It is to be noted that the ablative embraces the more specific senses expressed in other languages by the *instrumental* and the *locative.*

(2) *The instrumental case,* occurring in some Indo-European languages, expresses agency (the notion "by means of"). English once had an instrumental case of which there are a few petrified remains (e.g., the expression *the more the merrier*).

(3) *The locative,* or the case referring to the place of an action (He came *from West Virginia*).

(4) *The vocative,* or the case for direct address. The noun *David* in the following sentence would be inflected as a vocative: *David,* bring me the paper.

Some modern English grammars may refer, on occasion, to cases for which the language no longer has distinct inflectional forms. In such instances the reference is really to the *function*, not the *form*, of a noun in a sentence. For example, in the sentence "He went to the *store*," the word *store*, in its form is in the common case, but in its function it could be labeled a *dative* because it is used in a context which, in an inflected language, would require a dative form.

Cedilla

A small hook on the bottom of a *c* before *a* or *o* to indicate the pronunciation /s/ rather than /k/, as in the word *façade*.

Circumlocution

A term used in some style manuals to describe cumbersome, involved, and roundabout phrasing. Circumlocutions occur often in business and legal jargon.

> With respect to the case of Orville Higginbottom, we find ourselves required to take the position of foreclosing his mortgage.
> Improved: We have to foreclose Orville Higginbottom's mortgage.

Clause

A clause is a group of words which contains a subject and a predicate. Traditionally, clauses are identified as *independent* (or *main*) and *dependent* (or *subordinate*). Independent clauses occur in simple, compound, complex, and compound-complex sentences. They can, as their name implies, stand by themselves. *Dependent* clauses can only occur in complex or compound-complex sentences. They usually do not stand by themselves as sentences in editorial English; however, they are sometimes set off by periods as a stylistic departure. Dependent clauses can be introduced by subordinators like *after, although, since;* by interrogators like *which, what, who;* and by relative pronouns like *that, which, who.*

> *When* the game was over [dependent clause introduced by a subordinator], we slowly made our way to the exit [independent clause].

In all but the most formal English, relative pronouns introducing a dependent clause are occasionally left out.

> The road [formal *that*] I usually take home was snowed in.

Cliché

A worn-out word, phrase, or sentence. *Clichés*, also known as *trite* or *hackneyed* expressions, occur most often as figures of speech. Some are similes (*old as the hills, dumb as an ox, blind as a bat*); some are metaphors (*to work one's fingers to the bones, bright and shining faces*); some are personifications (*Father Time, Mother Nature*); but no matter what their rhetorical form, all clichés are expressions which have been used too often. The identification of clichés is a subjective matter; it cannot be accomplished with a list of pat expressions. Nor is it possible for any writer to avoid the use of clichés entirely. It is, however, wise to avoid any of the following: figurative comparisons which are archaic (*fend for oneself, at one fell swoop*); jargon which reveals chumminess or fatuousness (*the little lady, the good ol' U.S.A., age before beauty*); hackneyed proverbial wisdom (*money doesn't grow on trees, children should be seen but not heard*); overused, and often misquoted, literary allusions (*something is rotten in the State of Denmark, damn with faint praise*); dull formulas (*last but not least, first and foremost, history tells us*); images that give the illusion of vividness (sports jargon like *twin bill, splitting the uprights, the penalty stripe*); and pompous rhetoric (*point with pride, this great land of ours, the awesome responsibilities of the Presidency*). The only quality that all clichés have in common is a dullness resulting from overuse.

Cognate

The term *cognate* describes two or more words which are derived from the same source word. The German word *Hund* (dog) is cognate with English *hound;* both, in turn, are cognate with Latin *canis.* All of these words had a common ancestor in Indo-European.

Coherence

A term referring to style. Writing which has *coherence* flows smoothly and easily from point to point, and from sentence to sentence. In the marking of papers, some instructors use the word *coherence* (or an abbreviation like *coh.*) to indicate that a passage needs smoother connection with what precedes and follows. (See also **Transition,** p. 194.)

Colloquial English

Colloquial English refers to the spoken language. As a usage label, it appears in many dictionaries to identify expressions that occur primarily in familiar conversation. *Colloquial* is often taken erroneously as a synonym for *local* or *dialectal* language. Because of this confusion and also because it is difficult to sort out words which occur only in the spoken language, *Webster III* does not use the term as a label.

Comma Fault, Comma Splice

These terms are used interchangeably with reference to two independent clauses joined by only a comma (The game was boring, I could hardly wait to go home). *Comma faults* can be corrected by the substitution of a semicolon in place of the comma, the insertion of a connective (*and, but, for, so,* etc.) after the comma, or the use of two separate sentences in place of one. A sentence with a comma fault is often called a *run-on sentence*.

Comparative Linguistics

The study of language relationships. Comparative linguists are concerned with classifying languages into families usually by tracing existing linguistic systems to their origins. Modern American English can thus be traced through a series of phonological and environmental changes all the way back to Old English, which in turn can be traced to a language called Germanic, and ultimately to a still older language called Indo-European. Both Germanic and Indo-European are hypothetical languages; that is to say, there are no extant records of them. All that is known of them has been acquired through the rigorous searchings of comparative linguists. Their labors have determined that such different languages as modern English, German, Swedish, Dutch, and indeed even Russian and Sanskrit when traced back far enough can be proved to have sprung from one parent language. It was mainly through the work of such nineteenth-century comparative linguists as Rasmus Rask, Jacob Grimm, Franz Bopp, and Karl Verner that the Indo-European and Germanic languages were reconstructed and classified. At present, comparative linguists are at work in studying the relationships of many languages outside the Indo-European family, especially the native languages of Africa and America.

Comparison of Adjectives

In English, adjectives can be modified or inflected to express three degrees: the *positive* degree (*kind, tall, large*), the *comparative* degree (*kinder, taller, larger*), and the *superlative* degree (*kindest, tallest, largest*). As is evident from the illustrations cited, degree can be expressed structurally by the addition of inflectional suffixes (*-er, -est*). It can also be expressed syntactically by the use of the function words *more* and *less* for the comparative and *most* and *least* for the superlative. Generally in editorial English, inflectional suffixes are used with adjectives of one or two syllables (*larger* instead of *more large*), and function words are used with adjectives of more than two syllables (*more furious* instead of *furiouser*). The comparative usually involves the comparison of two ideas or objects (*the better of the two*), and the superlative involves more than two (*the best of the war novels*). A few adjectives in English are irregular, having different stems to express the three degrees (*bad, worse, worst; good, better, best*). (See also **Double Comparative, Superlative,** p. 131.)

Comparison, Illogical

The use of the superlative with *any* in phrases like *the brightest of any*, *the smallest of any,* appears frequently on all levels of editorial English. Objections have been raised against this construction on grounds of logic: the superlative, being unique, cannot logically be part of something else. But, as is true of so many other expressions, logic does not necessarily guide usage. For another form of a so-called illogical comparison, see **Unique,** p. 56 (see also **Adjective,** p. 106).

Complement

In its broadest sense, *complement* refers to any words or phrases which appear after the verb and which complete its meaning. The italicized words in the following sentences are complements:

He killed *six chickens.*
Marietta had *a date with the principal's oldest son.*
She was formerly *a good friend of mine.*

In a more restricted sense, one may also speak of *subject* and *object complements.* A subject complement is a noun, noun-equivalent, or adjective which typically follows a linking verb and describes the subject (He is *my brother;* She was *delighted*). An *object complement* describes or renames the object of a sentence (The orchestra was under the direction of Arturo Toscanini, *the famous conductor;* The grade made her *angry*).

Complementary Distribution

Linguists consider two elements of the same class to stand in *complementary distribution* when they are not interchangeable in their contexts. The /p/ sounds in the words *pill* and *lip* stand in complementary distribution. They are not interchangeable because the /p/ in *pill* requires an explosion of the breath stream, while the /p/ in *lip,* being final, is not exploded.

Complex Sentence

A *complex sentence* is made up of one independent clause and at least one dependent clause (He quivered all over [independent clause] when Jane took his hand [dependent clause]).

Compound-complex Sentence

A *compound-complex sentence* is made up of two or more independent clauses and at least one dependent clause (Although the weather bureau announced that the hurricane had passed on [dependent clause], the floodwaters still raged [independent clause], and the winds blew fiercely [independent clause]).

Compound Predicate

A *compound predicate* is made up of two or more verbs. A coordinating conjunction (see p. 125) usually precedes the last verb. When there are more than two verbs in the compound predicate, commas should be used after each verb or verb phrase.

She didn't go out with boys who *smoked, drank,* or *swore.*

She *lit* the stove, *set* the pan on it, and *fried* the most delicious trout you ever ate.

Compound Sentence

A *compound sentence* is made up of two or more independent clauses. Several devices may be used for joining the clauses of a compound sentence: semicolons, coordinating conjunctions preceded by commas, correlative conjunctions, and conjunctive adverbs preceded by semicolons.

Stand up; speak up; shut up.

He *not only* stumbled indelicately across the threshold, *but* he *also* called his hostess by the wrong name.

There were a few empty seats in the balcony; *however,* the main floor was filled to capacity.

Compound Subject

A *compound subject* is made up of two or more nouns or noun-equivalents. A coordinating conjunction (*and, but, or,* etc.) usually precedes the last part of the compound subject. When there are more than two parts in the compound subject, commas should be used as marks of separation.

The President, the Secretary of State, and the United States Ambassador to Great Britain were among the dignitaries at the reception.

Compound subjects usually take a plural verb. For exceptions see **Agreement, p. 110.**

Compound Word

A *compound word* contains two or more elements of which one must be an independent word. Compounds may thus combine a prefix and a free form (*ex-President*), a free form and a suffix (*childish*), or any number of free forms (*redhead, feet-first, quick-order counter*). Compounds are written in one of three forms: as one word (*dustbin*), with a hyphen (*teen-ager*), as two words (*beef cattle*). Since usage alone is responsible for the spelling of compounds, one should consult a reliable dictionary to determine which form of a given compound is conventionally used in writing. A glimpse through several pages of a dictionary will demonstrate how totally arbitrary is the spelling of compounds in editorial English (*e.g., Webster III* lists *ferry car, ferry-house* [hyphenated], and *ferryman* in quick succession).

Concrete Word
See **Abstract and Concrete Words,** p. 105.

Conjugation
The term *conjugation* refers to all the inflectional variations (forms of every person, tense, and mood) of a given verb. The conjugation of the verb *to be* in the present tense is as follows: I *am,* you *are,* he *is,* we *are,* you *are,* they *are.* The terms *conjugation* and *declension* are not interchangeable: one *conjugates* a verb and *declines* a noun. (See **Declension,** p. 127.)

Conjunction
In traditional grammar a *conjunction* is defined as a word which connects sentence parts. Structural linguists, while recognizing the fact that conjunctions do serve as connectors, consider the traditional definition inadequate because it fails to differentiate conjunctions from other connecting words like prepositions and relative pronouns. In structural grammar, therefore, conjunctions are identified by their connective function as well as their sentence position. Basically, there are two types of conjunctions: *coordinators* and *subordinators.*

    Coordinators are all connectives which join syntactically equal units (words, phrases, clauses) in a sentence. They must stand between the parts they connect. Classified as coordinators are the *coordinating conjunctions* of traditional grammar (*and, but, or,* etc.) and such compound connectors as *together with, rather than, along with,* and *as well as. Correlative conjunctions* (*not only . . . but also, neither . . . nor,* etc.) are also classified as coordinators; however, they differ from other coordinators in their sentence placement at both the beginning and the middle of a structure (*Not only* is Los Angeles badly overcrowded, *but* it is *also* frequently paralyzed by indescribable traffic jams).

    Subordinators, in contrast, do not connect syntactically equal units. They stand at the head of dependent, or subordinate, clauses, and they never serve to join individual words or phrases. Among the most frequently used subordinators are the following: *after, although, as, because, before, how, if, since, so that, through, till, unless, when, while, why.*

    One other type of connective, the *conjunctive adverb,* is often included in a definition of conjunctions. However, since the conjunctive adverb has much greater flexibility in its sentence placement than the connectors classified as *coordinators* or *subordinators,* it is treated separately in this book (see immediately below).

Conjunctive Adverb
The term *conjunctive adverb* applies to sentence connectors like *how-*

ever, moreover, therefore, consequently, furthermore, nevertheless, indeed. Conjunctive adverbs can be used to join two independent clauses (The office was closed; *however,* the manager was still there). In this usage, editorial English requires a semicolon after the first clause and a comma after the conjunctive adverb. The most important difference between conjunctive adverbs and coordinating conjunctions, which also connect independent clauses, is the movability of the conjunctive adverb. Like any other adverb, a conjunctive adverb can occupy many sentence positions, while a coordinating conjunction can appear only at the head of an independent clause.

COORDINATING CONJUNCTION: The sinking of the Lusitania was not the underlying cause of America's entry into World War I, *but* it was one of the immediate causes.

CONJUNCTIVE ADVERB: (*however* can fit any of the slots): The sinking of the Lusitania was not the underlying cause of America's entry into World War I; [_____,] it [_____,] was [,_____,] one [,_____,] of the immediate causes [,_____].

The advantage to the writer of using conjunctive adverbs is their potential to provide sentence variety. Conjunctive adverbs can also be used in simple sentences as transition words. When they appear in the middle of a sentence, they are usually set off by commas. (See also **Transition,** p. 194.)

Connective

A term used loosely to apply to such function words as conjunctions, prepositions, and conjunctive adverbs. As a special grammatical classification, the term *connective* is too general to be useful.

Connotation

The emotional overtones of meaning which attach to a word. Sometimes various people attach different connotative values to the same word. Even so prosaic a term as *chair* can evoke one kind of emotional response from a senator who has just been asked to chair an important committee and another, entirely different, from a death-row prisoner. More commonly, however, we generally agree about the favorable or unfavorable connotations of a word. The words *spy, flatfoot, nigger, squealer,* and *swabjockey* possess unfavorable emotional overtones which are not attached to their synonyms *government agent, policeman, Negro, giver of information,* and *sailor.* Other words almost always possess a favorable connotation: *hero, sweetheart, baby, beautiful, heaven.*

The rich stock of synonyms in the English language results in part from the fact that words develop distinct connotative meanings. We often create new words with neutral or favorable connotations to serve as synonyms for words which have developed unfavorable connotations (see also **Euphemism, p. 132**). For example, the motel owner caters to *guests* rather than *customers;* an auto dealer sells *preowned* rather than *secondhand* cars; a *janitor* calls himself a *custodian;* a worker chooses to be *terminated* or *nonreappointed* rather than be *fired* or *canned.*

Consonant

A sound formed by the occlusion or near-occlusion of the breath stream. *Consonants* differ from vowels by the audible friction with which they are produced. For a subclassification of consonants, see **Phonemic Alphabet, p. 165.**

Context

The surroundings of a word or other units of language. *Context* is an important determinant of meaning; to define words, therefore, requires a knowledge of the context in which they are used. Only the context can tell us the difference between a *breakfast roll, a roll of film,* and *a roll call.* Context is also of great importance in direct quotation. The writer must always be sure that he is not distorting a person's meaning by quoting a statement out of context.

Continuant

Any consonant which does not require stoppage of the breath stream (e.g., /s/, /f/, /w/, /n/). Consonants that do require stoppage are called *plosives* (see p. 168) or *stop consonants.*

Contractions

Contractions are often loosely defined as shortened forms of words. In their most frequent usage, however, they are more accurately described as combinations of two lightly stressed words, in one of which the vowel is muted. American English has two types of light stress combinations: the combination of personal pronoun and auxiliary (*I've, he's, you'd*), and the combination of auxiliary and negative particle (*wouldn't, hasn't, can't*). Some style manuals advise against the use of contractions in formal editorial English. However, usage studies indicate that contractions are widely used on all levels of editorial English.

Coordinating Conjunction

In traditional grammar, *coordinating conjunctions* are defined as words that join syntactically equal units (words, phrases, clauses) in a sentence. The most widely used coordinating conjunctions are the following: *and, but, for, nor, or,* and *yet.* Occasionally *only* and *while* are also used as coordinating conjunctions (He gave the orders, *while* I followed them; David enjoys outdoor sports, *only* he never goes out in cold weather). For a fuller discussion of coordinating conjunctions, see **Conjunctions,** p. 123. For the view that a coordinating conjunction should not come at the beginning of a sentence, see **And,** p. 8.

Coordination

The use of syntactically equal parts to form a sentence, a paragraph, or an outline. According to some style manuals, heavy coordination, which implies reliance on compound sentences, is a mark of immaturity in expression. It is well to bear in mind, however, that some of the most widely admired prose writers in English literature—among them Samuel Johnson, John Henry Newman, and Matthew Arnold— relied strongly on coordination in their sentence movement. In outlining, coordinate elements are generally phrased in similar syntactic structures (see **Outline Form,** p. 91).

Copula, Copulative Verb

See **Linking Verb,** p. 151.

Correlative Conjunctions

A type of coordinator illustrated by such words as *either . . . or, neither . . . nor, not (only) . . . but (also), both . . . and.* (See **Conjunctions,** p. 123.)

Current

See **Archaic, Current, Obsolete,** p. 114.

Dangling Modifier

The term *dangling modifier,* or *misrelated modifier,* has been widely applied by style manuals to participial or infinitive phrases which seem erroneously to modify the subject headword in the main clause of a sentence. For example, in the sentence *"Emerging from the last tunnel on the highway,* Switzerland came into view," the italicized phrase is considered a dangling modifier because it seems to modify *Switzerland,* the subject headword which immediately follows it. Though nobody would seriously assume that the writer intended Switzerland to emerge from a tunnel, the sentence nevertheless fails to communicate effectively if only for the distraction caused by the ludicrous interpretation to which it is open. Because the risk of such distraction is great, dangling modifiers should be avoided in editorial English.

ORIGINAL: While playing on these courts, tennis shoes must be worn.

REVISED: While playing on these courts, you must wear tennis shoes.

ORIGINAL: Opening the door, the dead body was immediately visible.

REVISED: Opening the door, I immediately saw the dead body.

ORIGINAL: Hoping to make another touchdown, my grandmother cheered from the stands.

REVISED: Hoping that I would make another touchdown, my grandmother cheered from the stands.

ORIGINAL: To prepare for retirement, common stocks should be purchased.

REVISED: To prepare for retirement, you should purchase common stocks.

Dative Case

The case of the indirect object. (See **Case,** p. 117, **Object,** p. 159.)

Deadwood

A descriptive term found in many style manuals referring to super-fluous words or phrases, such as the italicized portions of the following sentences:

It will be ready *at the time* when you will arrive.

The dimensions of the room were nine *feet in length* by seven *feet in width.*

Declarative, Exclamatory, Imperative, Interrogative Sentence

A *declarative sentence* primarily conveys information and ends in a period (Mountains surround Pocatello.). An *exclamatory sentence,* also known as an *interjectional sentence,* expresses an emphatic statement and ends in an exclamation point (Let the buyer beware!). An *imperative sentence* is a command and may end either in a period or an exclamation point (Dumbwiddie Dunkle, you come here!). An *interrogative,* or *interrogatory, sentence* is a question and ends in a question mark (When will this job finally be done?).

Declension

As it applies to English, the term *declension* refers to all the inflectional variations of a given noun or pronoun (in more highly inflected languages, adjective declensions also exist). To decline a noun, one must therefore list all its inflectional variants (*stone, stone's, stones, stones'*). The term *declension* is also used to refer to specific groupings of nouns in English according to the way in which classes of nouns form their plural: the *-s* declension (*stone, stones*), the declensions with root vowel changes (*foot, feet*), etc. The terms *declension* and *conjugation* are not interchangeable: one *declines* a noun or pronoun and *conjugates* a verb. (See **Conjugation,** p. 123.)

Demonstrative Adjective, Pronoun

The demonstrative forms most often used in English are *this, these, that, those,* and *such.* Demonstratives are used to point to substantives which precede or follow them (*This* book is an authoritative guide for tourists; *that* is a parody of travel books). In traditional grammar, demonstratives are called adjectives when they modify a noun which follows them (*this* book); they are pronouns when they stand alone (*This* is my book). Structural grammar classifies demonstrative adjectives in the broader category of *determiners* (see below). Sometimes, the demonstratives are differentiated according to their meanings: *this* and its plural *these* are called "near-demonstratives"; *that* and its plural *those* are called "far-demonstratives."

Denotation

The literal or essential meaning of a word stripped of its emotional overtones of meaning (see also **Connotation,** p. 124). Thus the word *cop* denotes a member of the police force, regardless of the unfavorable connotation which is attached to it. Many words, particularly scientific terms, possess only denotative meaning: *trochelminth, merbromin, volt, hypotenuse.* The dictionary definition of a word is often restricted to its denotation.

Derivation, Derivational Suffix

Derivation is a linguistic term which refers to a process of word formation. By means of certain suffixes and prefixes (*-able, -ment, pre-, en-,* etc.), our language is able to make new words from existing ones. Thus the verb *love* with the addition of a *derivational suffix* can become the adjective *lovable.* Derivational suffixes differ from *inflectional suffixes* (see p. 146) in several ways: (1) they usually change the form class of a word (making a verb out of a noun, etc.); (2) they are the inner layer in words that have both derivational and inflectional suffixes (in the word *establishments,* the inner suffixes *-ish* and *-ment* are derivational and the outer suffix *-s* is inflectional); (3) they attach to relatively few words within a class (the ending *-th* in nouns like *width* is much more restricted than the inflectional *-s* to show plurality).

Determiner

In structural grammar a *determiner* is a function word which signals the occurrence of a noun. Determiners are able to fit into the blanks of the following contexts: _____ dog; _____ men. Examples of the most common classes of determiners are the following: *one, my, the, a, an, no, this, these, any, another.* Some grammars classify determiners as *definite* (*the, this,* etc.) and *indefinite* (*a, no, any,* etc.).

Dialect

In the broadest sense, *dialect* refers to any form of a language spoken by a group of people within a larger linguistic community. Basically, the origin of dialects is geographic; that is to say, a dialect is the distinctive language of people who come from the same region. Dialect is spoken language; one encounters it in editorial language only when it is consciously imitated in dialogue or when it is used facetiously to underscore a point. The essentially oral character of dialect is demonstrated by differences in pronunciation, which are considered to be more reliable criteria for identifying regional speech than differences in vocabulary choice (*bag, poke, sack; bull, critter, toro, gentlemen cow*). It should be added that dialect speech is not necessarily substandard. As a matter of fact, all users of a language speak in a dialect, even the most educated. The major dialects in the United States, as represented by *Webster III*, are the following: Northern, New England, Midland, South, West, Southwest, Northwest.

Diction

The term *diction* refers to word choice. Faulty diction is marked by inexact or inappropriate language. The expression "to flaunt the law," for example, is faulty diction because it is inexact: *flaunt* means "to make a gaudy display." The word which fits into the context is *flout,* not *flaunt.* Faulty diction is usually the result of cloudy thinking.

Dictionaries

Dictionaries can be classified according to their size or their coverage. Labeled according to size, they may be either *abridged* or *unabridged.* The best known abridged dictionaries are desk-size, with a vocabulary of about 150,000 words; they include the following: *The American College Dictionary* (Random House); Funk and Wagnalls *Standard College Dictionary; The Webster New World Dictionary* (World Publishing Co.); *Webster's New Collegiate Dictionary* (G. & C. Merriam Co.). All four of these dictionaries are reputable, and any one of them is satisfactory as a quick reference tool. At present the only up-to-date unabridged dictionary is *Webster's Third New International Dictionary* (labeled *Webster III* in this book) with a vocabulary of approximately 450,000 words. Despite many unfavorable reviews in the popular press, *Webster III* is a monument of scholarship and, by all odds, the most authoritative current record of the English language.

In terms of coverage, dictionaries may be put into the following major categories, each illustrated with the best-known examples of its type:

HISTORICAL DICTIONARIES: *The Oxford English Dictionary (OED)*; *The Dictionary of American English (DAE)*

DICTIONARIES OF SYNONYMS: *Webster's Dictionary of Synonyms;* Roget's *Thesaurus of English Words and Phrases*

DICTIONARIES OF USAGE: Margaret M. Byrant's *Current American Usage;* Bergen and Cornelia Evans's *Dictionary of Contemporary American Usage;* H. W. Fowler's *Modern English Usage;* Eric Partridge's *A Dictionary of Slang and Unconventional English*

ENCYCLOPEDIC DICTIONARIES: *Century Dictionary* (though not revised since 1909, still the best of its kind)

ETYMOLOGICAL DICTIONARIES: W. W. Skeat's *An Etymological Dictionary of the English Language*

There are also dictionaries in specialized areas unrelated to language. These include biographical dictionaries, dictionaries of music, art, religion, mathematics, and numerous other fields.

Digraph, Diphthong, Ligature

These three terms are often confused because they refer to roughly similar concepts. A *diphthong* is the combination of two vowel sounds which are glided together and pronounced as one: the *i* in *chime* represents a diphthong which is recorded phonemically as /ay/. A *digraph* is the combination of two letters to represent one sound: the *ch* in *chime* is a digraph for the phoneme /č/. A *ligature* is a combination of two letters into one symbol: the letters *a* and *e* combine into the ligature æ.

Direct Address

Words or phrases used to indicate the person, group, or thing spoken to are said to be in *direct address* and are set off from the rest of the sentence by commas.

What do you think we should order for dinner, *Carol?*

Ladies and gentlemen, America needs your help now.

Well, *old horse,* we've covered a lot of ground together.

The term *vocative* (the case for direct address in Latin and other inflected languages) is sometimes used as a synonym for *direct address.*

Divided Usage

When two or more words or pronunciations are used with approximately equal frequency by educated speakers and writers, they are said to be in *divided usage.* The pronunciations /iyther/ and /ayther/ for *either,* and the past tense forms *dreamed* and *dreamt* are in divided usage.

Double Comparative, Superlative

These terms describe the use of *more* or *most* together with -*er* or -*est* to form the comparative and the superlative, respectively (*more harder, most tallest*). Neither the double comparative nor the double superlative should be used in editorial English, despite the fact that both were at one time employed by the most respectable writers. Shakespeare, for example, calls the wound inflicted by Brutus "the *most unkindest* cut of all."

Double Genitive, Possessive

The *double genitive* construction is one in which two signals of possession are used together (a friend *of John's;* this love *of mine*). Double genitives occur on all levels of usage and are acceptable even in the most formal editorial English. Generally, double genitives do not occur with inanimate nouns (the cover *of* the *book* [not *book's*]), and they are less likely to follow the definite than the indefinite article (*a* friend *of mine*).

Double Negative

The combination of a negative verb (*cannot, hasn't,* etc.) with a negative pronoun (*nobody, none,* etc.), a negative adverb (*scarcely, hardly,* etc.), or a negative connective (*neither, nor,* etc.) is known as a *double negative*. There is no truth in the notion that the double negative is wrong because "two negatives make an affirmative." Quite to the contrary, the double negative is, in fact, an emphatic negative construction. However, it is none the less unacceptable in editorial English, where it is rigorously avoided by force of usage. Certain constructions in editorial English do contain two negative words or particles (*not unfriendly, not without cause,* etc.), but they are not double negatives according to the terms of the foregoing definition.

Dual Number

A grammatical term denoting a plural of only two. Old English, besides having singular and plural numbers, also had a *dual number* for first and second person pronouns (*wit* for "we two," *git* for "you two," etc.).

Early Modern English

A label used by some linguists to designate the English language between ca. 1450 and ca. 1700. The works of Shakespeare and Milton, therefore, are written in *Early Modern English* (abbreviated *E.Mn.E.*). (See also **Modern English,** p. 153.)

Editorial English

Used as a label in this book to describe the language encountered in the writing of educated people. It ranges from the loosely informal style of the newspaper column to the highly formal and specialized style of the scholarly monograph. Where the distinction is necessary, the terms *formal editorial English* (see p. 134) and *informal editorial English* (see p. 146) appear in this book.

Editorial We

The use of *we* by a writer to refer to himself. The *editorial we,* as its name implies, often appears in newspaper columns. It should be avoided, especially in informative writing, where its only apparent purpose is to camouflage the writer's views. A related usage to the editorial *we* is that of the *royal we.* The use of *we* as a singular reference by royalty is a time-honored one. Heads of state, including American Presidents, have frequently resorted to the royal *we* in public speeches and proclamations. In Early Modern English the singular *ourself* was used to refer to the royal *we.*

Elliptical Constructions

A shortened construction in which one or more words have been left out. Editorial English contains many such constructions, but probably the most widely recurring ellipses are the omission of the relative pronoun (France is one of the few countries [*which*] he didn't see) and absolute phrases (Though [*they are*] indeed rare, whooping cranes are still found in this country). Elliptical constructions also occur frequently in answer to questions (When do you plan to be back? *Not until twelve*) or as sentence transitions (New and more serious consequences result. *Indeed, some tragic ones*). Elliptical sentences of this type are sometimes called *fragments* by style manuals. However, when executed successfully, such ellipses lend sophistication to a prose style. (See **Fragment,** p. 26.)

Etymology

The study of word origins or derivations. Most desk dictionaries give etymological information about their entry words.

Euphemism

A mild word substituted for one which may give offense or which may have strong emotional connotations. *Euphemisms* are often demanded in social situations where more direct language may irritate, injure, or offend people. The word *died* may be too stark for one who has just suffered a bereavement. The word *salesman* may be too commonplace for one who makes his living selling (he may prefer *sales representative* or *agent*). The words *false teeth* may give discomfort to the wearers of *dentures.* There is, however, a point beyond which the use of euphemisms can become a matter of squeamishness or obscuration. To call a *shroud* a *slumber robe,* or to call a *funeral home* (already a euphemism for *mortuary*) a *memorial chapel* is to tax the afflicted with a mawkish and commercial sentimentalism. Advertisers frequently use euphemisms to deflect a customer's attention from the less attractive features of a product: beer and liquor are referred to as *packaged spirits;* plastic products are called *polyethelene;* a coal furnace is dignified by the label *bituminous thermal mechanism.* Advertisers also use euphemisms to enhance the value of their products: a bar of soap becomes a *beauty bar;* an air-conditioned house is *autumn-breezed;* a record player is a *home entertainment center.* The opposite of a euphemism—i.e., the substitution of a harsh word for a milder one—is called a *dysphemism.* The words *cop* for *policeman* or *mutt* for *dog* are illustrations of dysphemisms.

Euphony

A term used to describe the agreeableness or smoothness of sounds and sound combinations. *Euphony* may be illustrated by Shelley's sonorous description of the calm, slumbering Mediterranean lying "Beside a pumice isle in Baiæ's Bay." In written composition, a sense of euphony will guide the writer away from using infelicitous sound patterns like accidental rhymes (a s*lick* tr*ick,* an interes*ting* undertak*ing*).

Exclamatory Sentence

See **Declarative, Exclamatory, Imperative, Interrogative Sentence, p. 127.**

Expletive

The words *there* and *it* are often used as *expletives,* which is to say as "fillers." When expletives *there* or *it* appear as subjects of a sentence they are usually followed by a linking verb and a predicate nominative or a predicate adjective (*There* seem to be some outside agitators in this crowd; *It* was his wish to be cremated). In such constructions, *there* and *it* are anticipatory subjects (see p. 113), while the logical subjects are usually the words that make up the predicate nominative or the predicate adjective. Expletive *it* also occasionally occurs in object position (He knew *it* to be true).

Exposition

One major form of prose composition, the others being persuasion and narration. *Exposition* or *expository writing* conveys information or attitudes. Its purpose is to inform a reader.

Figures of Speech

The following *figures of speech* are defined, each in its appropriate alphabetical place, in the section on Literary Terms: anacoluthon, antithesis, apostrophe, hyperbole, irony, metaphor, metonymy, oxymoron, paradox, periphrasis, personification, pun, simile, synecdoche, synesthesia, understatement.

Finite Verb

A verb form which shows distinctions in number and person and which stands in grammatical agreement with its subject. Finite verbs are sometimes said to complete or limit the meaning of their subjects (The farmhand *worked* till sundown; He *wrote* most of the book during his sabbatical). *Nonfinite* forms are sometimes called *verbals* (see p. 197); they include gerunds, infinitives, and participles.

Fluency

A term referring to style. *Fluency* is achieved by the apt use of transitions (see p. 194), by variation in sentence movement, and by the employment of a large working vocabulary.

Folk Etymology

A false derivation resulting from the confusion by naive speakers of an unfamiliar word with a more familiar one suitable for the context. *Cold slaw* is derived from the Dutch words *kool,* meaning "cabbage," and *sla,* meaning "salad." It became *cold slaw* because native speakers assumed wrongly that its name was derived from the fact that it was served cold. A *folk etymology* records a blunder which is widespread enough to influence either the spelling or the pronunciation of a word (*woodchuck* is so spelled because native users of the word misunderstood its Algonquian source *otcheck* as a compound for *wood* and *chuck*). Another name for a folk etymology is *popular etymology.*

Formal Editorial English

Used as a label in this book to describe the language found characteristically in the expository prose of scholarly books and periodicals as well as most professional and corporate reports.

Form Class

A term in structural linguistics to designate any set of words which can occupy the same position in a construction and which shares a pattern of morphologic or syntactic features. The words *name, tooth,* and *apple* belong to the same form class because they can fill the same phrase positions (such blanks as the following: of the _____; _____ is; my _____) and because they can undergo morphological change to express grammatical relationships (plurality, possession).

Structural linguists agree that there are four form classes in English, but they do not agree what to name them. Some refer to these four classes simply by using numbers. Others prefer the traditional terms *noun, verb, adjective,* and *adverb* for classes one through four, respectively, though they hasten to explain that the terms do not retain their traditional meaning. Thus, in structural grammar, the *noun* is a form class which includes many words known as pronouns in traditional grammar. The four form classes make up one major classification of words; the other is composed of *function,* or *structure, words* (see below).

Form-class words differ from structure words in that they have lexical meaning. Whereas a structure word (*and, of, the*) can only be defined by the function it performs in a construction, a form-class word has a dictionary meaning. Form-class words make up the bulk of our vocabulary, while structure words are relatively few—a rough estimate puts them in the vicinity of 300—though they also are the most frequently recurring words in the language. When new words are coined, they are almost certain to be form-class words. To recognize the stability of English structure words we need only note that the list of present-day structure words is almost identical with that used in Shakespeare's time.

Fragment
See p. 26.

Free Form
See **Bound Form, Free Form,** p. 116.

Fricative
Any consonant which is articulated with audible friction. The sounds represented by the italicized letters in the following words are *fricatives*: *ch*amp, *s*ee, *f*arm, *J*oe. Fricatives are sometimes referred to as *spirants*.

Front Vowel
The vowels for which the blade of the tongue is used to constrict the breath stream. Examples are the vowels in *meet* /iy/, *mate* /ey/, *mat* /æ/.

Functional Change
A word is said to undergo *functional change,* or a *functional shift,* when it is used as more than one part of speech. *Train* exemplifies functional change because it is capable of being used as a verb (*train, trains, trained, training*) and as a noun (*train, trains*).

Function Word
A word which has no lexical meaning and which can only be defined

by the function it performs in a phrase or sentence. According to the classification of structural linguists, *function,* or *structure, words* make up one of two basic classes of words, the other being *form-class words.* Among the most important groups of function words are *determiners* (*a, the, their*); *auxiliaries* (*is, can, do*); *prepositions* (*in, on, with*); *subordinators* (*which, since, after*); *coordinators* (*and, but, or*); *interrogators* (*who, which, what*); *intensifiers* (*very, more, rather*); *expletives* (*there, it*); and *sentence starters* (*well, oh, now*). For a differentiation of function and form-class words, see **Form Class,** p. 134.

Gender

A grammatical term which refers to the inflectional distinction of nouns, pronouns, and adjectives as masculine, feminine, or neuter. Modern English has only very few remnants of gender inflections or derivations. A few nouns show masculine or feminine gender by derivational suffixes (wait*er,* seamstr*ess,* aviat*rix*), and all third person singular pronouns show gender in all cases (*he, his, him; she, hers, her; it, its, its*). For the use of third person pronouns, therefore, there must be agreement in gender between the pronoun and its antecedent (Last Saturday *Cynthia* [antecedent] went on *her* first date). Modern English has *natural* gender; that is to say, the gender of given nouns and pronouns is determined by the sex of the referent. Occasionally a gender which is best designated as *poetic* occurs in English; hence one may refer to a ship or a favorite automobile as *she.* In contrast to the grammar of Modern English, Old English had *grammatical* gender, as do also most modern European languages. In German, for example, the word for *pencil* (*Bleistift*) is masculine. It must, therefore, be referred to with the masculine pronoun for *him* (*er*). Grammatical gender was a feature of Germanic, the ancestor of all Germanic languages.

General Semantics

The study of language as it relates to reality. General semanticists are concerned with the accuracy by which our language reflects events and ideas. They maintain that most human maladjustments are the result of distortions in communication. Among the better known general semanticists are S. I. Hayakawa and Alfred Korzybski.

Generative Grammar

See **Transformational Grammar,** p. 192.

Genitive Case

Another term for the possessive case. (See **Case,** p. 117.)

Germanic

The ancestor language of present-day English. No records are extant of *Germanic;* consequently, all of our knowledge of the language has been acquired through the inferential process of comparative linguistics (see p. 120). Germanic gave rise to several branch languages as a result of migrations. *East Germanic,* which is now extinct, was the language of the Goths (the eventual conquerors of Rome), the Vandalians, and the Burgundians. *North Germanic* was the language which later subdivided into Danish, Swedish, Norwegian, and Icelandic. English is directly traceable to *West Germanic,* which is also the parent language of Dutch, Frisian, and High German. The oldest records of the Germanic language are from North Germanic, of which certain runic inscriptions date to the second century A.D. The Germanic language is variously estimated to have had its origin between the years 2000 and 1500 B.C. Its subdivision into North, East, and West Germanic occurred sometime between the first and fifth centuries A.D. (See also **Indo-European,** p. 145.)

Gerund

A verbal, ending in *-ing* and used as a noun. Gerunds, like all other nouns, can be used as (1) subject (*Eating* is my favorite pastime), (2) direct object (Though he is not very good at it, Chuck likes *writing*), (3) predicate nominative (Mark's duty is *cleaning* the car), (4) object of a preposition (We were unprepared for their *coming*), and (5) appositive (The more serious charge, *breaking* and *entering,* was dismissed by the court). In formal editorial English, possessive forms of pronominal adjectives are preferred over objective forms immediately preceding gerunds (We were unaware of *his* [colloquial: *him*] *opening* the door). When proper names precede a gerund, the possessive form is usually used if the gerund is a subject or a predicate nominative (*Burnwell's driving* makes me intensely nervous). Either the possessive or the uninflected forms of nouns can precede gerunds that occur as objects; the choice is dictated by observation of prevailing usage (I can't concentrate with *David hammering* in the background; I abhor *Mantovani's playing* of Strauss waltzes). When they precede gerunds, nouns or pronominal adjectives are sometimes referred to as the *subject of the gerund* (*John's* humming; *his* playing).

Glide

A term in phonetics referring to intermediary speech sounds. In the flow of speech, some sounds are produced on a recurring basis by the movement of the tongue toward or away from certain pure vowels. These sounds are known as *glides*. The front glide /y/ is the first sound we hear in *yes* and the last sound in *stay*. The center glide /h/ occurs as the first sound in *house* and the last in *law*. The back glide /w/ is heard initially in *wish* and finally in *cow*. Glides in initial position are sometimes referred to as *on-glides,* while those in final position are known as *off-glides.* American English diphthongs usually consist of a pure vowel and an off-glide /aw, ow, ay/, though they may also be preceded by an on-glide (the /yuw/ sound in *you* or *news*). The glides, because they can appear in the position of consonants or vowels, are sometimes referred to as *semivowels.*

Glottal

Any sound articulated in the glottis, or the space between the vocal folds. The /h/ sound in American English is a *glottal* consonant.

Gradation

A systematic variation of vowels in a root form as a result of changes in stress and pitch. Gradation, or *Ablaut* as it was called by Jacob Grimm, is best exemplified for us by its occurrence in English strong verbs (see p. 184). The fact that we say *sing* in the present tense, *sang* in the past tense, and *sung* for the past participle is ultimately explained by vowel gradation which operated in the parent Indo-European. That is to say, very early in the development of our language, separate stem vowels developed for present and past forms of verbs probably because of systematic stress and pitch variations in their pronunciation. An illustration of a similar present-day variation in which the influence of stress and pitch can still be perceived is the vowel change in the auxiliary *can* when it is pronounced emphatically and unemphatically (I can /kæn/ go; I can /kɨn/ go). To a greater or lesser degree, all Indo-European languages retain vestiges of early vowel gradations.

Grammar

The term *grammar* has been defined as possessing three general meanings (see W. Nelson Francis, "Revolution in Grammar," *Quarterly Journal of Speech, XL* [October, 1954], 299–312). The first of these constitutes the complex sets of formal patterns which the average person learns by imitation and practice in his early childhood and over which he has mastery by the time he is six years old. Grammar in this sense has to do with the use of language, not its description or its analysis. The average user of the language knows this "grammar" intuitively.

A second general meaning for *grammar* relates to the formal study of the structure of language. Grammar in this sense is the description of the phonology (see p. 167), the morphology (see p. 155), and/or the syntax (see p. 189) of a language. It is in this signification that linguists are concerned with grammar. Linguistics attempts to describe all facets of language operation. As Nelson Francis has pointed out, this second type of grammar puts into a systematized scheme the behavioral patterns that constitute the first meaning of grammar.

A third meaning of *grammar* is what Francis calls "linguistic etiquette." It is only in this third sense that grammar can be described by qualitative adjectives like "good" or "bad." Grammar of this type is what one encounters in stylebook proscriptions and rules, like "Don't split infinitives" or "Be sure to use a plural verb after *one of those who.*" Most of these rules were formulated during the eighteenth century, at a time when literary men were concerned with regulating the English language to keep it, in their estimate, from degenerating into barbarism. This third type of grammar is rarely of direct interest to the linguistic scholar. It is rather of interest to the teacher of composition who is more concerned with the felicity of expression than with the abstract behavior of language. In recent times the term *grammar* in this sense has been giving way to *style* or *rhetoric.*

The separation of these three meanings is of great importance for objective study and for successful teaching. Most of the controversial commentary about *Webster III* resulted from a failure by critics to keep apart the second and third meanings. *Webster III* set out to describe as completely as possible the word usage and the pronunciation of American English; its grammar, therefore, belongs to the second category. The critics in turn wanted the dictionary to make rules; they judged it by the canons that apply to linguistic etiquette. In this *glossary,* by and large, the entries in the section entitled "Common Usage Problems" reflect the canons of the third, while the entries in the present section reflect the canons of the second definition.

Grapheme

A term describing significant units of written symbols. *Graphemes* are usually indicated by angle brackets, thus <p>. The grapheme<p> stands as a unit for any graphic variation of *p* (for example, *p*, p, P, pp). Graphemes are like phonemes (see p. 165); they represent any number of *allographs* which are nonsignificant variations of letters appearing in given contexts. The symbol *pp*, for example, never occurs in initial or final position in English spelling; it does occur medially between vowels (su*pp*er, co*pp*er). Consequently, *pp* is an allographic variation of the grapheme <p>. It stands in complementary distribution (see p. 121) with other allographs (p, P) because it cannot be interchanged with them. Modern English does not have close correspondence between phonemes (sound units) and graphemes (writing units). This fact accounts for the difficulties native speakers often encounter in learning to spell.

Great Vowel Shift

At the close of the Middle English period, or roughly in the middle of the fifteenth century, English underwent a wholesale sound change known as the *Great Vowel Shift,* which affected all the long vowels then in the language. Though the cause of this shift is not known, linguists have been able, by means of inference, to establish the general nature of the change. In Chaucer's day, as also before his time, all but one of the long vowels had what is known as "continental" value; that is to say, *i* was pronounced as in *see, e* as in *say, u* as in *sue,* and *o* as in *so.* The only long vowel which had already undergone a change from its continental value was *a,* which in Old English had been pronounced as in *father* but which had already shifted to the vowel sound of *saw* before Chaucer's time. The Great Vowel Shift involved the change of these continental sounds to what are approximately their Modern English values. In technical terms, the Great Vowel Shift, by and large, consists of a raising and fronting of the long vowels. It might be schematized in somewhat oversimplified terms as follows:

LATE MIDDLE ENGLISH	MODERN ENGLISH
ǫ (pronounced as in "saw")	ow (pronounced as in "so")
o (pronounced as in "so")	uw (pronounced as in "sue")
u (pronounced as in "sue")	aw (pronounced as in "sow")
e (pronounced as in "say")	iy (pronounced as in "see")
i (pronounced as in "see")	ay (pronounced as in "sigh")

Grimm's Law

A general statement—not really a law—describing a series of systematic consonant shifts which took place in the Germanic languages for a period of roughly three hundred years, beginning ca. 300 B.C. Named after Jacob Grimm, *Grimm's Law* is a more popular name for the phenomenon described by linguistic scholars as the *First Germanic Consonant Shift.* It explains such regular consonant correspondences as the following: English *f*ather : Latin *p*ater; English *f*oot : Latin *p*es; English *f*ish : Latin *p*iscis; English *f*ee : Latin *p*ecu. One must realize that this correspondence, as well as the others covered by Grimm's Law, does not indicate a direct relationship between Latin and English. Instead it shows that English and Latin once had a common ancestor called Indo-European (abbreviated I.E.; see p. 145), and that in the course of time this parent language branched off into dialects which still later became separate languages. Germanic was one of these languages, while Italic, Hellenic, and Celtic were others. English derives from Germanic, and Latin derives from Italic. It was in the formation of Germanic that the consonant change described by Grimm's Law took place. In other words, a series of consonants from the Indo-European language underwent a gradual and systematic shifting into Germanic, but not into Italic or the other newly formed languages. It follows, therefore, that in the examples cited the Latin *p* reflects the original Indo-European pronunciation while English *f* shows the consonant shift which took place in Germanic. The illustrations from the Latin were cited for the sake of convenience and familiarity; one could as well cite illustrations from such other Indo-European languages as Persian, Sanskrit, Greek, Lithuanian, or Gaelic. By the same token, one could show the operation of Grimm's Law from such other Germanic languages as German, Dutch, Gothic, or Icelandic. It is well to bear in mind, further, that the regularity of Grimm's Law is not always discernible at first from modern examples. The fact is that many sound changes have taken place, and sometimes these changes have obscured the descent of the consonants covered by Grimm's Law.

The particulars of Grimm's Law are too complicated to be shown here in detail. They may, however, be briefly summarized by the diagram on p. 142. Because some of the I.E. consonants underwent changes of their own (unrelated to Grimm's Law), notations have been made to indicate their development in Latin. It is to be emphasized that the illustrations show correspondences not genealogies. The Latin words are not the source for the English; instead, they are non-Germanic cognates.

The importance of Grimm's Law to comparative linguistics and the study of language in general cannot be emphasized enough. With the discovery of such far-reaching consonant correspondence, scholars learned what has since become a fundamental premise of linguistic study: the oral language has primacy over the written. To learn of the history and development of languages, one must first reconstruct their sound systems. The pioneering work done by Jacob Grimm, and even more fundamentally by the Dane Rasmus Rask, whose work preceded the publication of Grimm's second edition of his *Deutsche Grammatik* in 1822 (the source of Grimm's Law), set the tone and established the guidelines for all subsequent studies in philology. One such subsequent study led to the formulation of an exception to Grimm's Law. For a discussion of it, see **Verner's Law,** p. 197.

I.E. bh (Lat. *f*)	dh (Lat. *f*)	gh (Lat. h)
↓	↓	↓
Ger. b	d	g
(Lat. *f*rater: Engl. *b*rother)	(Sanskrit *dh*ogos: English *d*ay)	(Lat. *h*ortus: Engl. *g*arden)
I.E. p	t	k
↓	↓	↓
Ger. f	þ (as in *th*ief)	h
(Lat. *p*ater: Engl. *f*ather)	(Lat. *t*enuis: Engl. *th*in)	(Lat. *c*anis: Engl. *h*ound)
I.E. b	d	g
↓	↓	↓
Ger. p	t	k
(Greek kanna*b*is: Engl. hem*p*)	(Lat. e*d*ere: Engl. ea*t*)	(Lat. *g*enus: Engl. *k*in)

Group Genitive

A term given to a construction in which *'s* is added to a phrasal modifier as if it were a possessive noun (*the man across the street's* house; *the Chief of Police's* testimony). *Group genitives* are generally avoided in editorial English.

Headword

The word which is modified in a phrase. For example, *house* is the headword of the phrase *the old house*. Members of all four form classes (see p. 134), can perform the function of headwords as can also some function words (see p. 135): the *new book* (noun headword); *drives* fast (verb headword); bright *green* (adjective headword); very *slowly* (adverb headword); exactly *on* (preposition headword).

Historical Present

The use of the present tense to describe events which clearly occurred in the past. The *historical present* is a stylistic device which endows narrative writing with vividness (Chaucer next *turns* his attention to the Italian novella, a form he *is about to* employ with unrivaled artistry in his *Canterbury Tales*).

Homonym

A word which, though spelled differently, sounds exactly like another (*hare, hair; steel, steal*). *Homonyms* often cause spelling problems, as witness their appearance in lists of words most frequently misspelled (*there, their, they're; wright, right, write; two, too, to,* etc.). When homonyms are deliberately confused to create a humorous effect, they are called *puns* (see p. 227).

Idiolect

The language of one individual as differentiated from all other speakers, especially in terms of pronunciation. The ability of recognizing a familiar, unidentified voice over the telephone is a matter of recognizing the speaker's *idiolect*.

Idiom

An expression peculiar to one language. Usually the meaning of an *idiom* cannot be adduced from the literal meanings of its component words (*to take up smoking, to break in a horse,* or the German *Mach schnell* for "hurry up," literally "make quick").

Immediate Constituents

According to structural linguistic analysis, any sentence in the language can be cut into two parts; these parts, in turn can be cut in two, and so on, until ultimately the most basic elements in the language are isolated. The parts adduced from this method of analysis are called *immediate constituents* (or IC's), and the process of cutting structures in two is called *binary analysis*. Typically, the largest immediate constituents in a sentence are the subject and the predicate. These IC's can often be further reduced into other binary structures: phrases, words, morphemes, and finally phonemes. Immediate constituent analysis is, in a sense, a new diagrammatic method to reveal the linear structure of the English sentence down to its smallest constituent parts.

The following steps illustrate binary analysis into immediate constituents down to the level of words:

SENTENCE

John ate a ripe peach.

SUBJECT   PREDICATE

John   //   ate a ripe peach

VERB OBJECT

ate // a ripe peach

DETERMINER   NOUN PHRASE

a   //   ripe peach

ADJECTIVE   NOUN

ripe   //   peach

Binary analysis of this type has been an important feature of the modern school of structural linguistics (see p. 184). In recent times, some of the underlying assumptions of binary analysis have been challenged by exponents of transformational grammar (see p. 192). The latter have argued convincingly that certain sentence types are incapable of binary analysis. For example, questions beginning with question markers do not allow linear cuts to separate subject and predicate constituents. Thus, in a question like "Where did you put the keys?" no one line can separate subject and predicate. According to transformational theory such sentences are "transforms" of more basic sentence types known as *kernel sentences* (see p. 149). Transformation theory further argues that mere separation of parts, as seems to be the purpose of immediate constituent analysis, yields, little, if any, insight into the operation of language.

Imperative Mood

See **Mood,** p. 153.

Imperative Sentence

See **Declarative, Exclamatory, Imperative, Interrogative Sentence,** p.127.

Incoherence

The failure to connect ideas properly. Incoherent writing is marked by the absence of transitions and logical connection. (See **Transition,** p. 194.)

Indefinite Pronoun

A term in traditional grammar for any of the following words when they are used as substantives. Actually, the label *indefinite* is inaccurate when applied to some of the words listed (e.g., *both, nobody*).

all	anyone	each one
another	anything	either
any	both	every
anybody	each	everybody

everyone	nobody	other
everything	none	several
few	no one	some
many	nothing	somebody
much	one	someone
neither	oneself	something
		such

Indicative Mood
See **Mood,** p. 153.

Indo-European
The original or parent language from which most present-day European languages, including English, ultimately derive. *Indo-European* is a totally hypothetical language. No records remain of it, and all that is known about it has been reconstructed through the prodigious labors of comparative linguists, especially in the nineteenth century. Indo-European was a heavily inflected language with free accent. In these respects, Modern English differs from it, because in the course of time English has very much reduced its inflectional endings and has, like all other Germanic languages, developed a fixed accent on initial syllables.

Scholars now seem to agree that Indo-European was spoken in north-central Europe (earlier, the theory was held that it originated in southeastern Europe, and earlier still, in Asia). Recent scholarship quite ingeniously traces the original homeland of the Indo-Europeans to an inland region between the Vistula and the Elbe rivers, hence somewhere in the location of East and West Germany. Migrations, moving first in a southeasterly direction, probably began in the third millennium B.C. In the course of time, the isolation of tribes from the parent community brought about such wholesale linguistic changes that speakers from different regions no longer understood each other. Gradually a group of independent languages developed: Germanic (see p. 137), Hellenic, Italic, Celtic, Hittite, Tocharian, Balto-Slavic, and Indo-Iranian. These languages, in turn, developed into new dialects and eventually once more into new languages. Thus, modern Greek is traceable to Hellenic, Hindi to Indo-Iranian, Russian to Balto-Slavic, French to Italic, and English to Germanic.

Infinitive
A verbal form used as a noun. The *infinitive* may or may not be preceded by *to* (He likes *to sleep;* He may *come*). The infinitive without the sign *to* is used regularly after such auxiliaries as *can, do, may, must, shall, should, will, would* (must *know*, will *eat*, would *try*).

Infinitive Phrase

A group of words headed by an infinitive. The words following an infinitive and forming part of its phrase are known as its *complement* or its *subject*. *Infinitive phrases* can appear as substantives or modifiers (*To learn German* [substantive] is his first concern; Old Faithful is a wonder *to behold* [adjective modifier]).

Inflection, Inflectional Suffix

Inflection is a grammatical term referring to patterns of changes which a word can undergo in order to show *case, gender, mood, number, person, tense, voice,* etc. In English, inflectional distinctions are made primarily by means of suffixes (punishment*s*, write*s*, ox*en*, tremble*d*), though some few are made by internal changes (*foot, feet,* etc.) Inflectional systems involving nouns, pronouns, or adjectives are called *declensions* (see p. 127) and those involving verbs are called *conjugations* (see p. 123). (See also **Derivation, Derivational Suffix**, p. 128.)

Informal Editorial English

Used as a label in this book to describe the language found characteristically in the expository prose of mass-circulating magazines, non-fiction books addressed to the general reader, and popular columns in · newspapers.

Intensifier

A class of function words (see p. 135) used to modify descriptive adjectives or certain types of adverbs. Words like *quite, very, rather, extremely, more,* and *most* are *intensifiers* when they appear before adjectives or adverbs and when they specify degree (*very* ill, *quite* unhappy, *most* infrequently). Some grammars refer to intensifiers simply as adverbs; others call them *adverbs of degree* or *intensives*. Many structural linguists prefer the label *intensifier*.

Interdental

Any sound articulated by the placement of the tongue tip between the front teeth. The initial sounds in *thin* /θ/ and *then* /ð/ are *interdental* consonants.

Interjection

In traditional grammar, considered one of the eight parts of speech. An *interjection* is a word of exclamation registering emotion (*My,* was I ever happy! *Help!* My shirttail is caught in the wringer!). Structural linguists classify interjections as function words (see p. 135) called *sentence starters*.

International Phonetic Alphabet

Often referred to by its initials *IPA*, the *International Phonetic*

Alphabet was adopted by the International Phonetic Association in 1888. As its name implies, the IPA is a list of symbols standing for individual speech sounds occurring in any language in the world. A general adaptation of the IPA is used by John S. Kenyon and Thomas A. Knott in their *Pronouncing Dictionary of American English,* second edition (Springfield, Massachusetts, 1949). Because the IPA is no longer used widely by American linguists, this book employs the Trager-Smith phonemic alphabet, which is a modification of the IPA. (See **Phonemic Alphabet,** p. 165.)

Interrogative Pronoun

A term in traditional grammar referring to words which can stand as substantives while signaling the appearance of a question. Structural linguists call these words *question markers* and classify them among function words. Frequently used *interrogative pronouns* are the following: *who, whose, whom, which, what,* and their compounds in *-ever.*

Interrogative Sentence

See **Declarative, Exclamatory, Imperative, Interrogative Sentence,** p.127.

Intonation

In a broad sense, *intonation* refers to three features of speech: stress, pitch, and juncture. These features have to do with the relative loudness, quality, and finality of utterance. They can be transcribed with the help of certain suprasegmental symbols (so named because they are written in superscript). The intonation pattern of the question "Your name is Garth?" is transcribed as follows: ^{2}yuwr neym iz^3 gár$\theta^{3\#}$. For a discussion of these symbols, see **Stress,** p. 183; **Pitch,** p. 167; and **Juncture,** p. 148. In a narrow sense, intonation is used to refer to pitch alone. However, in present-day linguistic studies, this usage is infrequent.

Intransitive Verb

A verb which does not take a direct object (He *lept* and *fell;* The ashes are still *smoldering*). Some verbs can be used either transitively or intransitively according to the contexts in which they appear (He *writes books* [transitive] for a living; He *writes* [intransitive] for a living). (See also **Transitive Verb,** p. 196.)

Inversion

A rhetorical term referring to the placement of sentence parts in unnatural order (verb before subject, object before subject, etc.). Though certain statement and question patterns require *inversion,* it can be used in other instances as a stylistic device to bring variety and emphasis to a passage ("Help, Help!" he screamed as he dangled precariously from the edge of the cliff). For further discussion see **Word Order,** p. 201.

Isogloss, Isomorph, Isophone

In dialect studies, these are boundary lines to separate regional linguistic traits. *Isoglosses* are linguistic boundaries which separate different word usages (e.g., in the United States, the dialectal provenience of *brook, creek, run,* or *branch*). *Isomorphs* separate inflectional variations (e.g., the regional distribution of *you-all, you'ns,* and *mongst-ye*). *Isophones* separate variant pronunciations (e.g., *greasy* with /s/ or /z/). A dialect atlas for the entire United States showing isoglosses, isomorphs, and isophones is gradually being completed. At present, only the *Linguistic Atlas of New England* has been published. (See also **Dialect,** p. 129.)

Jargon

As a stylistic term, *jargon* refers to vague and abstract writing marked by fuzzy wording and overworked phrases (e.g., *in the case of, in light of* the circumstances). In linguistics, *jargon* most often refers to the specialized vocabulary associated with particular vocations (business jargon, legal jargon, etc.).

Journalese

A term for newspaper jargon. Though academic critics tend to overuse the term to refer to any sort of popular writing, *journalese* does occur widely in the daily press and in mass-circulating news magazines. In its attempt to be vivid, journalese is frequently marked by tarnished phrases and by overstatement. At its worst, it is "formula writing"; that is to say, a ready-made language is used to fit almost any report or summary. *Timestyle,* as the style of *Time* magazine is called by some of its critics, is perhaps the most notorious illustration of formula writing in the popular press. Because it aims for drama on every line, *Timestyle* resorts to inversions, blends (like *cinemactress*), action verbs (one critic observes that in *Time* people never *walk,* they *stride*), and a variety of special effects to create a packaged vividness.

Juncture

A feature of English intonation (see p. 147). *Juncture* refers to certain kinds of breaks (or, more accurately, pitch-pauses) which occur in the flow of speech. There are four juncture phonemes in modern English:

(1) *Plus juncture* is a phonological break which enables us to differentiate the pronunciation of "I scream" /ay + skriym/ and "ice cream" /ays + kriym/. These two phonological phrases, it will be noticed, would be identical were it not for the slight interruption of

the breath streams which marks the limits of the two words. Plus juncture occurs between words which are uttered on the same level of pitch and stress.

(2) *Single-bar juncture* appears in conjunction with primary stress. It is easily recognized in contexts within sentences where words are given unusual stress: "Nowadays *boys* are the ones who are clothes-conscious" (i.e., not girls) /nawɔdeyz bɔ́yz / ar ðə wanz huw ar klowz kǝnšɨz/.

(3) *Double-bar juncture* is sometimes referred to as the "comma juncture." It usually features a slight rise in pitch. The most dramatic demonstration of double-bar juncture is probably in sentences with nonrestrictive modifiers such as the following: "The students, who were protesting, were ordered to disperse." In such a sentence, it is double-bar juncture (marked //) which shows that "who were protesting" is nonrestrictive and, therefore, applies to all the students. Without double-bar juncture "who were protesting" would become restrictive thus implying that of all the students, only those who protested were ordered to disperse. Double-bar juncture also occurs after adverbial sentence openers in the speech of most people (As soon as Mark comes home // he raids the refrigerator).

(4) *Double-cross or terminal juncture* denotes finality. It is used conventionally at the end of sentences (We moved into our new house yesterday#).

Kernel Sentence

A term used in transformational grammar to describe basic or elementary sentence types, as contrasted with all other sentence types derived from them, known as *transforms*. *Kernel sentences are basic in the sense that they cannot be derived from other sentences.* Thus, for example, the simple noun-verb sentence "The stars shine" is a kernel sentence because no other sentence can inhere in it. In contrast, the question "Do the stars shine?" is a transform. Kernel sentences must be made up of a noun or noun phrase and a verb or verb phrase. (See also **Immediate Constituents,** p. 143 and **Transformational Grammar,** p. 192.)

Labiodental

Any sound made by the contact of the upper front teeth with the lower lip. The /f/ and /v/ sounds in American English are *labiodental* consonants.

Late Modern English

A label used to designate the English language since ca. 1700. (See also **Modern English,** p. 153.)

Lateral

A sound resulting from the placement of the tongue tip against the palate and the emission of the breath stream to the sides of the tongue. The /l/ sound in American English is a *lateral* consonant.

Levels of Usage

A term referring to a range of social dialects in a given language. This book differentiates words and locutions only as *formal* or *informal* because, in its concern with usage, it is limited to a description of editorial English. Linguistic sociologists who are concerned with the spoken language of the uneducated sometimes describe that *level of usage* as *popular* (see p. 168) or *vulgate* (see p. 200). These labels, or any other devised by linguists to delineate levels of usage, are meant to be descriptive, not evaluative. For a fuller discussion of levels and varieties of usage, particularly as these terms are used in this book, see pp. 1–3.

Lexicography

The compiling of dictionaries (see **Dictionaries,** p. 129).

Ligature

See **Digraph, Diphthong, Ligature,** p. 130.

Linguistic Geography

The study of the spatial distribution of dialects and languages. It is the task of the linguistic geographer to make maps for the provenience of regional pronunciations, word forms and meanings, and grammatical forms (see **Isogloss, Isophone, Isomorph,** p. 148). A *Linguistic Atlas of the United States and Canada* is now being prepared by linguistic geographers; however, only the part covering New England has thus far been published.

Linguistics

In its most general sense, the systematic study of language. Specialties in *linguistics* include the study of speech sounds, of usage, or grammatical systems, dialects, vocabulary and lexicography, writing systems, etymology, and the history and genealogy of languages. In recent times, many universities have added departments of linguistics for interdisciplinary study of languages and linguistic methodology as well as for the teaching of non-Indo-European languages. The more traditional course in the history, usage, or grammar of a single language is still being offered by such established academic departments as English, French, and German. The study of purely written language, as differentiated from oral, is now rarely classified as *linguistics;* instead, it is called the study of *composition* or *stylistics.* For special application of linguistics, see **Comparative Linguistics, p. 120; Structural Linguistics, p. 184; and Transformational Grammar, p. 192.**

Linking Verb

A verb which links a subject with a predicate nominative or predicate adjective. The most widely used linking verbs are forms of *be, become,* and *seem* (Mr. Lauderale *is* the best teacher I ever had; The ocean *seemed* calm). Another term for *linking verb* is *copula* or *copulative* verb.

Liquid Sounds

The consonants /r/ and /1/ are sometimes referred to as *liquid sounds* or *liquids.* They are so named because they are produced without friction. (See **Phonemic Alphabet, p. 165.**)

Loanword

As its name implies, a word borrowed from another language. Because English had close contact with a good many continental languages in its early history, its native word stock has been augmented by a large number of *loanwords.* When a word is first borrowed from another language, and while it is still pronounced and spelled as it was in its native language, it is considered a foreign word and should be underlined when written, or italicized when printed (*esprit de corps, Weltanschauung*). As the word comes to be used with more and more frequency, it gradually merges with the native word stock (e.g., *mercy* from Old French *merci, poppycock* from dialectal Dutch *pappekak*).

Localism

A regional usage of a word or phrase. *Critter* is a *localism* for a domestic animal in many rural areas of the United States. *Shinny* is a Canadian localism for *pond hockey.* Except to record dialogue or to add unusual color, localisms should be avoided in formal editorial English.

Loose Sentence

A sentence in which modifying words, phrases, and clauses are put after the verb in the main clause. A *loose sentence* is, therefore, one which could be brought to a grammatical end at one or more points before its actual ending (A hundred-story skyscraper will be built in Chicago [possible end] according to a report [possible end] just released by the UPI [actual end]). Loose sentences are characteristic of spoken English. The opposite of a loose sentence is a *periodic sentence* (see p. 163). For another major rhetorical sentence type, see **Balanced Sentence,** p. 116.

Macron

In linguistics, a line made over a vowel to show that it is long. Editors have traditionally used the *macron* to show vowel length in Old English words (O.E. *mīn, stān, hām,* for Mod. E. *mine, stone,* and *home*).

Metathesis

The transposition of adjacent sounds. *Metathesis* of /r/ and /i/ occurred in the change from Old English *bridd* to Modern English *bird*. A more recent illustration is the pronunciation of *preform* for *perform*.

Middle English

A label used to describe the English language between ca. 1100 and ca. 1450. *Middle English* (abbreviated *M.E.*) featured many more inflectional endings than the language of the present day. The literature and documents which survive from the Middle English period are written in various dialects, the most important of which represented the following regions: Kent, the South of England, the East Midlands, the West Midlands, and the North. Chaucer wrote in the dialect of the East Midlands, which was also the dialect of London and which eventually became the standard dialect of England. In literary history, the West Midlands dialect of Middle English is also of great importance, since it was the medium of such widely admired poems as *Sir Gawain and the Green Knight, Pearl,* and *The Vision of Piers Plowman.* Among the more notable sound changes which took place during the Middle English period were the silencing of final *-e* and the **Great Vowel Shift** (see p. 140). The following is an illustration of East Midland Middle English of the late fourteenth century:

> Jason, which sih his fader old,
> *Jason, who saw his old father,*
> Upon Medea made him bold
> *Upon Medea made (himself) bold*
> Of arte magique, which sche couþe
> *Of magic art, which she knew,*
> And preiþ hire, þat his fader ȝouþe,
> *And prayed her, that his father's youth,*
> Sche wolde make aȝeinward newe.
> *She would again make new.*

Misrelated Modifier

A phrase which is not clearly associated with its headword. *Misrelated modifiers* are likely to arise from the misplacement of sentence parts, often with unintended humorous effect (Room wanted by girl with bay window). (See also **Dangling Modifier, p. 126.**)

Mixed Metaphor

The joining of two or more incongruous metaphors, as in the following two illustrations:

> Never putting his eggs in one basket, Eisenhower used a double-edged attack to stem the tide of the German air force.

> Computer technology is a virgin field pregnant with opportunity.

Modal

A *modal* or a *modal auxiliary* is the name given to such "helping verbs" as *can, could, may, might, will, shall,* etc. For further discussion, see **Auxiliary, p. 115.**

Modern English

A term used to describe the English language from the period ca. 1450 to the present time. Some linguistic histories differentiate between *Early Modern English* (see p. 131) and *Late Modern English* (see p. 149); however, all linguists seem to agree that in its essential characteristics, the present-day language is the same as that of the late fifteenth century, by which time most major phonological and morphological changes had taken place. It is erroneous, therefore, to call Shakespeare's language *Old English*; instead, it should be referred to as *Early Modern* or *Modern English.*

Modifier

A word or word group which qualifies or limits the meaning of another word or word group. In traditional grammar, two parts of speech, the adjective and the adverb, are defined primarily on the basis of their use as *modifiers* (to speak *well,* the *long* letter). Words or word groups which modify the meaning of an entire statement are sometimes called "sentence modifiers" (In the evening [modifier], we visited the Culpeppers). The word which is modified is usually referred to as the *headword* (see p. 142).

Mood

A grammatical term referring to the speaker's attitude toward an utterance. Traditional grammar recognizes three *moods*: (1) the *indicative* for statements of fact; (2) the *subjunctive* for statements of probability, concession, desire, or condition; and (3) the *imperative* for statements of request or command. Originally, grammatical moods were differentiated by inflectional forms. There are, however, few formal signals left to indicate mood in modern English; that is to say, our language rarely differentiates an indicative from a subjunctive by form alone. Therefore, the term *mood* finds little of its original structural significance in English. To call such usages as *I may* or *I could* subjunctive simply because they name conditions is illusory and misleading. Neither of these verbs is inflected; hence, neither contains a structural indication that it expresses contingency.

There are only a few vestiges of a formal subjunctive left in modern English. The most widespread is the present subjunctive, third person singular form without -*s* (if he *make;* that he *write*). Another is the use of *be* in the present subjunctive and *were* in the first and third person singular of the past subjunctive (if he *be;* if I [or he] *were*). However, even these forms are limited in use, occurring primarily in formal editorial English. The more common usage is that of the indicative (if he *makes;* if I *am*) or the conditional as expressed by a modal auxiliary (if he *should make*).

The imperative mood is identified syntactically in modern English by the omission of its controlling subject pronoun (*Bring* me the newspaper; Please *call* back in the morning). In traditional stylebooks, this usage is sometimes called "*you* understood." Structural linguists object to this label because, they point out, it was invented to accommodate the notion that all proper sentences must have a subject and a predicate. However, a more recent school of linguistics known as *transformational grammar* implicitly upholds the concept of "*you* understood" by maintaining that imperatives occur in derived sentences, being "transforms" of *kernel sentences* (see p. 149) which contain a noun phrase and a verb phrase (thus, *Open the door* is a transform of the kernel sentence *You open the door*).

Morpheme

The smallest meaningful unit of language. A *morpheme* may consist of a single phoneme (*a, I*), of a multisyllabic word (*Massachusetts*), of a word root (*speak* in *unspeakable*), of a prefix or a suffix (*un-* and *-able* in *unspeakable*), or even of a unit as inconspicuous as a stress phoneme (the word root *tent* in *cóntent* [noun] and *contént* [adjective]). To determine the morphemic structure of a word, one must reduce that word to its minimal units of meaning. For example, the verb form *hangs* consists of two morphemes: the base morpheme *hang* and the inflectional suffix for the third person present singular, -*s*. Morphemes are usually inserted between brackets. Thus, the morpheme $\{-Z_1\}$ stands for all variant inflectional forms that signal plurality in nouns: road*s* /z/, hit*s* /s/, churche*s* /ɨz/, ox*en* /ɨn/, etc. The morpheme

{-Z₂} stands for all variant inflectional forms that signal the singular possessive cases in nouns: Syd's /z/, Matt's /s/, church's /ɨz/. These variant forms, because they stand in *complementary distribution* (i.e., they are not interchangeable; see p. 121), are called *allomorphs.* *Morphemes* must not be confused with *syllables,* which are strictly phonological units, not meaning units. The word *puts* has one syllable but two morphemes. In contrast, the word *Connecticut* has four syllables but only one morpheme.

Morphology

A basic branch of linguistic study concerned with the structure of words. *Morphology* concentrates on the analysis of parts of speech, inflectional forms, word roots, and affixes. It complements the other major area of grammatical study, that of *syntax* (see page 189).

Mutation

A sound change which took place in the Old English period. *Mutation* affected accented vowels or diphthongs which were followed by an /i/ or a /j/ in the next syllable. The difference between *man* and *men* is traceable to this phenomenon. Singular *man* was originally not followed by /i/ or /j/, but plural *men* was, deriving from a prehistoric form *manni.* The influence of /i/ in *manni* eventually changed the root vowel to /e/. Most present-day plurals which change their root vowels are the results of mutation in the Old English period (*goose, geese; mouse, mice; foot, feet; tooth, teeth*). Another word for *mutation* is *umlaut.*

Narration

One major form of prose composition, the others being exposition and persuasion. *Narration* involves the telling of an incident or series of incidents, usually in chronological arrangement and usually accompanied by description. For a discussion of a narrative with plot, see **Plot,** p. 225.

Nasal Consonants

Consonants which are articulated by means of closure of the oral passage and emission of the breath stream through the nasal passage. English has three *nasal consonant* phonemes: /m/ as in *m*an, /n/ as in *n*est, and /ŋ/ as in si*ng*. The last of these, called the "velar nasal," is not generally recognized because our alphabet lacks a letter for it. It can occur by itself in words that are spelled with a medial *ng* (si*ng*er, sti*ng*er) or a final *ng* (lo*ng*, ha*ng*, eveni*ng*), but it may also be the first phoneme in a consonant cluster as in /si*ng*k/ or /fi*ng*ər/. (See also **Phonemic Alphabet,** p. 165.)

Neologism

A newly coined word. As institutions grow and technology advances, many new words will, of needs, be introduced into the language (for example, *multiversity* to refer to large and complex universities; *blab-off* to refer to a mechanism that turns off the sound during TV commercials). New words lose their status as *neologisms* when they appear in a dictionary.

Nominative Absolute

See **Absolute Phrase,** p. 105.

Nonce Word

A word coined for a particular occasion (the billing of a suggestive movie as *sexcitement*). Literally, *nonce* means "the once," a construction which is traceable to Old English.

Nonrestrictive Modifier

See **Restrictive** and **Nonrestrictive Modifiers,** p. 177.

Noun

Traditionally a *noun* is defined as the part of speech which names a person, place, or thing. Structural linguists consider this definition inadequate and misleading because it fails to differentiate nouns from other parts of speech. For example, adjectives can also name persons (the *Kennedy* smile), places (a *New York* attorney), or things (a *copper* penny). Moreover, many nouns do not name a person, place, or thing; instead, they may name a quality (*heat*), a condition (*poverty*), a state of mind (*happiness*), an emotion (*fear*), and countless other concepts. In fact, so diverse are the words that function as nouns that a notional classification (one based on meaning) is unwieldy and unproductive.

Structural linguists, therefore, discard the notional definition found in traditional grammars. In its place they put a definition based on function and form. Nouns make up a large part of one of the four basic *form classes* (see p. 134) of English. This class, designated as Class I by some linguists, consists of any word (noun or pronoun) which has the potential to influence the behavior of a verb. Thus, in the frame

_____ speaks

any word which can fill the blank belongs to Form Class I (*Clarissa, she, humanity, money,* etc.). It is the word that fills the blank which determines the presence of inflectional *-s* in *speaks*. To find all the nouns in the language, one would have to make appropriate test frames for a wide variety of meanings, but even then an exhaustive list of nouns would be impossible to compile. Suffice it to say, then, that a noun (or a noun phrase) has the potential, when it appears in a basic or *kernel sentence* (see p. 149), for influencing the inflectional form of a verb.

Nouns can, furthermore, be differentiated from other parts of speech (as well as from pronouns which are grouped in one class with nouns by structural linguists) by the function words which are capable of introducing them. Those function words which signal the occurrence of a noun are known as *determiners* (see p. 128). Hence, the appearance of such words as *the* or *their* indicates that a noun will follow, though not always immediately. Determiners can be used with all classes of nouns, though they are used only in a demonstrative function with certain *proper nouns,* which are names of places, people, products (The home of the Paddock Bar—that is *the* New Orleans I remember).

Nouns, moreover, form a paradigmatic class, having distinct endings to indicate the possessive case in the singular and all cases in the plural. The possessive singular inflection is shown in writing by *'s* for all nouns except those that end in *-s* and a very few that end in *-ence* or *-ance* for which *'s* or simply an apostrophe may be used (James' or James's; conscience' or conscience's). Generally the choice is dictated by the pronunciation: if the suffix is pronounced /ɪz/, the spelling is *'s*; if, however, it is pronounced /z/, only the apostrophe is used. For plural possessives ending in *-s,* the standard spelling is the apostrophe alone (dogs', sailors'). For observations on the usage of the inflectional and phrasal possessive, see **Apostrophe,** p. 65.

The plural of English nouns is formed in various ways:

(1) By means of inflectional *-s* or *-es* (church*es,* father*s*). The ending *-es* occurs regularly in words ending with *-ch, -s, -sh, -x,* or *-z.* The *-s* or *-es* class of nouns is the productive class in English. New loanwords adopt this ending.

(2) By mutation of the root vowel (g*oo*se, g*ee*se; m*ou*se, m*i*ce).

(3) By means of inflectional *-n.* In Old English this class of plurals was the productive class, but today ox*en* is the only pure *-n* plural left in the language.

(4) By zero inflection (sheep, sheep; deer, deer). In colloquial usage nouns of measurement are frequently left uninflected (sixteen *head* of cattle, five *gallon* of gas, six *foot* tall). Nouns ending in *-ics* also form their plural by zero inflection (athle*tics*).

(5) By the retention of foreign plurals:

(*a*) From Latin
singular *-um,* plural *-a* (dat*um,* dat*a*)
singular *-a,* plural *-ae* (alumn*a,* alumn*ae*)

singular *-us*, plural *-i* (alumn*us*, alumn*i*)
singular *-is*, plural *-es* (analys*is*, analy*ses*)
singular *-ex*, plural *-ces* (vort*ex*, vort*ices*)
singular *-ix*, plural *-ces* (matr*ix*, matr*ices*).
(*b*) From Greek
singular *-ion*, plural *-a* (criter*ion*, criteri*a*)
singular, *-a*, plural *-ata* (stigm*a*, stigm*ata*)
(*c*) From French
singular *no ending,* plural *-x* (beau, beau*x*)
(*d*) From Italian
singular *no ending,* plural *-i* (bandit, banditt*i*)
(*e*) From Hebrew
singular *no ending,* plural *-im* (cherub, cherub*im*)

Many of these plurals, however, are dropping even from formal English, being replaced by native plural forms in *-s* or *-es* (index, index*es*; syllabus, syllabus*es*).

Certain spelling practices occasionally cause difficulties in the formation of plurals.

(1) Nouns ending in a consonant followed by *y* take plurals in *-ies* (beaut*y*, beaut*ies*; dand*y*, dand*ies*). Exceptions are proper nouns (Mar*ys*) and isolated common nouns (empt*ys* with reference to bottles).

(2) Nouns ending in a consonant followed by *o* vary in plural formation. Some simply add *-s* (solo*s*, banjo*s*, piano*s*), some add *-es* (Negro*es*, potato*es*, veto*es*), and some can take either ending (zero*s* or zero*es*, hobo*s* or hobo*es*). In case of doubt about the plural spelling of words in this class, one should consult a dictionary.

(3) Many nouns ending in *-f* or *-fe* change to *-ves* in the plural (lea*f*, lea*ves*; kni*fe*, kni*ves*; thie*f*, thie*ves*). A few nouns in this class can end in *-s* or *-ves* (wharf*s* or whar*ves*, hoof*s* or hoo*ves*).

Noun Adjunct

A noun which, in traditional terms, is used as an adjective. A *noun adjunct* appears in attributive position directly before the noun it modifies (the *telephone* booth, the *butcher* knife, a *roof* garden). Many compound nouns have developed from frequently used phrases composed of a noun adjunct plus a noun (*bookstore, classroom, timekeeper*).

Noun Clause

A dependent clause used as a simple noun. *Noun clauses* can occupy any sentence position available to one-word nouns:

SUBJECT: *That he had too much to drink* was obvious to everyone.

APPOSITIVE: His promise, *that he would never cross the street without looking,* won't mean much.

OBJECT: It is a well-known fact that children always want *what they can't have.*

COMPLEMENT: One advantage was *that we had helpful neighbors.*

Noun Phrase

A group of words used as a noun in any of its sentence functions:

SUBJECT: *The Third Symphony of Beethoven* is my favorite.

APPOSITIVE: John, *the little boy in the dirty overalls,* is my nephew.

OBJECT: Mark forgot *to clean his room.*

COMPLEMENT: Last Tuesday was *the unluckiest day of my life.*

Noun phrases, though not in themselves made up of a subject and a verb, can contain subject-verb structures (i.e., clauses) as subordinate elements (*The little old man who sat next to us* was once a jockey).

Number

A term referring to singular and plural in modern English. Subjects and verbs must agree in *number,* as must pronouns and their antecedents. For example, in the sentence "Everyone knew his place," the singular antecedent *everyone* agrees in number with the singular pronoun *his.* At one time English had a *dual number* (see p. 131) in addition to singular and plural.

Object

A term from traditional grammar referring to the part of the sentence which is affected by or receives the action of the verb. Four terms are used to differentiate the function of *objects* in English sentences.

(1) *The direct object* follows a transitive verb (see p. 196). Some grammars call the direct object a *complement* because it completes the action of the verb. The italicized words of the following sentences are direct objects:

After signing the contract, he threw *the pen* out the window.

Secret Agent Balthazar ate *the poisoned pudding.*

The coach sent *Dumper* into the game at quarterback.

(2) *The object of a preposition* is a noun or pronoun which usually follows a preposition (on the *hill,* after the *game,* with *her*). Occasionally, English syntax is scrambled, the preposition appearing

after its object. Some grammars suggest unscrambling such sentences so that the object of the preposition appears in its regular position.

The trade is a subject which baseball writers are still excited *about.* Unscrambled: The trade is a subject *about* which baseball writers are still excited.

What are you laughing *about?* Unscrambled: *About* what are you laughing?

(3) *The indirect object* follows verbs like *give, ask, lend,* and is traditionally defined as "the receiver of the action." In the sentence "She gave *her boyfriend* a good-night kiss," *her boyfriend* is the indirect object and *a good-night kiss* is the direct object. The indirect object in modern English cannot occur alone; it must precede the direct object. Indirect objects can be made the object of a preposition simply by being placed after the direct object and by following a preposition (She gave a good-night kiss *to her boyfriend*).

(4) *The object complement* usually follows and refers to a direct object. Object complements are likely to occur after verbs like *make, choose, name, designate, consider.* In the sentence "I consider Charles a dishonest poker player," the object complement is *a dishonest poker player* because it follows the verb *consider* and the direct object *Charles,* for which it is also a notional substitute. Object complements cannot occur alone in a sentence. Occasionally, ambiguities arise in the use of object complements and indirect objects. In a sentence like "They called Miss Jones a taxidermist," if *Miss Jones* and *a taxidermist* are meant to refer to the same person, they are direct object and object complement, respectively. However, if the reference is to two persons (They called a taxidermist *for* Miss Jones), *Miss Jones* is an indirect object and *a taxidermist* is a direct object.

Object Complement

See paragraph immediately above and **Complement,** p. 121.

Oblique Case

A term sometimes used by linguists to denote any grammatical case except the nominative. In modern English the objective and the possessive cases can be called *oblique.*

Obsolete

See **Archaic, Current, Obsolete,** p. 114.

Old English

A label used to describe the English language from its earliest surviving literary documents of approximately 700 A.D. to ca. 1100. The latter date marks the beginning of the Middle English language (see

p. 152), which differed from *Old English* primarily in the reduction of its inflectional endings and in its widespread adoption of French loanwords. Old English was a highly inflected language, featuring distinct forms in many of its declensions for the various cases of nouns, pronouns, and adjectives. It also had a fully inflected verbal system with distinctive endings to show number, tense, and mood. Old English is actually a collective term for several dialects: Kentish, West Saxon, Mercian, and Northumbrian. Of these, West Saxon is by far the most important to the student of Old English culture, since virtually all important surviving literary documents of the Old English period were either originally composed or copied by scribes in the West Saxon dialect. Perhaps the most important fact about West Saxon culture is that it nurtured King Alfred, who became the central figure of the revival of learning in the ninth century.

In reproducing the Old English language, many editors today "normalize" literary texts into the language of King Alfred. It is, however, a fact that the language of most surviving manuscripts is that of the tenth and eleventh centuries—a period often referred to as *Late Old English* or *Classical Old English*. The most important poem of the Old English period is *Beowulf,* an epic of almost 3,200 alliterating lines. *Beowulf* survives in a single manuscript copied by a scribe in the West Saxon dialect of approximately the year 1000. Scholars believe that the poem was originally composed sometime in the eighth century, probably in the Northumbrian dialect.

For modern readers without specialized training, Old English looks like an entirely foreign language. The term *Old English,* however, emphasizes the fact that it is simply an older version of the language we speak, not a foreign one. It is to stress the fact of this continuity that the term *Old English* rather than its synonym *Anglo-Saxon* is now generally used by scholars and literary historians. The following passage is the Old English version of the Lord's prayer:

> Fæder ure þu þe eart on heofonum, si þin nama gehalgod. Tobecume þin rice. Gewurþe þin willa on eorþan swa swa on heofonum. Urne gedæghwamlican hlaf syle us to dæg. And forgyf us ure gyltas, swa swa we forgyfaþ urum gyltendum. And ne gelæd þu us on costnunge, ac alys us of yfele. Soþlice.

Palatal

Any sound produced by the contact of the front of the tongue with the hard palate. The vowel in *see* /iy/ and the consonant in *she* /š/ are *palatal.*

Paradigm

A term in grammar referring to all the forms of a word that make up its declensions or conjugations. The *paradigm* of the noun *foot* is *foot, foot's, feet, feet's.*

Parallelism

A stylistic term referring to sentence balance. A *parallel* construction consists of two or more sentence parts which are similar in grammatical form and equal in importance.

A bird *in the hand* is worth two *in the bush.*

Mother bought *a sack of potatoes, a box of cereal,* and *a quart of milk.*

Tolerance without understanding is as irrational as *prejudice without hate.*

Faulty parallelism results when sentence parts of equal importance have not been cast in parallel grammatical structure.

FAULTY: Many sportsmen enjoy *catching* trout in the summer and also *to hunt* elk in the fall.

REVISED: Many sportsmen enjoy *catching* trout in the summer and *hunting* elk in the fall.

FAULTY: We are constantly aware of the *great expense* and *how difficult* it is to be admitted to Siwash University.

REVISED: We are constantly aware of the *great expense* and the *difficult admissions policy* of Siwash University.

FAULTY: A government career demands such qualities as *honesty, intelligence, efficiency, being loyal,* and *not to neglect one's duties.*

REVISED: A government career demands such qualities as *honesty, intelligence, efficiency, loyalty,* and *dependability.*

Paraphrase

See p. 223.

Participle

A verbal form which can be used in the function of a verb after an auxiliary (I have *known,* he is *coming*) or as an adjective (the *singing* nuns, the man *seen* on the street corner). English has a *present participle,* which ends in *-ing,* and a past participle, which ends in *-ed, -d,* or *-t* (as well as a few strong-verb forms which end in *-en* and/or which change their root vowel: driv*en,* s*u*ng). The *past participle* is conventionally listed as the third principal part of verbs.

Participial Phrase

A group of words headed by a present or a past participle (The

student *coming toward us* just won a Woodrow Wilson fellowship).
The function of a *participial phrase* is most commonly adjectival.

Partitive Genitive

The type of *of-genitive* in which a part of the whole is named (*a piece of pie, a share of stock*).

Parts of Speech

This term refers to the major grammatical classes into which the vocabulary of a language can be divided. The identification and sorting out of *parts of speech* is the major concern of the branch of grammar known as *morphology* (as differentiated from the other major branch, *syntax*). Traditional grammars customarily list eight parts of speech: the noun, pronoun, adjective, verb, adverb, preposition, conjunction, and interjection. The basis of this classification, however, is justifiably questioned by structural linguists, who point out that the classes were formed by the application of unlike criteria. For example, nouns are usually put in one class because they *name* something, but adjectives are put in another because they *modify* something. To remove this difficulty, the linguist has redefined the parts of speech in terms of their forms and functions. The conventional eight parts have consequently been regrouped: first into the major classifications of *form classes* (see p. 134) and *function words* (see p. 135), and then into various subordinate classifications. In this book the familiar names of the various parts of speech are used as entry words. The definitions, however, are based on the discoveries and observations of structural linguists.

Passive Voice

See **Voice,** p. 199.

Period Fault

The use of a period at the end of an unintentional non-sentence. Most *period faults* in student writing occur after an introductory dependent clause, and they may be easily corrected by changing the period to a comma and combining the dependent clause with the following clause if it is independent.

> PERIOD FAULT: After a long, fatiguing march to the top of the steep hill at the edge of town. We ate our lunch.
>
> CORRECTED: After a long, fatiguing march to the top of the steep hill at the edge of town, we ate our lunch.

Periodic Sentence

A sentence in which modifying words, phrases, and clauses are put before the verb in the main clause. A *periodic sentence* is, therefore, one which cannot be brought to a grammatical end before its actual ending (According to a report just released by the UPI, the astronauts have landed). Periodic sentences are more characteristic of written than of spoken English. The opposite of a periodic sentence is called a *loose sentence* (see p. 151). For another major rhetorical sentence type, see **Balanced Sentence, p. 116.**

Periphrasis
See p. 224.

Person
A grammatical term which serves to differentiate the three subjects of discourse: first person (the speaker), second person (the person spoken to), third person (the person spoken about). English pronouns are fully inflected for *person* (*I, you, he,* etc.), as is the verb *to be* in the present singular (I *am,* you *are,* he *is*). Most other verbs are inflected for person only in the third person present singular (I speak, he speaks).

Personal Pronoun
Words which specify first person (speaker), second person (person spoken to), third person (person spoken about). *Personal pronouns* may be singular or plural; they may, further, be subjective, possessive, objective, or reflexive. In addition, third person personal pronouns may be masculine, feminine, or neuter. The following are the major classes of personal pronouns in English.

SINGULAR	*subjective*	*possessive*	*objective*	*reflexive*
First person	I	my, mine	me	myself
Second person	you	your, yours	you	yourself
Third person	he, she, it	his, her, hers, its	him, her, it	himself, herself, itself
PLURAL				
First person	we	our, ours	us	ourselves
Second person	you	your, yours	you	yourselves
Third person	they	their, theirs	them	themselves

Persuasion
One major form of prose composition, the others being exposition and narration. *Persuasion,* as the name suggests, attempts to convince a reader of a particular belief usually leading to a definite course of action (e.g., vote for Joe Blow, spend the summer in Europe).

Responsible persuasive writing demands a greater emphasis upon rational than upon emotional argument. Persuasion as a form of discourse is often called "argumentation."

Philology

Until recent years, the term *philology* referred to the study of both language and literature. Its meaning has narrowed, however, and it is most often used today with reference to the study of historical and comparative linguistics.

Phoneme

The smallest unit of language by which utterances can be differentiated. The sounds /t/ and /d/ are separate phonemes in English because when placed in identical surroundings they produce different meanings: e.g., *t*ip and *d*ip, *t*uck and *d*uck. A phoneme represents only the general traits of a speech sound; it is an abstraction of many nonsignificant sound variants. The phoneme /t/, for example, is a generic symbol for all the minor variations of the sound that English speakers regularly use. These variations are many, and ordinary speakers of the language are seldom conscious of them. Note for example that the /t/ in *butter,* as it is usually pronounced, is heavily voiced; the /t/ in *hit* is not exploded or released, the /t/ in *Thames* is aspirated (or uttered with a puff of breath). Such variations are usually the result of phonetic surroundings. The variants that make up one phoneme are known as *allophones.*

As yet there is no precise agreement over the total number of phonemes in American English. However, most linguists seem to accept the classification by George L. Trager and Henry Lee Smith (in *An Outline of English Structure,* Norman, Oklahoma, 1951), who list 24 consonant phonemes, 9 vowel phonemes, and 3 semivowel phonemes. The vowel and consonant phonemes are known collectively as *segmentals.* In addition to the segmentals, American English has 12 *suprasegmentals* or phonemes which indicate gradations of pitch, stress, and juncture. The recording of segmentals and suprasegmentals is known as *phonemic transcription.* Customarily, phonemes are placed between slant lines, whereas allophones are placed within square brackets.

Phonemic Alphabet

A set of symbols representing phonemes. For American English, the most widely used *phonemic alphabet* is that devised by Trager and Smith (see **Phoneme,** p. 165). Phonemic transcriptions are customarily placed between slant lines, thus /fowniym/.

CONSONANTS

plosives

/p/	*p*ill, sto*p*
/b/	*b*ill, stu*b*
/t/	*t*ime, hi*t*
/d/	*d*ime, hi*d*
/k/	*c*ould, lu*ck*
/g/	*g*ood, lu*g*

continuants

fricatives	/f/	*f*ast, rou*gh*
	/v/	*v*ast, lo*v*e
	/θ/	*th*in, loa*th*
	/ð/	*th*en, loa*the*
sibilants	/s/	*s*ip, hi*ss*
	/z/	*z*ip, hi*s*
	/š/	*sh*ip, mi*ss*ion
	/ž/	bei*g*e, vi*s*ion
affricates	/č/	*ch*ur*ch*, pun*ch*
	/ǰ/	*j*u*dg*e, spon*g*e
nasals	/m/	*m*ine, Ti*m*
	/n/	*n*i*n*e, ti*n*
	/ŋ/	si*ng*, so*ng*
liquids	/l/	*l*ove, te*ll*
	/r/	*r*ank, tea*r*

VOWELS AND DIPHTHONGS

/i/	h*i*t, sp*i*ll
/iy/	h*ea*t, st*ea*l
/ɨ/	h*i*s, entertainm*e*nt
/u/	b*oo*k, h*oo*d
/uw/	r*oo*m, y*ou*
/e/	m*e*t, b*e*g
/ey/	m*a*te, st*a*y
/ə/	sof*a*, *u*p
/o/	cl*o*se, n*o*te
/ow/	g*o*, *o*pen
/æ/	h*a*t, *a*sk
/a/	h*o*t, *o*x
/ah/	c*a*lm, f*a*ther
/ay/	m*i*ne, st*y*
/aw/	h*ou*se, *ou*r
/ɔ/	b*ou*ght, c*ou*gh

/ɔh/	saw, paw
/ɔy/	boy, choice

SEMIVOWELS

/y/	yellow
/w/	work
/h/	house

Phonetics, Phonemics, Phonology

All three of these terms have to do with the study of speech sounds. *Phonetics* deals with the description and classification of speech sounds. There are two special branches of phonetics: *articulatory phonetics,* which deals with the physiological characteristics of speech sounds; and *acoustic phonetics,* which deals with the physical characteristics of speech sounds.

Phonemics is the study of minimum significant sounds in a language (see **Phoneme,** p. 165). Phonemics sets out specifically to describe the sound system of individual languages (e.g., the phonemics of American English). In contrast, phonetics has universal application; it is capable of describing the sound system of any language.

Phonology is the most general term of the three. In its broadest sense, it is simply any study concerned with speech sounds. In this sense, it embraces both phonetics and phonemics. Occasionally, however, phonology is used to describe a more specialized study—that of the history and development of the sounds in a language. It is in this latter sense that the term is generally used by historians of language.

Phrase

A group of words lacking a subject and a predicate. *Phrases* can function like single nouns (*Going to the movies* is his favorite recreation), like adjectives (the man *in the iron mask*), like adverbs (to walk *in long strides*), like prepositions (*because of, due to*). When not related to sentence function, phrases are named according to their structure:

PARTICIPIAL: The man *standing at the corner* knows you.
GERUND: *Writing letters* is a task I hate.
INFINITIVE: I want *to go to college.*
VERB: Pam *will be happy* to see Mark.
PREPOSITIONAL: We met *in the lobby.*

Pitch

A feature of English intonation (see p. 147). *Pitch* refers to the relative tone levels in speech. Linguists generally mark the highest level of pitch with a superfix[4], the next highest with a superfix[3], the next lowest with a superfix[2], and the lowest with a superfix[1]. The typical English statement pattern is a 2-3-1 pattern, which is to say, the sentence begins on a 2-level pitch, rises to 3-level on the word which receives sentence stress, and falls to 1-level at the end. The following sentence illustrates the pattern:

[2]This is my first trip to [3]Europe[1].

Because, typically, English drops to 1-level at the end of statements, it is said to be a language with falling pitch. In contrast, the lilt one hears in speakers with a Scandinavian accent is representative of rising pitch. The 4-level pitch in American English intonation is reserved for excessively high-pitched utterances, especially exclamations or harsh commands.

The phenomenon of pitch cannot really be understood in isolation. It needs to be analyzed in conjunction with *stress* (see p. 183) and with *juncture* (see p. 148).

Plagiarism

The practice of using as one's own, material written or spoken by another. *Plagiarism* is always a serious offense, both in or out of the classroom, and most schools impose severe penalties upon persons guilty of it. A student would be guilty of plagiarism if he practiced either of the following: (1) copied all or part of a paper from the manuscript or notes of another student; (2) copied, without giving due credit (see **Footnote,** p. 83), all or part of a speech, magazine or newspaper article, pamphlet, or book.

Plosive

Any consonant which requires stoppage of the breath stream. *Plosives* are also known as *stop consonants*. American English has six plosives: /p/, /b/, /t/, /d/, /k/ and /g/. All other consonants are continuants (see p. 125).

Plural

See **Number,** p. 159

Popular English

A label used by many linguists to refer to the spoken language of the uneducated and to dialect speech. (See **Levels of Usage,** p. 150.)

Popular Etymology

See **Folk Etymology,** p. 134.

Portmanteau Word

The blending of two words or parts of words into one (also referred to as *blends*). Advertisers frequently use *portmanteau words* (*chicken-burger, auto-rama, washeteria*), many of which have become standard items in the English language (*brunch, motel, cheeseburger, smog*). Some words, like *twirl,* have been in the language so long that they are rarely recognized as portmanteau words. Blending is one source of new words in a language.

Possessive Case

The grammatical case comprised of various personal pronouns (*mine, his, her, their, my, our*) and of nouns that end in *'s* (*woman's, women's,* etc.). The term *possessive* is somewhat of a misnomer since possession is not always shown (e.g., the *policemen's killer,* a *month's vacation,* a *children's library*). (See **Case,** p. 117.)

Possessive Form with Gerund

In editorial English, possessive forms of pronouns (*my, your, his,* etc.) are preferred over objective forms (*me, you, him*) before gerunds (I never objected to *his* working). In colloquial English the objective form frequently occurs in this context. For a fuller discussion, see **Gerund,** p. 137.

Précis

An abstract or summary of another piece of writing. A good *précis* maintains the order of ideas and the tone of the original. Unlike a *paraphrase* (see p. 223), a précis is always shorter than the original work.

Predicate

The part of the sentence which contains the verb (see p. 196), its modifiers, and its complements. Basic, or kernel, sentences must have a subject and a predicate.

Predicate Adjective

An adjective which follows a linking verb (The summers in Columbus are *hot* and *humid*).

Predicate Nominative

A noun or noun-equivalent which follows a linking verb (Deborah is my *niece*). A *predicate nominative* is sometimes referred to as a *predicate noun* or a *subject complement.*

Prefix

A *prefix* is a bound morpheme (see p. 116) which modifies the meaning of the root word it precedes. Modern English has only *derivational* prefixes, though Old and Middle English had *inflectional* prefixes as well (for a definition of the terms *derivational* and *inflectional* see

Suffix, p. 187). The use of prefixes allows a language to expand its vocabulary without departing from familiar root words. The following list contains the prefixes most commonly used in English:

PREFIX	MEANING	EXAMPLES
a-	not, without	*a*typical, *a*moral
ab-	off, away from	*ab*sent, *ab*normal
ad-	to, for	*ad*measure, *ad*venture
anti-	against, opposed to	*anti*-Catholic, *anti*thesis
co-	with, jointly	*co*operation, *co*existence
com- (con-)	with, jointly	*com*mingle, *con*descend
de-	deprive, reverse prohibit, away from	*de*louse, *de*bunk, *de*limit, *de*bark
dis-	reversal	*dis*compose, *dis*comfort
en- (em-)	put in, thoroughly	*en*wrap, *em*bitter
ex-	out of, former	*ex*communicate, *ex*-wife
in- (im-)	in, on, not	*in*put, *im*pression, *im*pure
mis-	wrong	*mis*print, *mis*manage
non-	not	*non*-Mormon, *non*sense
per-	thorough, utterly	*per*colate, *per*oration
pre-	prior to	*pre*fix, *pre*suppose
pro-	favor, forward	*pro*-American, *pro*create
pseudo-	false	*pseudo*nym, *pseudo*-doctor
re-	repetition	*re*search, *re*birth
semi-	half, partly	*semi*final, *semi*darkness
sub-	under	*sub*standard, *sub*conscious
super-	greater	*super*market, *super*charge
trans-	across	*trans*form, *trans*port
ultra-	excessive	*ultra*violet, *ultra*-ambitious
un-	not, reversal	*un*zip, *un*readable

Preposition

In traditional grammar the *preposition* is considered one of the eight parts of speech, and it is customarily defined as any word which relates a noun or a noun-equivalent to other parts in a sentence. Structural linguists classify the preposition as a function word (see p. 135) which serves as a *phrase marker* (*of* the boy, *in* the house). Generally, prepositions precede nouns, which are called the object of the preposition (for prepositions that follow the nouns they govern, see **Prepositions at End of Sentences,** p. 171). There are only some seventy prepositions in the English language, but, as might be expected, they occur with great frequency. The following are among the most widely used: *about, above, across, after, against, ahead of, along,* *among, around, as, at, because of, before, behind, below, beside, between, by, down, during, except, for, from, in, inside, into, like, near, of, off, on, onto, out, out of, over, past, since, through, throughout, till, to, toward, under, until, unto, up, upon, with, within,* and *without.* It should be noted that some prepositions also serve as adverbs (for example, *about, after, before, in*). They can usually be differentiated without trouble, since adverbs pattern with verbs, and prepositions pattern with nouns. Thus, in the sentence "He asked *about* Anne," *about* is an adverb patterning with *asked* (the whole verb is to *ask about* and *Anne* is the direct object). Sometimes, however, an ambiguity can develop in a context which would permit a word to pattern either as an adverb or a preposition (for example, "He drank *in* the air" where *in* can pattern with *drank* or as part of the phrase *in the air*). To insure clear communication, sentences containing such ambiguities should be rewritten entirely.

Prepositional Phrase

A group of words headed by a preposition. The noun or noun-equivalent which follows the preposition is known as the *object of the preposition.* Generally *prepositional phrases* function as adjectives (He drank a cup *of coffee*) or as adverbs (Cindy rode *in the back seat*).

Prepositions at End of Sentences

The stylebook rule that a sentence must not end with a preposition is as widely repeated as it is misunderstood. Actually, there are few constructions in English that can end in a preposition. As its name implies, a preposition is a word which normally occurs in "pre" position, or, to put it more familiarly, in the position before a substantive. In colloquial and informal editorial English, however, a preposition can occur after the substantive it governs in two constructions:

(1) At the end of a relative clause, whether or not the clause is marked by a relative pronoun (He is the boy [*whom*] *I talked to;* You would never guess *what the package was wrapped in*). Such a construction is a transformation of the more formal sentence in which the relative clause follows the preposition that governs it (He is the boy *to whom I talked*).

(2) At the end of a question which is signaled by an interrogative pronoun (Where did you come *from?* Which class does it belong *in?*). This question pattern occurs basically in oral English, a type which has rarely been successfully governed by the proscriptions of stylebooks. Except in dialogue, such questions almost never appear in

expository writing. For this reason, it is gratuitous and pedantic to suggest that the preposition be moved to the beginning of the question (*From* where did you come?).

In nearly all other instances, the so-called preposition which ends a sentence turns out actually to be an adverb. Many common words like *in, out, around, near,* and *down* can function as prepositions or adverbs, depending on their context. They are prepositions when they govern a substantive; they are adverbs when they combine into a unit with a verb (*bring up, drink down, speak out, putter around*). Thus, in the sentence "He asked us to come in," *in* is an adverb, not a preposition. So is the word *up* in the following sentence, even though it is separated from the verb with which it usually combines: "It was John who *brought* the point *up.*" Obviously, the prohibition against ending a sentence with a preposition should not be made to apply to an adverbial construction.

Preterit-present Verb

A class of verb in Old English from which most Modern English *modals* (see p. 153) are derived (including *can, could, shall, should, may, might, ought, will, would,* and *must*). These verbs were called *preterit-present* because their original preterit (or past tense) forms became present tense forms in Old English. This fact accounts for the absence of inflectional -*s* for the third person singular of these verbs. A new past tense was formed by the addition of a dental suffix as in coul*d,* shoul*d,* migh*t,* ough*t,* woul*d,* and mus*t.*

Principal Parts of Verbs

A verb is said to have three *principal parts:* the infinitive (*talk, drink*), the past (*talked, drank*) and the past participle (*talked, drunk*). Most verbs in English are called "weak" or "regular" verbs; that is, they change forms in the past tense and the past participle by the addition of -*ed,* -*d,* or -*t* to the infinitive (walk*ed,* dream*t*). Fewer than a hundred of our most frequently occurring verbs change an internal vowel to form the past tense and the past participle (dr*i*nk, dr*a*nk, have dr*u*nk) and are called "strong" or "irregular" verbs.

The list which follows is composed largely of irregular verbs and includes most of those which are troublesome.

INFINITIVE	PAST TENSE	PAST PARTICIPLE
arise	arose	arisen
awake	awaked, awoke	awaked, awoke
bear	bore	borne, born (see p. 14)
bid (offer)	bid	bid

INFINITIVE	PAST TENSE	PAST PARTICIPLE
bid (command)	bade	bidden
bite	bit	bit, bitten
blow	blew	blown
break	broke	broken
burst	burst	burst
catch	caught	caught
choose	chose	chosen
cling	clung	clung
come	came	come
dig	dug	dug
dive	dived, dove	dived (see p. 20)
do	did	done
drag	dragged	dragged
draw	drew	drawn
dream	dreamed, dreamt	dreamed, dreamt
drink	drank	drunk
eat	ate	eaten
fall	fell	fallen
find	found	found
flee	fled	fled
fly	flew	flown
forget	forgot	forgot, forgotten
freeze	froze	frozen
get	got	got, gotten
give	gave	given
go	went	gone
grow	grew	grown
hang	hung, hanged	hung, hanged (see p. 29)
know	knew	known
lay	laid	laid
lead	led	led
lend	lent	lent
let	let	let
lie (recline)	lay	lain
lie (speak falsely)	lied	lied
light	lighted, lit	lighted, lit
loan	loaned	loaned
lose	lost	lost
pay (debt)	paid	paid
pay (rope)	payed	payed

INFINITIVE	PAST TENSE	PAST PARTICIPLE
plead	pleaded, pled	pleaded, pled
prove	proved	proved, proven (see p. 46)
raise	raised	raised
ride	rode	ridden
ring	rang, rung	rung
rise	rose	risen
run	ran	run
say	said	said
see	saw	seen
set	set	set
shake	shook	shaken
shine	shone, shined	shone, shined
show	showed	shown, showed
shrink	shrank, shrunk	shrunk, shrunken
sing	sang, sung	sung
sink	sank, sunk	sunk
sit	sat	sat
slide	slid	slid, slidden
sow	sowed	sown, sowed
speak	spoke	spoken
spit	spit, spat	spit, spat
spring	sprang, sprung	sprung
stand	stood	stood
steal	stole	stolen
sting	stung	stung
stink	stank, stunk	stunk
strive	strove, strived	striven
swim	swam	swum
swing	swung	swung
take	took	taken
tear	tore	torn
throw	threw	thrown
tread	trod	trodden, trod
tread (tires or water)	treaded	treaded
wake	waked, woke	waked, woken
wear	wore	worn
weave	wove, weaved	woven, wove
wring	wrung	wrung
write	wrote	written

Pronoun

In traditional grammar a *pronoun* is defined as a substitute word for a noun or a noun-equivalent. Though this definition is not fully sufficient to differentiate pronouns from other parts of speech, it is in a very general sense an accurate statement. Pronouns are capable of filling the same sentence positions as nouns, and they are also capable of governing the inflectional forms of verbs (*I am, you are, he is*). To be completely accurate, however, one would have to say that pronouns fit as exact substitutes only for proper nouns. Unlike common nouns, neither pronouns nor proper nouns are signaled by determiners (we say *the man,* but we cannot say *the Tom* or *the you*).

Occasionally, the possessive forms *my, your, his, her, its, our,* and *their* are called pronouns. However, it is more accurate to call them either by their traditional label, *pronominal adjective* or by the label used by structural linguists, *determiner*. It should be noted, that the forms *his, her,* and *its* are only determiners when they are used as noun modifiers (*his* book, *its* rattle); when used as noun substitutes, they are pronouns (The book is *his;* It belongs to *her*).

The following are the major classes of pronouns: *demonstrative pronouns, indefinite pronouns, interrogative pronouns, personal pronouns, reflexive pronouns,* and *relative pronouns.* Each of these classes is defined as a separate entry in this book.

Pronunciation

See **Articulation,** p. 114.

Punctuation Marks

The written form of most languages develops a system of *punctuation marks,* signals used to assist the reader's ease of comprehension. The appropriate use of these marks within any language community is governed largely by editorial practice. The conventions of American usage are discussed for each of the following in its appropriate alphabetical position in the section on the "Conventions of Editorial English."

'	Apostrophe	-	Hyphen
[ ]	Brackets	( )	Parentheses
:	Colon	.	Period
,	Comma	?	Question mark
—	Dash	" "	Quotation marks
. . .	Ellipsis	;	Semicolon
!	Exclamation point	_____	Underlining (Italics)

Quotation

A *quotation* may be either *direct* or *indirect*. Direct quotations record the exact words of a writer or speaker, and they are set off by quotation marks (see also **Quotation Marks,** p. 94). Indirect quotations summarize or paraphrase the words of a speaker or writer; no special punctuation is required.

DIRECT: The coach shouted, "All of you guys take three laps around the field."

INDIRECT: The coach said that he wanted us to take three laps around the football field.

Reading Rate

The average number of words a person reads per minute. To determine your *reading rate* on any given passage, divide the number of seconds it took you to read it into the number of words in the selection, then multiply by 60.

$$\frac{number\ of\ words}{number\ of\ seconds} \times 60 = reading\ rate\ in\ words\ per\ minute$$

Taken by itself, reading rate is a meaningless term. It would be better to read at 200 words per minute with maximum comprehension than to read at 700 words per minute with minimum comprehension. Also, some materials can and ought to be read much more rapidly than others. These factors considered, however, the college student ought to be able to read material of average difficulty (e.g., an article in *Time,* a newspaper editorial) at 250 to 275 words per minute. The student who reads such material at less than 200 words per minute will usually experience great difficulty with college work.

Reference of Pronouns

In unambiguous writing every pronoun must have a clearly established antecedent, the substantive for which it stands. If the reference of a pronoun is left unclear, ambiguity can result. For example, in the sentence "Labor leaders, government mediators, and top management officials failed to agree among *themselves,"* the pronoun *themselves* could refer to each group individually or to all three groups collectively. The reference of *themselves* is consequently vague or indefinite. Usually sentences containing reference errors need to be rewritten entirely. For further discussion see **Agreement,** p. 110.

Referent

The object or person to which a concrete word refers. The word *house,* for example, has a *referent* which can be pointed to or can be drawn. Dictionaries often include sketches of the referents of unfamiliar words.

Reflexive Pronoun

A compound form which combines a possessive or an objective pronoun with the suffix *-self* (*myself, yourself, himself*). *Reflexive pro-*

nouns are used either to refer the action of the verb back to the subject (I dressed *myself*) or to intensify (Professor Jones *himself* answered the question). In editorial English, reflexive pronouns are never used as subjects (Joe and I [not *myself*] saw the exhibit last year). The forms *hisself* and *theirself* are substandard dialectal variants of *himself* and *themselves*.

Relative Clause

A clause which is introduced by a relative pronoun (*that, which, who,* etc.). In the following sentences, *relative clauses* are italicized.

> During the summer, Debbie met a boy *whom she really liked.*
> We knew right away *that our request would be denied.*
> *Whoever participated in the prank* is guilty.

In informal editorial English as well as colloquial English, relative pronouns are sometimes omitted. The clause in such constructions is nevertheless called a *relative clause* (We didn't know [*that*] *the trains weren't running*).

Relative Pronoun

Words which introduce relative clauses and which are, therefore, called "clause markers" in some grammars. The most commonly used *relative pronouns* in English are the following: *that, which, of which, whose, who, whom, whoever, whomever, whichever, what* and *whatever.*

Several problems may arise in the usage of relative pronouns. In formal editorial English, *which* refers to "thing" words, *who* to "person" words, and *that* generally to "thing" or "animal" words. The use of *that* with reference to persons is discouraged by most style manuals. This usage, however, is frequent in colloquial and informal editorial English, and it is slowly finding acceptance even in formal editorial English.

The omission of the relative pronoun in certain constructions is another problem treated by many style manuals. For a discussion of it, see **Relative Clause,** p. 177, and **Elliptical Constructions,** p. 132.

Still another usage problem involving relative pronouns has to do with an old stylebook rule stating that relative pronouns must have single word antecedents. For a discussion of this problem, see **That, This,** p. 53.

Restrictive and Nonrestrictive Modifiers

A *restrictive modifier* is a phrase or clause which points out or identifies the person or thing modified. It is not set off by commas. A *nonrestrictive modifier* is a phrase or clause which is not essential to point out or identify the person or thing modified. It is set off by commas.

RESTRICTIVE: The candidate *who won a plurality* was elected.
NONRESTRICTIVE: James Buckner, *who won a plurality,* was elected.

The correct designation (indicated by use or nonuse of commas) of a restrictive or nonrestrictive modifier is absolutely essential to the meaning of many sentences. The sentences in the following pair differ in meaning.

RESTRICTIVE: Our relatives *who live in Nebraska* are Republicans. [Only the Nebraska relatives are Republicans.]
NONRESTRICTIVE: Our relatives, *who live in Nebraska,* are Republicans. [All our relatives are Nebraskans; all are Republicans.]

Retroflex

A term in phonetics referring to the type of /r/ sound for which the tip of the tongue is bent backward (as in fathe*r*, bi*r*d). In American English, the *retroflexed* /r/ is a nonsignificant, or allophonic, variation.

Rhetoric

The principles and rules which govern the effective presentation of ideas in writing or speech. Since ancient times, *rhetoric* has held an important place in the educational process. The Greeks emphasized the rhetoric of public address, particularly with regard to persuasion, and that emphasis persists in the training of forensic students in the modern university. In the medieval university, rhetoric joined grammar and logic in the *trivium,* a basic course of study in the liberal arts. Medieval rhetoric considered written as well as spoken composition. The written emphasis continues in collegiate English departments today. Under the influence of the Greek Sophists, who tended to emphasize the art of rhetoric more highly than the validity of the argument it was intended to support, the term developed an unfavorable connotation which many people still attach to it.

Rhetorical Question

The *rhetorical question* is one which is not intended to elicit a direct answer from the reader or listener (Could anyone have predicted that this awkward appearing rail-splitter would one day become President of the United States?). As a stylistic device, the rhetorical question is used primarily in formal speeches, though it occasionally appears in editorial English, where it may be punctuated either with a question mark or a period.

Root

See **Base,** p. 116.

Round Vowel

A vowel for which the lips are rounded or pursed. English contains several *round* or *rounded vowel* phonemes: /uw/ as in r*oo*m, /u/ as in h*oo*d, /ow/ as in t*o*ne, /o/ as in cl*o*se, /ɔ/ as in b*ough*t, and /ɔw/ as in s*aw*. Although only back vowels (see p. 116) are rounded in Modern English, front vowels are capable of rounding and, indeed, are rounded in such languages as German, French and Swedish. Front rounded vowels are sometimes referred to as "umlaut vowels" (e.g., German sch*ö*n or French s*u*d).

Run-on Sentence

The punctuation of two or more sentences as one. Failure to recognize the sentence as a stylistic unit is a serious shortcoming; it can lead alike to the writing of fragments (see p. 26) and of *run-on sentences.* A run-on sentence either has no punctuation separating its independent clauses, or it has a comma (see also **Comma Fault, Comma Splice,** p. 119) instead of a stronger mark of punctuation. Run-on sentences can be corrected in a number of ways, the most important of which are enumerated below:

(1) Separate the independent clauses with a mark of terminal punctuation (.!?).

RUN-ON: I am sorry that you failed chemistry you will have to work harder next semester.

REVISION: I am sorry that you failed chemistry. You will have to work harder next semester.

(2) Separate the independent clauses with a semicolon.

RUN-ON: There is no light in the room, Sally must have gone to bed.

REVISION: There is no light in the room; Sally must have gone to bed.

(3) Separate the independent clauses with a comma plus a coordinating conjunction.

RUN-ON: Barbara took the manuscript home she will work on it this evening.

REVISION: Barbara took the manuscript home, and she will work on it this evening.

(4) Separate the independent clauses with a semicolon plus a conjunctive adverb plus a comma.

RUN-ON: Russia does not need more heavy machinery, she does need food.

REVISION: Russia does not need more heavy machinery; however, she does need food.

(5) Convert one of the independent clauses into a dependent clause.

RUN-ON: The girls are still getting dressed, we will delay our departure for a half hour.

REVISION: Since the girls are still getting dressed, we will delay our departure for a half hour.

Segmentals
See **Phoneme**, p. 165.

Semantics
The study of the meaning of words and the changes which take place in their meaning. The related term *general semantics* refers to the study of the relationship between the words or symbols we use and the things or ideas we wish them to represent.

Semivowel
The phonemes /w/, /h/, and /y/ are known as *semivowels*. These sounds characteristically are of short duration; they have no precise point of articulation, being formed as the tongue shifts toward or away from pure vowels. As their name implies, *semivowels* are used in the position of vowels and consonants. For a fuller discussion of semivowels, see **Glide,** p. 137. According to some phonemicists, /r/ is also a semivowel.

Sentence
Because a *sentence* is an extremely complex unit, it is nearly impossible to define. Certain general observations, however, can be made. In traditional grammar, a sentence is customarily defined as a group of words containing a subject and a predicate and expressing a complete thought. Objections have been raised against this definition because certain sentence types—for example, the command or the response sentence—may not contain a subject and/or verb. Moreover, there can be no objectively based agreement on what constitutes a complete thought. Some maintain that completeness is achievable only in large rhetorical units, perhaps paragraphs or entire discourses. It follows,

therefore, that the traditional definition is too exclusive and too vague to serve as a useful general statement.

Perhaps the best solution toward defining a sentence is to recognize its different forms in oral and written English. The spoken sentence, being a unit in immediate utterance, is marked by a particular kind of juncture. It ends with a rise or fall in pitch indicating termination. A spoken sentence, therefore, is best defined as a unit of speech with *terminal juncture* (see p. 148).

The written sentence is too complex to define, but one can note its minimal characteristics. Basically, English which is written for a general reader (as differentiated from one particular reader like a recipient of a letter or a note) contains declarative sentences that do, in fact, have a subject and a predicate as a minimal distinctive feature. All other sentences in such written English are rhetorical departures from the subject-verb unit. Commands, interjections, questions, and elliptical answers to questions are simply stylistic variations of the declarative sentence and are used by the writer for the sake of variety and interest. It follows, therefore, that a basic sentence in written English addressed to the general reader consists of at least a simple subject and a simple predicate, both of which can be expanded in a wide variety of patterns. Such a sentence is capable, further, of transformations into certain subjectless and/or verbless rhetorical patterns and of expansion into compound, complex, or compound-complex units.

Shifted Construction

The failure to put two or more coordinate sentence elements in the same grammatical form. *Shifted constructions* violate structural consistency; they should be revised.

SHIFTED: *Flowers* bring cheer; *you* really appreciate them in a hospital room. (Shift of subject.)

REVISED: *Flowers* bring cheer; *they* are really appreciated in a hospital room.

SHIFTED: Our neighbors never really learned *to understand* the children nor *got* along with them. (Shift from infinitive phrase to finite verb.)

REVISED: Our neighbors never really learned *to understand* the children nor *to get* along with them.

Sibilant

A term in phonetics referring to any high-friction consonant which has a hissing quality. In English, there are four *sibilants:* /s/ as in *s*ip, /z/ as in *z*ip, /š/ as in *sh*ip and /ž/ as in bei*g*e.

Simple Sentence

A sentence consisting of one independent clause and any number of modifying words and phrases. The following sentence, despite its length, is a simple sentence of which *residents* is the subject headword and *began* the verb: After seeing the horrible destruction wrought by the worst floods in the last half century, the residents of Mankato, Minnesota, silently and resolutely began to work around the clock to wash away the debris and mud left in the wake of receding floodwaters and to rebuild their battered homes.

Singular

See **Number,** p. 159.

Slang

A generic term for colloquial language consisting of colorful words, often with taboo meaning, and of new uses for words from the standard vocabulary. Slang need not be bad English, though it is rarely appropriate in writing other than dialogue. Slang is difficult to illustrate because it changes as quickly as the seasons. Any fad will encourage the development of new slang words; for instance, during a recent sidewalk skateboarding craze, a "fall" or "spill" was termed a *wipe out.* At about the same time, a Kansas college reported the following slang usages: *cancer stick* for "cigarette," *dark* for a "studious girl," and *double ugly* for a "pretty girl." At one time, *slang* referred to the special language of criminals, constituting an underworld code. Later, it embraced as well the language associated with special occupations. Today, linguists generally refer to underworld language as *cant* and to languages associated with special occupations as *jargon, argot,* or *shoptalk.*

Solecism

A grammatical error or an unacceptable stylistic usage.

Spirant

See **Fricative,** p. 135.

Split Infinitive

A construction in which an adverb or an adverbial phrase occurs between *to* and the infinitive form of a verb (*to really answer* a question, *to at least eat* one good meal). Though *split infinitives* are regarded as poor style by most handbooks, they occur often in informal editorial English and occasionally in formal editorial English. Some constructions, in fact, demand the splitting of an infinitive for the sake of clarity or emphasis. For example, in the sentence "Many of the people we interviewed agreed to quickly register to vote," the adverb *quickly* can only be placed between *to* and *register* in order to convey the notion that it was the registering, not the agreeing or the voting, which had to be done quickly. Such constructions, however, do not occur often, and since they tend to be awkward no matter where the adverb is placed, they should be entirely rewritten in formal editorial English.

Spoonerism

A slip of the tongue, usually involving the transposition of sounds in a word (the *sex sickton* for the *sick sexton*). The term *spoonerism* was derived from the name of William A. *Spooner* (1844–1930), an English clergyman and educator who was notorious for his slips of the tongue.

Squinting Modifier

Another name for a *misrelated modifier* (see p. 152).

Stop Consonant

See **Plosive,** p. 168.

Stress

The technical term for the relative loudness with which statements are uttered. "Relative" here refers to variations in the speech of all people to differentiate the prominence of certain syllables in the flow of speech. Linguists customarily identify four stress phonemes in English:

(1) *Weak stress* (marked with the breve accent ˘) is placed on any vowel which is unstressed in running speech. Because unstressed vowels occur so frequently, many linguists do not mark weak stress at all in their transcriptions.

(2) *Tertiary stress* (marked with a grave accent ˋ) is the next softest phoneme of stress. It is easily recognized in its occurrence on nouns which are modified by other nouns; dóg càtcher (in which *dog* receives primary stress and the first syllable of *catcher* receives tertiary stress).

(3) *Secondary stress* (marked with the circumflex accent ˆ) occurs typically on the adjective in an adjective-noun construction: the whîte shóes (in which *white* receives secondary stress and *shoes* —as differentiated from such items as white gloves, white handbag, or white hat—primary stress).

(4) *Primary stress* (marked by an acute accent ´) identifies the most prominent syllable of a phonological phrase. Every utterance must have at least one primary stress. In the typical English sentence, it is likely to occur on the root syllable of the last word (He came to schóol). When words are spoken in isolation, they have primary stress on the root syllable.

Strong Verb, Weak Verb

Like other Germanic languages, English has two principal types of verbs: *strong verbs,* or those which form their principal parts by a change in the root vowel (*drive, drove; ring, rang; eat, ate*), and *weak verbs,* or those which form their principal parts by adding a dental suffix like *-ed, -d,* or *-t* (*trip, tripped; build built; love, loved*). In Modern English, there are many more weak verbs than there are strong; however, strong verbs comprise some of the most frequently used verbs in the language. When new verbs are taken into the language, they usually adapt to the pattern of weak verbs (*zero, zeroed, blitz, blitzed*). Because the English language has changed drastically since its earliest period, it is not always easy to differentiate weak from strong verbs in Modern English. One subclass of weak verbs is especially deceptive since it features what seems to be both root vowel change and inflectional suffixes (*teach, taught; bring, brought; catch, caught*). These verbs, however, did not originally form their past by means of a root vowel change. For a further discussion of strong verbs, see **Gradation,** p. 138.

Structural Linguistics

The special branch of linguistics, developed largely by twentieth-century American linguists, which concentrates on describing forms and patterns of language. Structural linguists have re-examined the means by which a language signals meanings. Beginning with the phoneme, which is the smallest significant unit of language, they have classified a hierarchy of complex linguistic units, including the morpheme, parts of speech, and sentence patterns. Many definitions of grammatical units in this book are derived from the discoveries of structural linguists.

Structural linguistics differs from traditional grammar in its attempt to define language units in terms of their form rather than their meaning. The analysis of structural linguistics is called *formal* (i.e., related to *form*) while that of traditional grammar is called *notional* (i.e., related to *notions*, or ideas). Structural linguistics also differs from traditional grammar in its insistence that the oral language has primacy over the written language.

In recent times, transformational grammar (see p. 192) has challenged the rationale and objectives of structural linguistics. Transformationalists contend that structural grammar does not reveal the operations of language, that indeed it merely lists an inventory of linguistic units. Moreover, they point out that the aim of structural grammar—to describe every possible utterance unit which appears in a language—is impossible of fulfillment. Structural linguistics is, thus, seen as an *analytic* study—one that is concerned with the separation of parts and not with their synthesis, or combination.

By and large, the interest of structural linguists has been in the description of living languages. This interest is unquestionably a reaction to the historical emphasis of linguistics in the nineteenth century. Recently, however, structural linguistic methods—that is, the classification of phonemes and morphemes—have been applied as well to extinct languages like Old and Middle English. The study of a language at a single particular time in its history is sometimes referred to as *synchronic* linguistics; the comparison of two historical stages in the development of a language is called *diachronic* linguistics.

Structure Words
See **Function Words,** p. 135.

Subject
In traditional grammar the *subject* is usually defined as the word or word group which names the actor or the concept about which the verb makes a statement. This definition, however, needs qualification. It applies, by and large, to kernel sentences (see p. 149), but it does not apply to all types of transformed sentences. For example, in the transformed sentence "The train was derailed by pranksters," the actor is clearly not the subject word *train* but the object word *pranksters.* And the verb *was derailed* clearly makes a statement about both *train* and *pranksters.* It is better, therefore, to define the subject as that sentence element which is capable of controlling the inflection of the verb. Thus, in the sentence cited, *train* is the subject because it governs *was.* If *pranksters* were the subject, the verb form would have to be *were.*

In Modern English the regular word order puts the subject word or phrase before the verb. Subject, or nominative, pronouns (*I, they*) must be used in subject positions.

Subject Complement
See **Complement,** p. 121.

Subjunctive Mood
See **Mood,** p. 153.

Subordinate Clause
See **Clause,** p. 118.

Subordinating Conjunctions
A class of function words, sometimes called "subordinators" or "clause markers," which introduce dependent clauses. The following words are the most frequently used *subordinating conjunctions*:

after	how	till
although	if	unless
as	in order that	when
as if	since	where
as long as	so	while
because	so that	why
before	though	

Certain function words, among them *that, which, who, whom,* and *what,* can appear either as subordinating conjunctions or as relative pronouns (see p. 177). They are subordinating conjunctions when they serve simply to connect a dependent clause with a main clause (He is the man *whom* I saw at the airport). They are relative pronouns when they serve as subject of the dependent clause which they introduce (Franklin D. Roosevelt was the President *who* had the longest term of office).

Subordination
The use of syntactical and grammatical arrangements which indicate the dependence of one sentence element to a larger or more important part of the whole. Proper *subordination,* therefore, is a matter of showing the appropriate relationship between ideas of unequal status. If we analyze the sentence "I saw the tall man," we discern that two ideas are involved in the object seen: it is *tall,* it is a *man.* Obviously, the fact that it is a *man* is more important than that it is *tall,* and that relationship is made manifest by placing the concept of tallness in adjectival position.

The matter of proper subordination, however, most commonly involves clauses. The *dependent* (or *subordinate*) clause is one which, except for such stylistic contexts as an answer to a direct question (When are you going home? *After the dance is over*), does not stand alone as a complete sentence. Such dependent clauses are generally introduced by a subordinating conjunction (e.g., *after, although, as, because, before, if, since, though, till, until, unless, when, where, while*) or a relative pronoun (e.g., *which, who, that, what*). Immature writers too often fail to use dependent clauses where they are appropriate, using independent clauses in their stead.

ORIGINAL: Joseph G. Mentor will speak at the Student Union next Thursday. He is presently Chairman of the California Civil Rights Commission. The speech is scheduled for 2 p.m.

REVISED: Joseph G. Mentor, *who is presently Chairman of the California Civil Rights Commission,* will speak at the Student Union next Thursday *at 2 p.m.*

ORIGINAL: We ate our breakfast at the hotel. Then we proceeded to the church for the wedding ceremony.

REVISED: *After having eaten* [or *we had eaten*] *breakfast at the hotel,* we proceeded to the church for the wedding ceremony.

In large part proper subordination of ideas results in the discriminating use of complex and compound-complex sentences, both of which are considered marks of greater sophistication in writing than simple sentences. (See also **Complex Sentence,** p. 125 and **Compound-Complex Sentence,** p. 125.)

Substantive

Any word or word group which functions as a noun. A *substantive,* therefore, may serve as a subject, a complement, or as an object of a preposition, those positions in a sentence occupied by nouns. Various types of substantives are italicized in the following sentences:

type of substantive	*example*
NOUN:	The *girl* ate *dinner.*
PRONOUN:	*She* liked *it* very much.
GERUND:	I never enjoyed *fishing.*
INFINITIVE:	I like *to ski* at Sun Valley.
NOUN CLAUSE:	*Whatever she said* was stupid.
DIRECT QUOTATION:	*"Get out!"* shouted the policeman.

Suffix

A *suffix* is a bound morpheme (see p. 116) which modifies the meaning of the root word it follows. There are two kinds of suffixes in English: *inflectional* and *derivational. Inflectional* suffixes are those which are added regularly to nouns (to form plurals and possessives), to verbs (to indicate tense and number), and to adjectives and adverbs (to indicate degree). Derivational suffixes are much more numerous than inflectional suffixes. The addition of a derivational suffix usually changes the form class (see p. 134) to which the word belongs (e.g., *free,* an adjective plus *dom* gives a noun). When both derivational and inflectional suffixes are added to a base, the inflectional suffix will come at the end of the word: e.g., *work* plus *-er* plus *-s* (*-er* is derivational, *-s* is inflectional). The use of suffixes allows a language to expand its vocabulary without departing from familiar root words. The following list contains the derivational suffixes most commonly used in English:

SUFFIX	MEANING	EXAMPLES
-able, -ible	ability, likelihood	perish*able*, collect*ible*
-ance, -ence -ancy, -ency	act, state, or quality of	further*ance*, infer*ence*, buoy*ancy*, tend*ency*
-ate	having, to make	affection*ate*, capacit*ate*
-dom	act, state, or quality of	free*dom*, official*dom*
-ed	having	beard*ed*, conceit*ed*
-eer, -ess (fem.)	doer, one who	auction*eer*, host*ess*
-en	having, to make	length*en*, black*en*
-er	doer, one who	learn*er*, work*er*
-ery	act, state, or quality of	trick*ery*, eat*ery*
-ful	full of	power*ful*, joy*ful*
-fy	having, to make	beauti*fy*, citi*fy*
-hood	act, state, or quality of	father*hood*, false*hood*
-ic, -ical	resembling	alcohol*ic*, poet*ical*
-ice	act, state, or quality of	just*ice*, coward*ice*
-ish	resembling	mann*ish*, book*ish*
-ism	act, state, or quality of	capital*ism*, Buddh*ism*
-ist	doer, one who	capital*ist*, Buddh*ist*
-ive	having	plaint*ive*, correct*ive*
-ize, -ise	having, to make	union*ize*, merchand*ise*
-less	without	wit*less*, child*less*
-like	resembling	life*like*, boss*like*
-ly	resembling, per	sad*ly*, month*ly*
-ment	act, state, or quality of	entertain*ment*, develop*ment*
-ness	act, state, or quality of	sad*ness*, truthful*ness*
-or	doer, one who	elevat*or*, act*or*
-ous	full of	poison*ous*, joy*ous*
-ship	act, state, or quality of	author*ship*, horseman*ship*
-sion, -tion	act, state, or quality of	propul*sion*, elec*tion*
-ster	one who is, makes, handles	young*ster*, song*ster*, team*ster*
-ulent	full of	fraud*ulent*, vir*ulent*
-y	resembling	creep*y*, church*y*

Superfix

The notation in phonemics to indicate stress, pitch, or juncture. *Superfixes* derive their name from being written above the line.

Suprasegmentals
See **Phoneme,** p. 165.

Syllable
A unit of sound constituting one vocal impulse. A *syllable* must contain one vowel; it can contain consonants or consonant clusters in initial and/or final position. Syllables which end in a vowel are called "open"; those which end in a consonant are called "closed." A *long* syllable is one which contains a long vowel or diphthong (*day, see, do, time*) or one which has a short vowel followed by a consonant cluster (d*u*sk, dr*i*nk, tr*a*pped).

Synonym
A word with nearly the same meaning as another (*friend, pal; chilly, cool; eat, devour*). Usually, synonyms differ in connotational meaning (see p. 124) but not in denotational meaning (see p. 128).

Syntax
A basic branch of linguistic study concerned with the interrelationships of words. Syntactical analysis concentrates on the examination of phrasal and clausal patterns in a language. It complements the other major area of grammatical study, that of *morphology* (see p. 155).

Synthetic Language
See **Analytic, Synthetic Languages,** p. 113.

Tenses of Verbs
The system of verbal inflections which indicates distinctions in time. English, like all other Germanic languages, has only two formal grammatical *tenses:* the present and the past. All other time distinctions are shown by function words.

The present tense for virtually all English verbs has two inflectional forms: the *-s* ending for the third person singular (he think*s*) and zero inflection for all other persons (*I, you, we, they think*). The past tense is formed essentially in one of two ways: by the addition of a dental sound (*-ed, -d,* or *-t* as in *minded, strived,* or *built*) and by the change of a root vowel (*drive, drove; sing, sang*). A small but important subclass of verbs shows both changes (*teach, taught; bring, brought*). For a discussion of these past tense formations, see **Strong Verb, Weak Verb,** p. 184.

Besides the simple present and the simple past tenses, English also has a number of *periphrastic tenses.* Tenses of this kind make use of one or more modal auxiliaries and an infinitive or a participle. The following list illustrates the various grammatical and periphrastic tenses in English:

	active voice	passive voice
SIMPLE PRESENT	I call	I am called
PRESENT PROGRESSIVE	I am calling	I am being called
PRESENT EMPHATIC	I do call	
SIMPLE PAST	I called	I was called
PAST PROGRESSIVE	I was calling	I was being called
PAST EMPHATIC	I did call	
PERFECT	I have called	I have been called
PERFECT PROGRESSIVE	I have been calling	
PAST PERFECT	I had called	I had been called
PAST PERFECT PROGRESSIVE	I had been calling	
FUTURE	I will (shall, 'll, am about to, am going to) call	I will (shall, 'll, am about to, am going to) be called
FUTURE PROGRESSIVE	I will be calling	I will be called
FUTURE PERFECT	I will have called	I will have been called
FUTURE PERFECT PROGRESSIVE	I will have been calling	

The use of these tenses presents few difficulties to native speakers of the language. The simple present generally expresses repeated action (I *eat* breakfast at 7:00 a.m.) or action for which time is not specified (Children never *tire* of playing). Actions which specify present time are usually expressed by the present progressive tense (I *am going* right now).

Past actions are expressed in several ways. Those that were completed in the past are indicated by means of the simple past or the past progressive (I *painted* yesterday; I *was painting* yesterday). It should be noted that these two tenses do not state identical concepts: usually, the simple past puts emphasis on the duration of the action (I *rested* from 12:00 to 1:00), while the past progressive emphasizes a more specific moment of past time (I *was resting* when the bell rang). The perfect tense indicates an action carried from the past into the present (The United States *has* never *lost* a war). The past perfect refers to an action completed before another action or point of time in the past (The United States *had* already *fought* one war against England when the War of 1812 erupted).

It is to be noted that English has no formal tense to express future action. Various verb phrases can be used to denote future time: *I may go, I will go, I'm about to go, I hope to go, I shall go, I'll go,* etc. The choice of the auxiliary or the verb is determined in essence by the modality, not the projected time of the action. To express determination, one chooses one kind of verb phrase; to express doubt, another; to express probability, still another. The simple present or the present progressive are used frequently to express reasonably definite future action (*I'm leaving* on the 7:15 plane; My plane *leaves* at 7:15 p.m. tomorrow).

The terms *preterit* and *imperfect* are rarely used to describe past action in English. They are, however, used regularly to classify grammatical past tenses in languages like Italian or Spanish, which formally differentiate between terminated action in the past (the preterit tense) and continued action in the past (the imperfect tense).

Consistency in the use of tense is a mark of mature style. One should not shift without good reason from the present tense to the past, or vice versa, in narrative writing. For a discussion of this point, see **Shifted Construction,** p. 181.

Topic Sentence

A sentence which focuses attention upon the unifying idea of a paragraph. A *topic sentence* often appears at the beginning of a paragraph and serves to prepare the reader for what follows. When, for example, the paragraph begins with the sentence "Skiing requires a considerable investment for equipment," the reader expects a discussion, accompanied with price estimates, of the necessary items, such as skis, bindings, boots, poles, stretch pants, parka. He does not expect to read about the writer's last vacation in Sun Valley or about a ski accident that took place on the slalom course last week.

Not all paragraphs contain a topic sentence. Particularly when they are short, paragraphs may need no specific sentence to achieve unity. Nevertheless, every well-constructed paragraph should be capable of being summarized in a single sentence.

The following examples illustrate the use of topic sentences at the beginning and end of paragraphs.

The new culture throve in Iceland. The immigrants were an exceedingly competent, and even a rather well-educated lot, as educated people went under the Arctic Circle in those days. They could fish, or fight, or farm, and they did all of these. Iceland became a key station in the settlement of Greenland and in the eventual discovery of the continent of North America. Icelanders developed a relatively representative government, a stable and prosperous community, and a great love of the culture they had brought with them. They went their own hearty way, too distant and too insignificant to be much bothered by the rest of Europe. Icelanders had gone west in order to get away from Harold Fairhair and all his works, and they did. (Charlton Laird, *The Miracle of Language.*)

Some are dinning in our ears that we Americans, and moderns generally, are intellectual dwarfs compared with the ancients, or even the Elizabethan man. But what is that to the purpose? A living dog is better than a dead lion. Shall a man go and hang himself because he belongs to the race of pigmies, and not be the biggest pigmy that he can? *Let every one mind his own business and endeavor to be what he was made.* (Henry David Thoreau, *Walden.*)

Transformational Grammar

A theory of grammar which attempts to account for every possible sentence and to exclude every non-sentence in a language by means of a systematic set of rules. *Transformational* (or *generative*) *grammar* is not concerned with making an inventory of all the sentences or sentence parts which are or have been in use, because such an objective would be impossible of attainment. Rather, it attempts to generate rules which will predict all the possible grammatical patterns which can occur in a language.

Transformational grammar is built by a series of *constituent-structure* rules which reveal the means by which units of language (phrases, words, morphemes, and phonemes) combine. These constituent structures are shown in formulas or *rewrite rules*. Thus, for example, a basic sentence is represented as follows:

$$S \rightarrow NP + VP$$

That is to say, a noun phrase (NP) and a verb phrase (VP) are constituent structures generated from a sentence (S). The left side of the arrow indicates the higher-level element; the right side indicates the lower-level constituents. One can proceed thus to smaller and smaller units in the constituent-structure analysis of a language. A noun phrase can be rewritten as

NP → Det + N

In this rewrite rule, the noun phrase of a particular sentence is said to be generated into a determiner (*a, the, their*) and a noun. A noun phrase in the view of transformational grammar could consist of a single word (for example the word *dogs* in "Dogs are domestic animals"). The formula NP → Det + N would apply even to such a context, for the determiner in this situation would be regarded as a zero form (see p. 202). The rewrite rule for the determiner would therefore look as follows (Ø being the symbol for zero form):

Det → Ø

The zero form in the rewrite rule is not a superfluous sign, for it makes a significant comment about English grammar. We do not ordinarily say "The dogs are the domestic animals," a point that must be observed by any grammar which attempts to describe the possible and available grammatical patterns in a language. The zero form in this instance is a form of the indefinite article (it is really the plural of "*A* dog is *a* domestic animal"). In the same way, all of the constituent structures can be subclassified by means of various rewrite rules. Ultimately, every unit which can combine into a noun phrase or a verb phrase will thus be revealed. Significantly, parts are then not seen in isolation, as is true of parts-of-speech grammars, but in their syntactical contexts.

Constituent-structure rules are concerned with the analysis of *kernel sentences*, that is to say, basic sentences (see p. 149). While there is not yet complete agreement as to the number and kinds of kernel sentences in the language, the following list taken from a popular transformational grammar is reasonably representative (see Paul Roberts, *English Syntax*, Harcourt, 1964, p. 62):

1. John is heroic (a hero).	NP + be + substantive
2. John is in the room.	NP + be + Adv-p
3. John worked.	NP + VI
4. John paid the bill.	NP + VT + NP
5. John became a hero (heroic).	NP + Vb + substantive
6. John felt sad.	NP + Vs + Adj
7. John had a car.	NP + Vh + NP

The following is a key for the unfamiliar symbols in Roberts' kernel types: VI, intransitive verb; VT, transitive verb; Vb, verbs like *become* (followed either by a noun phrase or an adjective); Vs, verbs like *seem* (followed only by an adjective); Vh, verbs like *have;* Adv-p, adverb phrase.

The term *transformation* applies specifically to the rules for the conversion of kernel sentences into more complex types, like passive-voice sentences, questions, imperatives, negative sentences, and many others. By means of systematic rules, one can thus study the structural changes that take place when a statement like "You went out" is converted into a simple yes/no question, "Did you go out?". Transformation rules, which are too complex to be discussed here, are usually shown by a double arrow, thus $\Rightarrow$.

Transition

Transition refers to the techniques for achieving a smooth flow of ideas from sentence to sentence or from paragraph to paragraph. The following methods are commonly used to accomplish successful transition:

(1) *Between sentences*

(*a*) Use of the same subject in successive sentences, employing identical words, synonyms, or pronouns.

Music appeals to more than man's ear. *Music* appeals to his soul.

(*b*) Repetition of some key words from the previous sentence; for example, the direct object of one sentence may be used as the subject of the second.

Money may provide material things. Yet *material things* are not life's greatest assets.

(*c*) Use of a pronoun to refer to a word in the previous sentence.
A true scholar is patient. *He* never hurries a conclusion.
The wise man seeks solitude. The fool avoids *it.*

(*d*) Use of parallel structure in successive sentences.
If we win, we will have found our victory. If we lose, we will have deserved our defeat.

(*e*) Use of enumerative devices.
Our dean has two remarkable traits. First, he never makes decisions without examining alternatives. Second, he is on friendly terms with his entire faculty.

(*f*) Use of transitional words or phrases. English has a rich stock of words and phrases which indicate relationships between ideas. The following list classifies the most common of these according to the nature of the relationship.

ADDITION: again, also, and, besides, equally important, finally, further, furthermore, in addition, last, lastly, likewise, moreover, next, to

CLARIFICATION: as a matter of fact, clearly, evidently, in fact, in other words, obviously, of course, too

COMPARISON: also, likewise, in like manner, similarly

CONTRAST: after all, although, at the same time, but, conversely, for all that, however, in contrast, in spite of, nevertheless, notwithstanding, on the contrary, on the one hand, on the other hand, still, yet

EXEMPLIFICATION: for example, for instance, that is, thus

PLACE: above, adjacent to, below, beyond, close by, elsewhere, inside, nearby, next to, opposite, within, without

RESULT: accordingly, as a result, because, consequently, hence, in short, therefore, thus, then

SUMMARY: in brief, in conclusion, in short, on the whole, to conclude, to sum up, to summarize

TIME: after, after a short time, afterwards, at last, at length, at the same time, before, during, immediately, in the meantime, lately, meanwhile, of late, presently, since, shortly, soon, temporarily, then, thereafter, thereupon, until, while

(2) *Between paragraphs*

(*a*) Repetition of key words from one paragraph in the first sentence of the following paragraph.

> The next great influence into the spirit of the scholar is the mind of the past in whatever form, whether of literature, of art, of institutions, that mind is inscribed. Books are the best type of the influence of the past, and perhaps we shall get at the truth—learn the amount of this influence more conveniently—by considering their value alone.
>
> The theory of books is noble. . . . (Emerson, *The American Scholar.*)

(*b*) Use of an opening sentence which summarizes the previous paragraph and establishes the subject of the new one.

> Now that we have examined Roosevelt's domestic policies, we are ready to consider his accomplishments in the field of foreign affairs. . . .

(*c*) Reference to the subject matter of the previous paragraph with relation to the idea which is to follow.

> In the midst of these hardships and persecutions, the powerful figure Brigham Young led his people on to the new Zion. . . .

(*d*) Use of a question at the end of one paragraph or at the beginning of the next.

. . . The facts being what they are, we cannot evade the painful question: what is the solution to the problem of farm surplus? The previous administration in Washington sought to answer the question by increased farm-support prices. . . .

(e) Use of enumerative devices.

First, we should determine the need for further hydroelectric development on the Columbia River. The Bonneville Power Authority has estimated that by the year 1975 there will. . . .

Second, we must examine the feasibility of cheap future power through atomic generators. . . .

(f) Use of the transitional words or phrases listed under (1f), p. 194.

Transitive Verb

A verb which takes a direct object (John *laid* the book on the table; He *took* it away). Some verbs can be used transitively or intransitively according to the context in which they appear (*I drove the truck* [transitive] for hours; I *drove* [intransitive] for hours). (See also **Intransitive Verb,** p. 147.)

Trite Expression

See **Cliché,** p. 118.

Umlaut

See **Mutation,** p. 155.

Velar

Any consonant produced by the contact of the back of the tongue with the velum, or the soft palate. The vowel in st*ool* /uw/ and the initial consonant in *cat* /k/ are *velar.*

Verb

The term *verb* is used in two senses. It may refer to a sentence function (as in the context "A sentence must have a subject and a verb"), or it may refer to a part of speech. In this book, the term *predicate* (see p. 169) is used to denote verb in the former sense, as a sentence function.

As one of the basic parts of speech, a verb is traditionally defined as a word that names an action or a state of being. However, like many other notional definitions, this statement fails to differentiate a verb from other parts of speech. Action, for example, can be expressed by nouns (*commotion, smash*), by adjectives (*stormy, vigorous*), or even adverbs (*fast, energetically*). It is better, therefore, to define a verb by its structural features.

Structural linguists consider the verb to be a *form-class* word (see p. 134). It is differentiated from all other form classes by adding *-s* (or, more accurately, the phonemes /s/, /z/, or /ɨz/) to designate third person singular, present indicative. From this definition, it follows that words like *can, may,* or *must,* which do not add *-s,* cannot be considered verbs; structural linguists, indeed, regard these as function words and call them "auxiliaries" or "verb markers."

Many other facts concerning the inflection, function, and derivation of verbs must be noted in a comprehensive definition. In this glossary, the most important of these details are discussed separately under the following headings: **Anomalous Verb; Aspect; Conjugation; Finite Verb; Intransitive Verb; Mood; Number; Person; Preterit-present Verb; Transitive Verb; Strong Verb, Weak Verb; Tense;** and **Voice.**

Verbal

A form of a verb which functions as an adjective, an adverb, or a noun. The present participle, the past participle, and the infinitive can be used as *verbals.* (See also **Gerund,** p. 137.) The following sentence illustrates various forms of verbals in their several functions:

The *singing* [present participle used as adjective] marchers were ordered *to stop* [infinitive used as noun], but, their protest *unheeded* [past participle used as adjective], they refused *to obey* [infinitive used as noun].

Verner's Law

A statement made by Karl Verner, a Danish philologist, in 1875 to explain certain apparent exceptions to the sound shifts covered by Grimm's Law (see p. 140). *Verner's Law* specifically accounts for the voicing of consonants in Germanic when the stress did not occur on the immediately preceding syllable. Thus, where Grimm's Law indicates that Indo-European /t/ (as in Latin *dentis*) regularly becomes /θ/ in Germanic (as in Old English *toþ,* Modern English *tooth*), Verner's Law covers such apparent exceptions as the /t/ in Latin *centum* which developed into the voiced consonant /ð/ in Germanic and ultimately into /d/ in Old English *hund* (Modern English *hundred*). Though the listing of all the sound changes covered by Verner's Law is beyond the scope of this book, it is important to note that Verner's Law was regarded by many linguists as evidence that linguistics is an exact science, one which is totally systematic and which permits no exceptions. Verner, and other *Junggrammatiker,* as these linguists were called, thus initiated a vogue of extremely precise linguistic analysis. In the twentieth century, the emphasis once more turned to the study of larger units of language (as witness the more recent study of phonemics contrasted with the earlier phonetics).

It should also be noted that Verner's Law accounted for a consonant change in the past tense plural and the past participle of a large number of English strong verbs because of a prehistoric shift in accent (reminders of this change in Modern English are *seethe* and *sodden,* or *lose* and *forlorn*). This variation was noted by Jacob Grimm, who was, however, unable to account for it. He called it "grammatical change" (*Grammatischer Wechsel*), a term still used on occasion as a synonym for Verner's Law.

Vocabulary

According to *Webster III,* the English language has a current general *vocabulary* of approximately 450,000 words. The sources of this vocabulary are many. A great many words are, of course, derived from Old English and, ultimately, from Germanic and Indo-European. Foreign languages have, at various times, added significantly to this native stock of words: Scandinavian in the age of the Viking invasions, French during the Norman Conquest, Latin throughout the Middle Ages; and in more recent times Italian, German, Dutch, Spanish, Portuguese, the languages of the American Indians, and countless others from all parts of the world. The native word stock together with loanwords, then, comprise the major source of the English vocabulary.

Vocabulary growth also takes place as a result of changes in meaning. Though there are many types of such changes, four can be cited here as particularly important:

(1) *Generalization.* Some words have broadened their meaning in the course of time. Generalization takes place whenever a word is used with a new referent or in a new sentence function. The word *Kleenex,* for example, though used as a commercial label for a specific brand, is often generalized to stand for any brand of facial tissue. *Boycott* is derived from a proper name, that of a certain Captain C. Boycott, who was himself the victim of what is now generally called a *boycott.*

(2) *Specialization.* The narrowing of word meanings is known as specialization. For example, the word *fowl* (like its German cognate *Vogel*) once referred to any bird, but now it is used in the more special sense to denote such domestic birds as the chicken, goose, duck, or turkey. Similarly, *starve* (like its German cognate *sterben*) once had the general meaning of "to die," whereas now it has the more specialized meaning of "perishing from hunger."

(3) *Degeneration.* Some words have developed unfavorable meanings in the course of time. For example, the word *crafty* once meant "skilfull"; now it means "cunning." Similarly, *silly,* which once meant "blessed," now means "foolish."

(4) *Elevation.* Other words have acquired favorable meanings. The word *fond* has been elevated since Shakespeare's time, when it meant "foolish." *Steward* once meant literally a "sty-warden" (or a "swineherd"); now it has the considerably more favorable meaning of "caretaker" or "manager."

The influences on the growth of the English vocabulary have been too varied and complex to be discussed here in detail. However, aspects and types of vocabulary growth are discussed in a number of entries in this glossary, including **Cognate, Connotation, Neologism, Nonce Word, Onomatopoeia, Portmanteau Word,** and **Slang.**

Voice

A grammatical term indicating whether a verb is *active* (I *hear,* he *robs,* they *give*) or passive (I *am heard,* he *is robbed,* they *are given*). Verbs occur in the active *voice* when the subject is the initiator or the performer of an action; they occur in the passive voice when the subject is the receiver or the goal of an action.

ACTIVE: Anne gave dancing lessons to Cindy. Mark dated Linda.
PASSIVE: Cindy was given dancing lessons by Anne. Linda was dated by Mark.

By and large, only transitive verbs can be put into a passive voice sentence. In recent times, passive constructions have been regarded as transformations of sentences in the active voice. The passive in English consists of a form of the verb *to be* and a past participle, though in colloquial usage, *get* sometimes occurs in place of *be* (The bike *got* stolen).

Many stylebooks recommend the use of the active voice wherever possible. Passive constructions can deprive one's style of vividness and animation. In some instances, however, the passive voice is necessary or desirable:

(1) When the performer of an action is unknown (John was wounded in the last battle of World War II).

(2) When the action rather than its performer is emphasized (The car was smashed by a train).

(3) When the identity of the performer is deliberately concealed (Smoking is prohibited).

Voiced, Voiceless

These terms are used in phonetics to differentiate types of consonants according to the presence or absence of vocalization as they are articulated. *Voiced* consonants are those in which the vocal folds vibrate; *voiceless* consonants are those in which the breath stream passes unimpeded through the larynx (the voice box). It is this voicing which gives a humming quality to /b/ as in *ball*—a quality which is absent in its voiceless counterpart /p/ as in *Paul*. English has the following consonant sets which are differentiated on the basis of voicing:

voiced	*unvoiced*
/v/ in *v*at	/f/ in *f*at
/b/ in *b*at	/p/ in *p*at
/d/ in *d*ot	/t/ in *tot*
/g/ in *g*ot	/k/ in *c*ot
/ð/ in clo*the*	/θ/ in clo*th*
/z/ in *z*ink	/s/ in *s*ink
/ž/ in bei*ge*	/š/ in ba*sh*
/ǰ/ in *jud*ge	/č/ in *ch*ur*ch*

Vowel

A sound formed by the relatively free passage of the breath stream over the center of the tongue. The tone of vowel sounds is formed by the vibration of the vocal folds. When the folds are tautly strung, the vowels produced are high-pitched, or *tense* (e.g., the vowels in *do* /uw/ or *he* /iy/); when the folds are relaxed, the vowels produced are low-pitched, or *lax* (e.g., the vowels in *calm* /ah/ and *man* /æ/). The resonance of vowel sounds is shaped by the modification of the oral and nasal chambers. Vowel sounds are free of audible friction.

Vowels are classified in several ways: as *long* or *short* (the vowels in *seat* /iy/ and *sit* /i/, respectively); as *high, mid,* or *low* according to the raising or lowering of the tongue (the vowels in *meat* /iy/, *mate* /ey/, and *mat* /æ/, respectively); or as *front, central,* or *back* according to the fronting or retracting of the tongue (the vowels in *mean* /iy/, *in* /ɨ/, and *moon* /uw/, respectively). A full description of a vowel will take into account all of these criteria; thus, an /iy/ is a long, high, front vowel.

For a list of American English vowels, see **Phonemic Alphabet,** p. 165.

Vulgate English

A label sometimes used by linguists to refer to the spoken language of the uneducated or to dialect speech. Many linguists avoid this label because *vulgate,* meaning "common" or "popular," is frequently confused by the uninitiated with *vulgar.* A synonym for *vulgate English* is *popular English* (see p. 168).

Weak Verb
See **Strong Verb, Weak Verb,** p. 184.

Word Choice
See **Diction,** p. 129.

Wordiness
A term used to describe flabby, inexact, and uneconomical writing. A *wordy* style lacks precision and is usually characterized by circumlocution, bloated diction, deadwood, anticipatory subjects, and other redundancies.

WORDY: There is in our institutions of higher learning a tendency toward greater seriousness of purpose on the part of college students, and I have recognized this phenomenon throughout our country.
REVISED: I have noticed that college students in America are more serious than they used to be.
WORDY: In our modern day and age of today, very few individuals pass to their reward because of the ravages of smallpox.
REVISED: Very few people die of smallpox today.

Word Order
The set patterning of words for the purpose of conveying grammatical relationships. Because Modern English is no longer a fully inflected language, its *word order* is *fixed* rather than *free,* as was that of Old English. Word order, therefore, is a device for grammatical analysis in Modern English. The standard placement of the larger sentence elements is subject-verb-object, a sequence which in itself signals the grammatical function of the several parts as follows: "The President (subject) greeted (verb) the ambassador (direct object)." In such a sentence, since neither noun contains an inflectional signal, only word order enables us to recognize "President" as subject and "ambassador" as object. Languages with free word order could easily change the placement of these sentence parts without affecting the intended meaning.

Although English word order is not entirely fixed, it does favor a regular placement of elements within a sentence and of words within a phrase. Native speakers quite unconsciously place indirect objects before direct objects (The office manager promised *me* [indirect object] *a raise* [direct object]), adverbs of place before adverbs of time (Pamela usually comes *home* [place adverb] *at lunchtime* [time adverb]), or adjectives before the nouns they modify (John never wears *brown* dungarees). Constructions like these rarely present any problems of usage.

There are, however, certain patterns in which the placement of words or phrases can be troublesome even to native speakers. For example, the use of two consecutively placed prepositional phrases can lead to such humorous ambiguities as the following: "Mortimer married the blonde with the beautiful figure from Hollywood." Since even an inversion of the two phrases would not entirely eliminate ambiguity in such a construction (the blonde from Hollywood with the beautiful figure), the best way to revise the sentence is to rewrite it in a different form altogether (Mortimer married the shapely blonde from Hollywood).

Inversion of elements within a phrase, clause, or sentence is obligatory in some constructions. For example, sentences beginning with expletive *there,* normally place the verb before the delayed subject (There *are* [verb] six vacant *apartments* [subject] in the building). Likewise, a sentence introduced by a negative adverbial modifier has verb-subject order (Nowhere in the world *can* [verb] retired *families* [subject] live so well on so little income). Most question formats also feature inversions (Where *is* [verb] *the bank* [subject]? *Are* [verb] *you* [subject] the dean's wife?).

Some inversion patterns are optional. Often these are used for rhetorical effect to achieve variety or emphasis (*A few of its most dramatic findings* [object], the committee will release to the public on Friday).

Zero Inflection

A term used by structural linguists to account for uninflected forms among English morphemes. For example, the plural noun form *sheep* is said to have *zero inflection*. Some linguists use the symbol Ø to indicate zero inflection or zero form.

LITERARY
TERMS

This list of literary terms does not pretend to be exhaustive. We have, however, attempted to define those terms most likely to be used in introductory collegiate courses in English. Students who become familiar with these terms will have mastered the basic vocabulary of literary analysis and will, as a result, have prepared themselves to discuss belletristic matters with clarity and precision.

We have included in the following list descriptive terms of general interest as well as major literary types and figures of speech. Not included are terms relating specifically to literary history, such as Augustan Age, Sturm und Drang, and Battle of the Books. Moreover, except for some widely used terms, this glossary does not define critical labels which are usually associated with a particular writer; hence, one will not find definitions for such terms as objective correlative, negative capability, and willing suspension of disbelief.

We have attempted to provide succinct definitions followed wherever possible by clarifying examples drawn from the work of well-known authors. In so doing, we hope to furnish the beginning student of literature with definitions he can easily understand.

Accent

See p. 105.

Alexandrine

A six-foot iambic line which in English poetry often occurs within or at the end of an iambic pentameter poem in order to achieve variety or finality. For example, the *Alexandrine* is used as the last line in the Spenserian stanza, which is otherwise iambic pentameter. The Alexandrine is a long line, and it tends to be heavy and slow moving. In his *An Essay on Criticism,* Pope criticizes and illustrates the use of the Alexandrine:

A needless Alexandrine ends the song
That, like a wounded snake, drags its slow length along.

Allegory

An *allegory* is a story which can be read on an abstract or figurative level. Commonly allegory embodies abstract (moral or social) concepts by means of personification or metaphor. The first book of *Gulliver's Travels,* for example, may be read as a straightforward story, as children have read it for centuries. It may also be read as a *political allegory* in which the Queen of the Lilliputians stands for England's Queen Anne and Gulliver stands at different times for Lord Bolingbroke (a British statesman) and for Jonathan Swift himself. Similarly, the island of Lilliput stands as a metaphor for England; the island of Blefuscu, for France. The Lilliputian adventure may also be read as a *moral allegory,* in one interpretation of which Gulliver stands for the vainglorious (and quite gullible) man of the Enlightenment who saw himself puffed up or "larger than life." The illustration from *Gulliver's Travels* makes an additional point: to be superior, allegories do not necessarily need to be totally consistent in their symbolism. They can shift their reference within one level of interpretation (Gulliver as Bolingbroke or Swift), and they can shift levels of interpretation themselves (*Gulliver's Travels* as political *or* moral allegory). English literature is rich in allegory; some well-known examples are *The Vision of Piers Plowman, The Faerie Queene, Everyman,* and *Pilgrim's Progress.* (See also **Fable,** p. 217, and **Parable,** p. 223.)

Alliteration

The repetition of the same initial letter or sound in words which are close together. In Old and Middle English poetry *alliteration* often served as the chief structural device throughout a poem, but it is now used only occasionally either to ornament or to achieve a particular effect. The alliteration of the breathy *b* or *f* sounds in the following lines of Coleridge suggest by their sound the brisk breeze and rapid movement that he is describing:

> The *f*air *b*reeze *b*lew, the white *f*oam *f*lew,
> The *f*urrow *f*ollowed *f*ree.

Though primarily a poetic device, alliteration is sometimes used in prose as well. Thoreau, for example, talks of *"w*inter evenings by my fireside, *w*hile the snow *w*hirled *w*ildly *w*ithout." Too frequent use of alliteration in prose, however, savors of affectation.

Advertisers used the device lavishly in order to make brand names and slogans stick in the minds of purchasers (*S*alem's *s*oftness freshens your taste; *M*arlboro, a *m*an's smoke; *B*etter *b*uy *B*uick).

Allusion

A reference to a well-known person or event from either history or literature. The following lines from Robinson's *Mr. Flood's Party* depend for their full meaning upon the reader's understanding the *allusion* to Roland, hero of the medieval romance *The Song of Roland.*

Alone, as if enduring to the end
A valiant armor of scarred hopes outworn,
He stood there in the middle of the road
Like Roland's ghost winding a silent horn.

Ambiguity

In its usual sense *ambiguity* is an undesirable quality which writers should avoid; this meaning of the term is discussed under the heading **Ambiguity** in the section on linguistic, stylistic, and grammatical definitions.

Applied to literature, however, the term has developed a favorable meaning. When a literary critic uses the word, he refers to a verbal nuance which allows multiple reactions or interpretations to the same word or statement. Literary ambiguity lends richness to a text. For example, when Wordsworth in his *Ode, Intimations of Immortality* refers to "The Youth, who daily farther from the east / Must travel," he allows a multiple interpretation of the image: (1) traveling from east to west represents the passage of time and, hence, the process of growing older; (2) the east represents spirituality and the seat of the godhead. Both these interpretations are compatible with the context of the poem.

The *pun* is a particular literary device which makes use of ambiguity (see p. 227).

Anachronism

An event which is "out of time"; one which did not take place as early as indicated. The medieval dramatist who lets one of the shepherds in the nativity swear by "Christ's cross" commits an anachronism. So does Shakespeare when he allows a clock to strike in *Julius Caesar*.

Anacoluthon

A figure of speech in which the structural plan is shifted in mid-sentence. Poets often use this construction to convey the effect of surprise or extreme emotion upon a speaker. Milton's Satan, for example, uses the figure *anacoluthon* upon first seeing Beelzebub in Hell:

If thou beest he; [structure shift] But O how fall'n! how
   chang'd
From him, who in the happy Realms of Light
Cloth'd with transcendent brightness didst outshine
Myriads though bright.

Analogue

Similar versions of the same story by different authors are called *analogues.* Thus, the story of Amleth, who in a Norse myth recorded by Saxo Grammaticus avenged his father's murder, is an analogue of Shakespeare's *Hamlet.*

Anapest

A metrical foot consisting of two unstressed syllables followed by a stressed syllable (see **Metrical Feet, p. 221**).

Anecdote

A brief narrative, usually of a biographical nature, dealing with a single incident. An *anecdote* does not contain complexities of plot and character; instead, it is a simple relation of the incident, often humorous. Aubrey's *Brief Lives* contains many anecdotes.

Antagonist

The character who is opposed to the protagonist, or chief character, of a story or play. The *antagonist* involves the protagonist in a conflict of one sort or another. Though he is usually a human being, the antagonist may in some stories be an animal, as in Melville's *Moby Dick,* or a natural force, as in London's *To Build a Fire* (see also **Protagonist, p. 227**).

Antithesis

A figure of speech in which two or more strikingly different ideas are expressed in balanced rhetorical units. This balance may consist of paired words, phrases, clauses, or even sentences. The effect of a successful *antithesis* is surprise. Pope employed antithesis when he wrote that a woman's screams of anguish occur equally "When husbands and when lap-dogs breathe their last." *When husbands* and *when lap-dogs* are balanced structurally, yet there is a striking contrast between them.

Aphorism

A concise statement of a profound truth or sentiment. An *aphorism* is usually restricted to one short and particularly effective sentence. In poetry it is often found in a couplet. Aphorisms share some of the properties of maxims and proverbs. Unlike maxims, however, aphorisms are not always directed toward improved conduct; unlike proverbs, which are usually anonymous, aphorisms are attributed to their authors. The poetry of William Blake abounds in aphoristic statements expressed either as single lines ("He who desires but acts not, breeds pestilence") or as couplets:

> A truth that's told with bad intent
> Beats all the lies you can invent.

Apostrophe

A figure of speech in which an object or a person not present is addressed by the speaker. Keats apostrophizes the Grecian urn in the following lines:

> O Attic shape! Fair attitude! With brede
> Of marble men and maidens overwrought . . .

Archetype

A recurrent pattern or model of experience encountered in literature of all types and all nations. According to Carl G. Jung, an *archetype* reflects a "collective unconscious" and embraces the typical experiences of all men in all ages. The concept of death is often represented archetypically as a return to nature (e.g., King Arthur's body being carried on a barge to the Vale of Avalon). So is the renewal of life, which might be viewed in a mythic tale of regeneration (e.g., the Green Knight who is able to grow a new head after it is severed by Gawayn). Archetypical themes are to be found in every work of imaginative literature (e.g., the recurrent narrative of the separation, initiation, and return of the hero).

Assonance

The repetition of identical or similar vowel sounds. The recurrence of *o* sounds in the first two lines of Poe's *The Raven* is a good example of *assonance*.

> Once upon a midnight dreary, while I pondered, weak and
>   weary,
> Over many a quaint and curious volume of forgotten lore . . .

Ballad

A verse intended to be sung or chanted and characterized by its simple narrative form. The *folk ballad* is anonymous, and it has probably been transmitted by oral tradition through many generations, gathering many variants as it aged. Oral transmission tends to eliminate nonessentials and subleties of characterization; hence most folk ballads deal rather starkly with a single episode of a highly dramatic, and usually tragic, nature. The most common ballad form is a quatrain with alternating lines of four and three stresses, rhyming *abcb*.

> Up and spak an eldern knicht,
>   Sat at the kings richt kne:
> "Sir Patrick Spence is the best sailòr,
>   That sails upon the se."

4

The *literary ballad* is a conscious attempt on the part of an author to imitate and capture the spirit of folk ballads. The common ballad quatrain often becomes modified, usually by the addition of another rhyme (*abab*) and the lengthening of the second line to four stresses.

> Why, William, on that old grey stone,
> Thus for the length of half a day,
> Why, William, sit you thus alone,
> And dream your time away?

Bathos

A comic quality in a literary work resulting from pathos which is so overdone as to become laughable, or from a sudden shift from the serious to the trivial. An example of unintentional *bathos* is Coleridge's *To a Young Ass, Its Mother Being Tethered Near It*, a poem which seeks unsuccessfully to evoke the reader's sympathy for young donkeys. The following lines from Byron's *Don Juan*, on the other hand, illustrate intentional bathos, achieving the comic effect by descending unexpectedly from the straightforward observations in the first line to the quip at the end of the second.

> He learned the arts of riding, fencing, gunnery,
> And how to scale a fortress—or a nunnery.

Beast Epic

A narrative made up of a series of episodes which feature animal characters. *Beast epics*, also known as *beast fables*, are often satirical as in Chaucer's *Nun's Priest's Tale*, perhaps the best-known example of the type in English literature. In medieval literature, one finds a number of beast treatises which make moral and religious interpretations; such collections of beast stories are known as *bestiaries*.

Belles Lettres

A term used to differentiate artistic and imaginative literature from that which has an immediately practical and informative purpose. Shakespeare's plays, Shelley's poetry, and Hemingway's novels, for example, would appropriately be called *belles lettres;* Parrington's *Main Currents of American Thought,* Darwin's *The Origin of Species,* and Paine's *The Age of Reason* would not.

Bildungsroman

A German word referring to a type of novel which focuses on the educational and spiritual development of its protagonist. Typical examples of the *Bildungsroman* are Goethe's *Sorrows of Young Werther,* Maugham's *Of Human Bondage,* and Salinger's *The Catcher in the Rye.*

Blank Verse

Unrhymed iambic pentameter lines. Since its introduction into England in the mid-sixteenth century by Surrey, *blank verse* has been commonly used in English literature for long narrative and philosophic poems as well as for drama.

> The World was all before them, where to choose
> Their place of rest, and Providence their guide:
> They hand in hand with wandering steps and slow,
> Through Eden took their solitary way.

Burlesque

Applied to literature, the term refers to deliberate ridicule by means of exaggeration and distortion. Its intended effect is always comic. Often a *burlesque* achieves its purpose through the trivial treatment of an essentially serious subject (see **Travesty,** p. 233). Thus Cervantes in *Don Quixote* pokes fun at the chivalric romance through the exaggerated and ridiculous chivalry of his errant knight protagonist. On the other hand, a burlesque may accord serious treatment to an essentially trivial subject (see **Mock-heroic,** p. 221). Thus Alexander Pope burlesques the conventions of epic poetry in his *Rape of the Lock.* Burlesque, since it ridicules conventions which characterize a type of literature, is broader than *parody,* which generally ridicules a particular author or literary work.

Caesura

A pause or break, usually marked with punctuation, within a line of poetry. In classical verse the *caesura* appeared near the middle of the line; many poets, however, seek diversity of rhythm by varying its position.

> No cloud,// no relique of the sunken day
> Distinguishes the West,// no long thin slip
> Of sullen light,// no obscure trembling hues.
> Come,// we will rest on this old mossy bridge.

Carpe diem

Phrase from the Latin of Horace meaning "seize the day." The *carpe diem* theme is particularly prominent in lyric poetry: live life fully today; tomorrow may never come. Usually the poet urges his lady to immediate love, as in Marvell's *To His Coy Mistress;* however, sometimes, as in the following stanza from FitzGerald's *Rubáiyát of Omar Khayyám,* there is a more general application of the theme.

Some for the Glories of This World; and some
Sigh for the Prophet's Paradise to come;
Ah, take the Cash, and let the Credit go,
Nor heed the rumble of a distant drum!

Catharsis

A Greek term with the literal meaning "purgation." According to Aristotle, the effect of tragedy upon the spectator was a *catharsis* of the emotions of pity and fear. Whether or not Aristotle intended the meaning "purgation" or "purification" is a matter of some scholarly dispute. Nevertheless, the term has gained wide currency in literary criticism to describe a mood of emotional serenity experienced by a reader or viewer after his contact with great tragic literature.

Climax

Traditionally the *climax* of a story or play is defined as the highest point of action or interest. That definition, however, often leads to confusion; not all readers will agree on the precise point in the narrative at which the action or interest was at its highest level. It is often more satisfactory to identify the point of climax by using one of the following definitions: (1) that point in the development of the major conflict at which the protagonist makes, or has made for him, an irrevocable decision; (2) that point in the development of the major conflict at which either the protagonist or the antagonist has won an irreversible victory.

Closed Couplet

See **Couplet,** p. 213.

Closet Drama

A play intended to be read rather than performed (e.g., Byron's *Manfred,* Browning's *Pippa Passes*). The term is also applied to some plays which, though meant to be performed, have survived primarily as literature (e.g., Browning's *Strafford,* Shelley's *The Cenci*).

Conceit

A figure of speech frequently employed by the metaphysical poets of the seventeenth century. A *conceit* is an ingenious, sometimes seemingly farfetched, analogy which shocks the imagination to perceive likenesses in objects and/or ideas that are commonly not associated with each other. John Donne uses a conceit when he pictures the separation of the souls of two lovers in terms of a pair of compasses:

If they be two, they are two so

As stiffe twin compasses are two;
Thy soule the fixed foot, makes no show
To move, but doth, if the other do.

And though it in the center sit,
Yet when the other far doth roam,
It leans, and harkens after it,
And grows erect, as that comes home.

Consonance

The poetic use of similar consonants in a group of neighboring words.
John Keats relies on *consonance* when he repeats the sounds *m* and *n*
in the opening of the *Ode to a Nightingale*:

My heart aches, and a drowsy numbness pains
My sense, as though of hemlock I had drunk,
Or emptied some dull opiate to the drains
One minute past, and Lethe-wards had sunk.

Couplet

Two successive rhyming lines of poetry. A *couplet* may be an entire
poem; more often, however, couplets are used as a verse pattern for
a larger poem. Though couplets may be written in lines of various meter
and length, the iambic pentameter couplet has been the most popular
in English poetry. An iambic pentameter couplet is called a *closed* or
heroic couplet when it contains a complete grammatical unit. A heroic
couplet is likely to end with a mark of terminal punctuation (a period,
question mark, exclamation point, semicolon, or colon). The following lines of Alexander Pope illustrate the use of the heroic couplet:

Whoever thinks a faultless piece to see,
Thinks what ne'er was, nor is, nor e'er shall be.
In every work regard the writer's End,
Since none can compass more than they intend;
And if the means be just, the conduct true,
Applause, in spite of trivial faults, is due;
As men of breeding, sometimes men of wit,
T'avoid great errors, must the less commit;
Neglect the rules each verbal Critic lays,
For not to know some trifles, is a praise.

An *open* couplet, on the other hand, makes use of enjambment (see
p. 215) to avoid the repetitive rhythm of the closed couplet. The following lines from Keats's *Sleep and Poetry* are open couplets which
comment upon the use of closed couplets in eighteenth-century poetry:

Yes, a schism
Nurtured by foppery and barbarism,
Made great Apollo blush for this his land.
Men were thought wise who could not understand
His glories: with a puling infant's force
They sway'd about upon a rocking horse,
And thought it Pegasus. Ah dismal soul'd!
The winds of heaven blew, the ocean roll'd
It's gathering waves—ye felt it not. The blue
Bared its eternal bosom, and the dew
Of summer nights collected still to make
The morning precious: beauty was awake!
Why were ye not awake?

Dactyl

A metrical foot consisting of an accented syllable followed by two un-accented syllables (see **Metrical Foot,** p. 221).

Dénouement

A French word with the meaning "unknot." As a literary term *dénouement* refers to that part of a narrative in which the mysteries or complications of the plot are solved or unraveled. In a typical Sherlock Holmes story, for example, the dénouement occurs when the famous detective discusses with Dr. Watson the method by which he solved the mystery and identified the villain. Sometimes the term is loosely used to refer to all the action which follows the climax of a story.

Deus ex machina

From the Latin meaning "god from a machine," the term was used originally to describe the practice in the Greek theater of lowering a god to the stage by means of ropes. Today, however, critics use the term to describe the improbable appearance of any character, god or otherwise, to bring a plot to a satisfactory conclusion. Since most critics believe that a plot should be resolved by probable and mo-tivated action, the *deus ex machina* is usually considered an inferior, unimaginative, and melodramatic way by which to resolve narrative conflict. An example of the deus ex machina would be the sudden and unexpected appearance of a repentant murderer who shouts out his confession at the very moment when the innocent hero is about to be hanged for the crime.

Didacticism

The instructional purpose in a literary work. Though the term *didacti-cism* is often used in an unfavorable sense, it would be difficult to find a literary work which does not, though perhaps indirectly, serve to instruct mankind on some aspect of life. A poem like Pope's *Essay on Man* is overtly didactic, while the didactism of Frost's lyric *Stopping by Woods on a Snowy Evening* is subtly imbedded in its action. Didactic elements need not degrade a literary work if they are subordinated to artistic considerations and if they avoid striking the reader as a mere catalogue of self-righteous moral platitudes.

Dimeter

A line of poetry consisting of two metrical feet (see **Metrical Foot,** p. 221).

Dramatic Monologue

A form of lyric poem which involves the speaker in a dramatic situation but records only his words. The other characters in a *dramatic monologue* participate only insofar as the words of the main speaker reveal their action or conversation. In this respect reading a dramatic monologue resembles listening to a person who is having a telephone conversation. The form was brought to perfection by Robert Browning, whose major work in it attempted a fourfold revelation: character analysis of the speaker, who is usually caught in a moment of crisis or decision; character analysis of the person or persons spoken to; analysis of the person or thing spoken about; a picture of the time in which the poem is set.

Elegy

In Greek and Roman poetry an *elegy* was simply a meditative poem written in a particular couplet form. Today, however, the term refers to a poem dealing with the subject of death. An elegy may commemorate the death of an individual (Whitman's *When Lilacs Last in the Dooryard Bloom'd* mourns Lincoln's death) or the fact of death as it applies to all mankind (Gray's *Elegy Written in a Country Churchyard*). The *pastoral elegy* (e.g., Milton's *Lycidas,* Shelley's *Adonais*) is a specific type of personal elegy in which the dead person, presented as a shepherd, is mourned by his fellows. Such elegies are characterized by dignified, serious language and by the observance of set pastoral conventions. Regardless of its type—personal, general, pastoral, or otherwise—a great elegy usually reaches beyond grief for an individual or for mankind and finds in the fact of death some reason for resignation, acceptance, and ultimate joy.

Enjambment

The practice of continuing one line of poetry to the next without a grammatical break at the end of the line. In English poetry *enjambment* is a common feature of blank verse, though it occurs in other poetic forms as well. In the following example from Browning's *My Last Duchess,* the enjambment of the second and third lines almost obscures the fact that the poem is written in couplets.

> That's my last Duchess painted on the wall,
> Looking as if she were alive. I call
> That piece a wonder, now: Frà Pandolf's hands
> Worked busily a day, and there she stands.

Epic

A long narrative poem in which the hero, sometimes part divine and always of high position, participates in a series of adventures which in their totality are important to the development of a national or racial history. Epics are divided into (1) *folk epics* (also called "primary" or "primitive" epics), which are written versions of the folk legends of a people, and (2) *literary epics* (also called "secondary," "classical," or "artificial" epics), which are conscious imitations by individual authors of earlier epics. Folk epics (e.g., *Gilgamesh, Beowulf*) are of anonymous authorship, and their plots are usually a composite of myths that have special ethnic significance. Literary epics (e.g., Virgil's *Aeneid,* Milton's *Paradise Lost,* Longfellow's *The Song of Hiawatha*) generally observe a fairly regular set of conventions, which include the following: invocation to the muse; beginning *in medias res* (see p. 219) and recounting previous events at a later point in the narrative; use of the supernatural; descriptions of heroic battles; lengthy catalogues of warriors or ships or battles, etc.; descent of the hero to the underworld; mysterious or miraculous birth of the hero; great single combat between the hero and his chief antagonist; formal and dignified style.

Epigram

Originally meaning "inscription," the term now refers primarily to a short and witty poem, often with a surprising or satirical twist at the end. The following epigram by Robert Herrick is addressed to his reader:

> Thou sayest my lines are hard,
> And I the truth will tell;
> They are both hard and marr'd,
> If thou not read'st them well.

Eulogy

Any literary work in which praise of a person's character and accomplishments is a dominant purpose. Eulogies may be written either in prose or verse. Ben Jonson's *To the Memory of My Beloved Master, William Shakespeare* is a famous example of a verse eulogy.

Euphuism

A stylistic term named after John Lyly's *Euphues: the Anatomy of Wit* (1579) and referring to an ornate prose style marked by the elaborate use of antitheses, alliteration, and allusions to mythology and unnatural "natural" history. The following sentence from *Euphues* illustrates some of the typical characteristics of the euphuistic style: "I see now that as the fish Scolopidus in the flood Araris at the waxing of the moon is as white as driven snow and at the waning as black as burnt coal, so Euphues, which at the first encreasing of our familiarity was very zealous, is now at the last become faithless."

Fable

A brief prose or verse tale which serves as moral instruction. *Fables* are often drawn from folklore, and animals frequently serve as characters. Aesop's *Fables* exemplify many of the possibilities of the form, while Orwell's *Animal Farm* represents a modern extension of the fable into the area of political morality.

Farce

A term from the Latin meaning "to stuff." Used originally to designate any insertion in the church liturgy, the term came to be applied to the low-comic situations in secular dramas. Today the word *farce* refers to comic productions, or parts of them, which achieve their effects through slapstick, buffoonery, mistaken identities, improbable situations, unmotivated action, and coarse wit.

Flashback

A term derived from the motion picture industry and now used in literary criticism to describe scenes which shift back to an earlier period of time in the lives of one or more characters. Miller's *Death of a Salesman* employs the *flashback* skillfully on the stage, and many modern novelists and short story writers make use of the device.

Free Verse

That form of verse which departs from the conventional patterns of uniform meter and rhyme and seeks its metrical effect instead from the cadences and rhythms of natural speech. *Free verse* provides the poet with an almost limitless variety of possible effects, many of which are achieved through the repetition of key words and phrases (often in successive stanzas) and the use of alliteration and other devices. Free verse, to be skillfully written, requires a talent just as acutely developed as that for the composition of conventional poetry. The following poem by Walt Whitman illustrates the form.

> When I heard the learn'd astronomer,
> When the proofs, the figures, were ranged in columns be-
> fore me,
> When I was shown the charts and diagrams, to add, divide,
> and measure them,
> When I sitting heard the astronomer where he lectured with
> much applause in the lecture-room,
> How soon unaccountable I became tired and sick,
> Till rising and gliding out I wander'd off by myself,
> In the mystical moist night-air, and from time to time,
> Look'd up in perfect silence at the stars.

Genre

A distinctive category or type of literary composition. The word *genre* is most often applied to broadly defined literary types (e.g., tragedy, comedy, novel, short story, epic, lyric); however, it is sometimes applied to such subtypes as the detective novel, ode, or sonnet. Another meaning derives from the use of the word in art circles, where a *genre painting* is one which portrays commonplace life in a realistic manner. Thus by analogy a literary work dealing realistically with common people is sometimes called a *genre study*.

Heptameter

A line of poetry consisting of seven metrical feet (see **Metrical Foot,** p. 221).

Heroic Couplet

See **Couplet,** p. 213.

Hexameter

A line of poetry consisting of six metrical feet (see **Metrical Foot,** p. 221).

Hyperbole

A figure of speech in which extravagant exaggeration arrests the reader's attention for either a serious or comic effect. Pope's "Belinda smiled, and all the world was gay" is *hyperbole* used for comic effect; Marlowe's "Is this the face that launched a thousand ships" is used for serious effect. (See also **Pathetic Fallacy,** p. 224.)

Iamb

A metrical foot consisting of an unaccented syllable followed by an accented syllable (see **Metrical Foot,** p. 221).

Image

A literary device which yields a sense impression. *Images* are produced by figurative language; they function to enrich the presentation of a subject often by reference to several or all of the five senses. For example, the crescent of the moon is represented in the traditional ballad *Sir Patrick Spens* by a verbal picture that appeals to the senses of both sight and touch:

> Late, late yestreen [yesterday] I saw the new moon
> Wi' the old moon in her arm.

In recent times, some literary studies have concentrated on isolating a poet's recurrent use of an image, thus showing the relationship between the subject, the theme, and the language of a literary work. In *Hamlet,* for example, Shakespeare repeatedly uses images of sickness and decay to emphasize that life at Elsinore is diseased, or, to put it in his own words, that "something is rotten in the state of Denmark."

In medias res

A Latin phrase meaning "in the middle of things." The phrase refers to the practice of beginning a narrative in the middle, but always before the climax, then recounting previous events at a later point of the story. It is conventional that epics (see p. 216) start *in medias res,* but the practice is widely used in prose fiction, drama, and movies as well.

Invective

Strong denunciation of a person or cause. If it is humorously oriented, *invective* may be satirical (see p. 228). Browning's abuse of Wordsworth in *The Lost Leader* is an example of invective.

> Just for a handful of silver he left us,
> Just for a riband to stick in his coat . . .

Irony

As a figure of speech, *irony* refers to a statement in which the literal meaning is exactly opposed to the intended meaning. In his oration over the body of the murdered Caesar, Antony repeats several times his ironical comment, "Brutus is an honorable man."

In its broader sense, however, irony refers to that pervading quality of a literary work best defined as an inability of the major characters to foresee the tragic consequences of their actions. Thus Othello's great love of Desdemona and his powerful sense of honor lead only to her death and his dishonor. The word is also applied to expository prose in

4

which an author assumes an ideological position opposed to that which he actually espouses. Swift's *A Modest Proposal,* in which he suggests with overwhelming mock seriousness the use of Irish children as gastronomical treats for English landlords, is an excellent example of sustained irony. The terms *cosmic irony* or *irony of fate* are often applied to a situation in which tragedy narrowly misses being averted. The hero who dies of thirst, not knowing the existence of a clear spring less than a hundred yards away, has been the victim of cosmic irony.

Lyric

Though the term was originally used by the Greeks to signify a song sung to the accompaniment of a lyre by a single member of the chorus, the word *lyric* has subsequently broadened in its application. As a literary term, *lyric* refers to any poem which records the emotions and personal meditations of a single author dealing with an essentially non-narrative subject. Most lyrics are relatively short, and the emphasis in a lyrical poem is upon the individual author's imaginative response to an isolated incident or idea. The sight of birch trees bending left and right, for example, inspired Robert Frost's well-known lyric poem *Birches.*

Both the subject matter and the form of the lyric are exceedingly varied. Love, particularly unrequited love, is the subject of many lyrics, yet patriotism (Tennyson's *Love Thou Thy Land*), politics (Coleridge's *France, an Ode*), unusual scenes (Wordsworth's *Westminster Bridge*), an exciting book (Keats's *On First Looking into Chapman's Homer*), and indeed any subject capable of imaginative personal treatment can furnish the point of departure for a lyric poem. Lyric poems may be written within recognized forms such as the sonnet, ode, elegy; they may also employ various stanzaic and metrical patterns, including free verse.

Malapropism

A confusion between words that sound somewhat similar. *Malapropisms* often occur when a person attempts to use a vocabulary that he has not completely mastered, and the result is often humorous (Never *oscillate* [for *osculate*] outside the *privation* [for *privacy*] of your own *orifice* [for *edifice*]). The term derives from Mrs. Malaprop, a comic character in Sheridan's *The Rivals.*

Meiosis

See **Understatement,** p. 233.

Metaphor

A figure of speech in which one thing is implicitly compared with another. A *metaphor* says that one thing *is* another (e.g., Wordsworth's line, "Our birth is but a sleep and a forgetting"). A *simile,* in contrast, says that one thing is *like* another; see p. 229.

The term *metaphor* and its adjectival and adverbial forms, *metaphorical* and *metaphorically,* are sometimes used broadly to refer to all figurative language.

Metonymy

A figure of speech in which the name of a thing closely associated with an object or person is substituted for that object or person. To say "I have read Golding" is to use *metonymy,* because the word *Golding* is allowed to stand for the books that he wrote.

Metrical Foot

A unit of rhythm which recurs regularly within a line of poetry. The various feet common to English poetry are identified by specific combinations of accented and unaccented syllables.

ANAPEST: two unaccented syllables followed by an accented syllable (ŭn·dĕr·stánd).

DACTYL: an accented followed by two unaccented syllables (súb·ši·dў).

IAMB: an unaccented followed by an accented syllable (dĕ·feát).

SPONDEE: two successive accented syllables (hańd·máde).

TROCHEE: an accented followed by an unaccented syllable (mí·sĕr).

Mixed Metaphor

See p. 153.

Mock-heroic

A literary form (also known as *mock-epic* or *high burlesque*) of burlesque in which a trivial subject is treated in a serious and lofty manner. Pope's *Rape of the Lock* is a well-known example of the *mock-heroic* poem. (See **Burlesque,** p. 211.)

Myth

A story, usually featuring gods or heroes, traceable to an early civilization. *Myths* are usually fantasy; they are fictional explanations for natural phenomena or complex social events. A famous myth in Western culture concerns Prometheus' stealing of fire from heaven and bringing it to earth, thus giving man the implement with which to become self-sufficient. The myth of Prometheus, like other famous myths from early Greek civilization, has been subjected to various interpretations in works of literature from different periods, such as Aeschylus's *Prometheus Bound* (470 B.C.) and Shelley's *Prometheus Unbound* (1814). (See also **Archetype,** p. 209.)

Octave

The term refers either to a complete poem consisting of eight lines or to an eight-line stanza or division within a longer poem. (See also **Sonnet,** p. 229.)

Ode

A lyric poem, often lengthy, dealing in a dignified and exalted style with a serious subject. The word comes from the Greek meaning "song," and the form was originally used as a choral interlude in dramatic productions. Its pattern was regular, divided into three sections: the *strophe,* during which the choral group moved toward one side of the stage; the *antistrophe,* during which it moved away on the other side; and the *epode,* during which the group stood in a center position. The strophe and the antistrophe had similar metric patterns; the epode differed. Such regular odes are called *Pindaric,* after the Greek poet Pindar.

Although the Pindaric ode has appeared infrequently in English poetry, a notable illustration of it is Gray's *Progress of Poesy.* In place of the Pindaric ode, English literature has developed two separate ode forms. The first, the *homostrophic ode,* contains a series of stanzas, identical in length and generally similar in both rhyme and meter (e.g., Keats' *Ode on a Grecian Urn,* Shelley's *Ode to the West Wind,* Coleridge's *France, an Ode*). The second type is called the *irregular ode.* Each stanza, often called a strophe, is developed independently according to the emotional needs of the subject; neither the length nor rhyme pattern need be repeated from strophe to strophe. Two excellent examples of the irregular ode are Tennyson's *Ode on the Death of the Duke of Wellington* and Wordsworth's *Ode, Intimations of Immortality.*

Omniscient Observer

See **Point of View,** p. 226.

Onomatopoeia

The formation or use of words which carry in their pronunciation a suggestion of their meaning. Such words (*hum, moan, murmur, zoom, hiss, chugged, thud*) are called *onomatopoeic words.*

Open Couplet

See **Couplet,** p. 213.

Ottava Rima

An eight-line stanza of iambic pentameter rhyming *ababababcc.* Originally an Italian form, it has been used importantly by such English poets as Milton, Shelley, Keats, Byron, and Yeats. The following stanza from Shelley's *Witch of Atlas* illustrates the form:

For she was beautiful—her beauty made
   The bright world dim, and everything beside
Seemed like the fleeting image of a shade:
   No thought of living spirit could abide,
Which to her looks had ever been betrayed,
   On any object in the world so wide,
On any hope within the circling skies,
But on her form, and in her inmost eyes.

Oxymoron

A figure of speech named from the Greek meaning "pointedly foolish."
An *oxymoron* combines two words or phrases of seemingly contradic-
tory meaning. The following speech from *Romeo and Juliet* abounds in
oxymoron:

Why then, O brawling love! O loving hate!
O any thing! of nothing first create.
O heavy lightness! serious vanity!
Mis-shapen chaos of well-seeming forms!
Feather of lead, bright smoke, cold fire, sick health!
Still-waking sleep, that is now what it is!

Parable

A short, simple narrative used to illustrate a moral lesson. *Parables* may
be allegorical (see p. 205), though they are not always so. Christ's
stories of the Prodigal Son and of the Good Samaritan are parables.

Paradox

A figure of speech in which an apparently self-contradictory statement
turns out, upon closer examination, to express a truth. John Donne
employed *paradox* twice in the following lines of a sonnet addressed
to God:

Take me to You, imprison me, for I
Except You enthrall me, never shall be free;
Nor ever chaste, except You ravish me.

The notions that Donne will be free when imprisoned, or chaste when
ravished seem to be false because they are self-contradictory. But they
turn out to be true in their spiritual contexts: a man's soul is free only
when it is subordinated to God's will; it is chaste and pure only when
it has submitted to God's power.

Paraphrase

A restatement of the meaning in another piece of writing. The purpose
of a *paraphrase* is to explain something either difficult or complex in

the original work. Unlike a précis (see p. 169), which is always shorter, a paraphrase often equals and sometimes exceeds the original in length.

Parody

A literary form of burlesque in which a particular author's language, style, or—though less commonly—his subject matter are imitated for the purpose of comedy or derision. Henry Fielding's *Shamela,* for example, parodied the moralistic subject matter as well as the sentimental style of Samuel Richardson's novel *Pamela.* Poems, however, are more frequently subjects of parody, especially when the original was marked by either an excessively simple or an excessively pompous style. The following two lines parody those of Joyce Kilmer's *Trees*:

> I think that I was never bid
> To eat more juicy food than squid.

Pastoral

A poem which deals with the idyllic life of shepherds. From its beginnings with Theocritus in the third century B.C., pastoral poetry has been highly conventional and highly artificial; it has never sought to present a realistic description of the rustic life. In English literature an important use of the pastoral has been for elegiac purposes, where a surviving shepherd, the poet, laments the death of another shepherd, the deceased friend (Spenser's *Astrophel,* Milton's *Lycidas,* Shelley's *Adonais,* Arnold's *Thyrsis*).

Pathetic Fallacy

A term coined by John Ruskin and much used in literary criticism to describe a poetic passage in which nature is so strongly personified that it responds in a human way to some human action. The following lines from Pope's *Summer* demonstrate the *pathetic fallacy*:

> Soft as he [a shepherd] mourned, the streams forgot to flow.
> The flocks around a dumb compassion show.

Pentameter

A line of poetry consisting of five metrical feet (see **Metrical Foot,** p. 221).

Periphrasis

The use of an elegant circumlocution (see p. 118) to avoid low or commonplace terms (*I perambulated to my edifice for evening repast* in place of *I walked home to supper*). In the following example Wordsworth uses *periphrasis* to avoid the commonplace term *ticktacktoe*:

> At evening, when with pencil, and smooth slate
> In square divisions parcelled out and all

With crosses and with cyphers scribbled o'er,
We schemed and puzzled, head opposed to head
In strife too humble to be named in verse.

Personification

A figure of speech in which inanimate objects (see also **Pathetic Fallacy,**
p. 224) or abstract notions are embodied with human qualities. Thomas
Gray uses personification in his *Elegy Written in a Country Churchyard.*

Let not Ambition mock their useful toil,
Their homely joys, and destiny obscure;
Nor Grandeur hear with a disdainful smile
The short and simple annals of the poor.

Plot

The arrangement of a series of incidents into a coherent narrative having a beginning, a middle, and an end. A *plot* differs from the straight
chronological relation of incidents that one might get, for example, in
a newspaper account. Instead, it is composed of artistically conceived
and selected incidents; those which are irrelevant to the main action
are expunged, and the action may violate straight chronology if the
author feels that his purpose is well served by jumping ahead or flash-
ing back in time. The aim of a well-constructed plot is to create order
out of the chaos of life; to do so, it focuses upon carefully selected
material.

A successful plot deals with a series of incidents having a causal
relationship one to another. These incidents involve a conflict of some
kind, traditionally represented by the protagonist (see p. 227) and the
antagonist (see p. 228), and a series of actions increasing in tension
to the point of climax (see p. 212), after which follows the dénouement
(see p. 214). Without conflict there can be no such thing as a plot in
the artistic sense. If, for example, little Red Ridinghood had carried
her basket of fruit to her grandmother and had returned home without
incident, we could not do more than narrate the passage of her time.
Only with the appearance of the wolf as antagonist can we say that
a plot exists.

It may well be said that all good plots begin with one kind of status
quo and end with another. Between them, however, something must
happen through the development of a conflict which drives the protagonist from his usual pattern. "Once upon a time there was a girl
named Red Ridinghood" represents an initial status quo. "And she lived
happily ever after" is a terminal status quo. The essentials of plot
concern those things which happen in the intervening period. Without
them the narrative would not engage our attention. Similarly we read

The Catcher in the Rye because of the things that happen to Holden between the status quo of a young boy leaving his prep school and the new status quo of his entry into a mental hospital.

A loosely constructed plot is one which contains incidents which have no relationship to the main action being portrayed. A *subplot,* on the other hand, is one which develops a relationship parallel to that of the main plot and, by so doing, clarifies or directs attention to it. In Shakespeare's *As You Like It* the farcical love affair between Touchstone and Audrey is a subplot which parallels the relationship between Rosaline and Orlando.

Point of View

All narratives are told by somebody, and the identity of the teller, along with his peculiarities of perception, constitute a literary work's *point of view.* Writers have always, of course, been somewhat concerned with point of view. Chaucer, for example, had his Canterbury pilgrims relate tales generally appropriate to their vocation or station in life. Within the last seventy-five years, however, authors have become particularly conscious of experimentation with and scrupulous following of consistent points of view. And literary critics have established names for the various possibilities.

A story may be told from the *first-person* point of view. The storyteller, differentiated from the author, may simply be an observer of the principal characters and action, as he is in Maugham's *The Razor's Edge,* in which case the point of view is called *first-person observer.* Logically, this point of view allows the storyteller no liberties beyond telling what he sees: he cannot probe the minds and emotions of the major characters, nor can he describe what is going on in places other than those in which he finds himself. The storyteller may, on the other hand, be the protagonist of the narrative, as he is in Camus, *The Stranger,* where the point of view is called *first-person participant* (see also **Stream of Consciousness,** p. 231). This point of view allows the teller to know what is going on within his own mind and to analyze his own perceptions. It is often difficult to differentiate clearly between the two first-person points of view, for some stories are told by persons who stand midway between passive observers and protagonists, as do the storytellers of Conrad's *Heart of Darkness* or Melville's *Moby Dick.* Some critics also isolate a third type of first-person point of view. When the storyteller is a child, an adolescent, or a mentally handicapped adult, the point of view is sometimes called the *innocent eye.* Salinger's *The Catcher in the Rye* employs this point of view. Whatever first-person point of view is used, the story must be filtered through the storyteller's eyes and told in a way that is consistent with his personality, education, character, and mental maturity. If he is a cynic, he will place a cynical construction on the actions he observes; if he is an old man, he will perhaps be forgetful of some incidents and repetitive with others; if he is a child, he will relate the story with intuitive clarity and without the complexities which often accompany mature understanding.

Most stories, however, are told from a *third-person* point of view. Here, although the author and the storyteller are the same, there are, nevertheless, varieties in technique. When the author enters into the thoughts of several or all his characters, and when he allows himself the liberty of describing simultaneous action in different places, the point of view is that of an *omniscient observer*. If in addition he interrupts the narrative to comment directly to the reader about his characters, as does Thackeray in *Vanity Fair,* the point of view is sometimes called *editorial omniscience*. When the author enters the thoughts and emotions of only one of his characters, as in Mansfield's *The Garden Party,* the point of view is called *limited omniscience*. Still another third-person point of view is that in which the author neither editorializes nor enters the thoughts and emotions of any of his characters, but instead restricts himself to a simple record of that which can be seen. This mode is very common in contemporary fiction and is called the *objective* or *clinical* point of view (also, though rarely, called *camera eye*).

Prosody

The theory underlying the principles of rhyme, meter, stanzaic pattern, and other components of poetic composition.

Protagonist

The chief character in a story or play. The word *hero,* which is sometimes used in place of *protagonist,* is a less satisfactory term, for it connotes admirable qualities in the character. Often, however, the chief character possesses many undesirable traits; he may even be a villain, as in Shakespeare's *Macbeth* (see also **Antagonist,** p. 208).

Pun

A play upon words having the same or similar sounds and more than one meaning. The assistant professor who, after he has been denied a promotion, claims to have been "a victim of *rank* discrimination" is punning upon the multiple meaning of the word *rank*.

Quatrain

The term refers either to a complete poem consisting of four lines or to a four-line stanza. The *quatrain* has been a popular stanza in English poetry, and it has accommodated various line lengths and rhyme patterns. The most frequently used quatrains, however, have been the ballad stanza (see **Ballad,** p. 209) and iambic tetrameter or pentameter quatrains rhyming *aabb, aaba,* or *abab.* The following quatrain illustrates the *abab* rhyme pattern:

> Seek out—less often sought than found—
> A soldier's grave, for thee the best;
> Then look around, and choose thy ground,
> And take thy rest.

Rhyme Royal

A seven-line stanza of iambic pentameter rhyming *ababbcc.* The stanza is so named because of its use by James I of Scotland; however, Chaucer and others had used it earlier. The following stanza from William Morris's *The Earthly Paradise* illustrates the form:

> Of Heaven or Hell I have no power to sing,
> I cannot ease the burden of your fears,
> Or make quick-coming death a little thing,
> Or bring again the pleasure of past years,
> Nor for my words shall ye forget your tears,
> Or hope again for aught that I can say,
> The idle singer of an empty day.

Satire

An attempt to improve human society by blending wit and humor with criticism. Satirists ridicule social institutions in the hope of making men aware of their ludicrous shortcomings, and hence to correct them. The most effective and lasting *satire* is that which rises above personal invective and deals instead with universal types. Satire has been written in many genres and verse forms: the drama, novel, mock-epic, sonnet, and heroic couplet, among others. In modern literature, however, the heroic couplet in poetry and the novel in prose have been the ones most effectively used.

Satire is often called *Horatian* or *Juvenalian* according to its tone. The Roman poet Horace satirized man's follies with genial laughter; good-natured satire, therefore, is called Horatian. Juvenal, on the other hand, attacked man's vices with trenchant and often bitter ridicule; forceful and indignant satire, therefore, is called Juvenalian.

Some well-known satires in English are Swift's *Gulliver's Travels,* Pope's *Rape of the Lock,* Byron's *Don Juan,* and Breckenridge's *Modern Chivalry.*

Sestet

The term refers either to a complete poem consisting of six lines or to a six-line stanza or division within a longer poem. (See also **Sonnet,** p. 229.)

Simile

A figure of speech in which the similarity between two objects (see also **Metaphor,** p. 220) is expressed with the words *like* or *as.* Addressing Milton, Wordsworth compresses three *similes* within as many lines.

> Thy soul was like a Star, and dwelt apart:
> Thou hadst a voice whose sound was like the sea:
> Pure as the naked heavens.

Soliloquy

A speech delivered by a character who is alone on the stage. The purpose of a *soliloquy* is to allow the audience to know what is going on in the mind of the character. Shakespeare's *Hamlet* has many famous soliloquys, of which the one beginning "To be or not to be" is the best known.

Sonnet

Originally an Italian verse form, the *sonnet* was introduced to England in the sixteenth century. A sonnet is a lyric poem of fourteen iambic pentameter lines. Two basic forms are recognized: (1) the *Italian* (or *Petrarchan*), which is divided into an octave (rhyming *abbaabba*) and a sestet (rhyming *cdecde, cdcdcd, cdedce,* or other combinations without a couplet at the end); (2) the *English* (or *Shakespearean*), which is divided into three quatrains and a couplet (rhyming *abubcdcdefefgg*). In addition to these two basic patterns, some critics identify the Spenserian pattern (rhyming *ababbcbcdedeff*), and the sonnet has developed numerous experimental forms as well. The following two sonnets by Milton and Shakespeare illustrate the Italian and English forms, respectively.

> How soon hath Time the suttle theef of youth,
>   Stoln on his wing my three and twentith year
>   My hasting dayes flie on with full career,
>   But my late spring no bud or blossom shew'th.
> Perhaps my semblance might deceive the truth,
>   That I to manhood am arriv'd so near,
>   And inward ripenes doth much less appear,
>   That som more timely-happy spirits indu'th.
> Yet be it less or more, or soon or slow,

It shall be still in strictest measure eev'n,
To that same lot, however mean, or high,
Toward which Time leads me, and the will of Heav'n;
    All is, if I have grace to use it so,
    As ever in my great task Masters eye.

That time of year thou mayst in me behold
When yellow leaves, or none, or few, do hang
Upon those boughs which shake against the cold,
Bare ruined choirs, where late the sweet birds sang.
In me thou see'st the twilight of such day
As after sunset fadeth in the west;
Which by and by black night doth take away,
Death's second self, that seals up all in rest.
In me thou see'st the glowing of such fire,
That on the ashes of his youth doth lie,
As the death-bed whereon it must expire,
Consumed with that which it was nourished by.
This thou perceivest, which makes thy love more strong,
To love that well which thou must leave ere long.

A *sonnet sequence* is a series of sonnets dealing with a unified theme. While some sonnet sequences do tell a story, they do not aim to tell a straight narrative; instead, they attempt a lyric record of a series of related incidents, usually dealing with love. Some well-known sonnet sequences in English literature are Rossetti's *House of Life,* Sidney's *Astrophel and Stella,* Shakespeare's *Sonnets,* and Elizabeth Barrett Browning's *Sonnets from the Portuguese.*

Spenserian Stanza

A nine-line stanza rhyming *ababbcbcc;* the first eight lines are iambic pentameter, the last an Alexandrine. The stanza was first used by Spenser in his *Faerie Queene,* and it has subsequently been used by such important English poets as Wordsworth, Byron, Shelley, Keats, and Tennyson. The following stanza from Keats's *Eve of St. Agnes* illustrates the form:

    St. Agnes' Eve—Ah, bitter chill it was!
    The owl, for all his feathers, was a-cold;
    The hare limp'd trembling through the frozen grass,
    And silent was the flock in woolly fold:
    Numb were the Beadsman's fingers, while he told
    His rosary, and while his frosted breath,

Like pious incense from a censer old,
Seem'd taking flight for heaven, without a death,
Past the sweet Virgin's picture, while his prayer he saith.

Spondee

A metrical foot consisting of two accented syllables (see **Metrical Foot,** p. 221).

Stream of Consciousness

A term first used by William James and now widely employed in literary criticism to describe that technique by which the author tries to record for a selected period of time the complete flow of thought in one of his characters. The *stream of consciousness,* in its attempt to approximate the chaotic nature of unorganized mental activity, is not bound by linguistic, syntactical, grammatical, and logical conventions. It features sudden shifts of thought, often triggered by a key word. With each appearance of the word *bottom,* for example, in Mrs. Bloom's interior monologue of Joyce's *Ulysses,* the flow of thought shifts to the erotic. In skillful stream-of-consciousness writing, a basic pattern evolves from the seeming discontinuity and the barrage of detail, much of which appears at first glance to be irrelevant. James Joyce's *Ulysses* is one of the most artful and sustained applications of the stream-of-consciousness technique in all modern literature, though other writers— among them Faulkner, Hemingway, Anderson, and Virginia Woolf —have also used it extensively.

Symbol

In literature, a word or a group of words which stands for a meaning other than the literal or the purely denotative. William Golding uses a conch as a *symbol* in his novel *The Lord of the Flies.* The conch is not merely a mollusk shell, as a dictionary might define it; instead, it is a device which the assembled children on a deserted island use to gain attention so that they can speak. On an abstract level, then, the conch stands for social order. Without the conch, there can be no rational deliberation; the decline of its use, therefore, symbolizes the gradual abandonment of the rules of civilization. Symbols appear widely in literature. The white whale is a complex, encompassing symbol in *Moby Dick;* a heap of gold coins symbolizes death in Chaucer's *Pardoner's Tale;* the unweeded garden symbolizes disorder in Shakespeare's *Richard II;* long tresses of hair symbolize femininity in Ibsen's *Hedda Gabbler;* a twitch on the face of a man symbolizes purposelessness in Robert Penn Warren's novel *All the King's Men.* The complexity of a work of literature is often the result of the various symbols it embraces and the multiplicity of interpretations to which these symbols can be put.

Synecdoche

A figure of speech in which the name of a part is used to signify its whole. When a captain calls, "All hands on deck!" he is using *synecdoche*.

Synesthesia

A figure of speech in which something belonging to one of the five senses is described in terms of another sense. *Synesthesia* occurs frequently in everyday speech in such expressions as *loud color* and *soft music*. Similarly, Shelley uses the figure when he speaks of the "soft breeze, green with spring."

Terza Rima

A verse form in which successive units of three lines each are interlocked by rhyme, the middle rhyme in each unit providing the rhyme for the first and third lines of the next unit, *aba bcb cdc ded,* etc. The following selection from Shelley's *Ode to the West Wind* illustrates the form:

If I were a dead leaf thou mightest bear;
If I were a swift cloud to fly with thee;
A wave to pant beneath thy power, and share

The impulse of thy strength, only less free
Than thou, O uncontrollable! If even
I were as in my boyhood, and could be

The comrade of thy wanderings over Heaven,
As then, when to outstrip thy skiey speed
Scarce seemed a vision; I would ne'er have striven . . .

Tetrameter

A line of poetry consisting of four metrical feet (see **Metrical Foot,** p. 221).

Theme

Used as a literary term *theme* refers to the abstract concept which is treated in a particular work. In highly didactic works the theme is stated directly. Many literary works, however, do not contain a direct statement of the theme; the reader must determine what it is that the author intended to say. What statement, in other words, does the author wish to make about the human condition? The theme of Golding's *The Lord of the Flies,* for example, might be stated as follows: man's primitive nature could very easily overcome the restraints of civilized society.

Tone

The general attitudes of an author toward his subject and audience as those attitudes are inferred from a literary work. Thus we may say that the *tone* of a passage or entire work is compassionate or cruel, formal or intimate, ironic or serious, earnest or playful, hard or gentle, etc. Often, particularly in longer works, the tone shifts. For example, while the general tone of Byron's *Don Juan* is comic, the poem contains passages or even entire cantos in which the tone is best described as intimate or serious or vindictive. Similarly, the cosmic seriousness of Shakespeare's *Hamlet* is occasionally interrupted by scenes in which the prevailing tone is comic.

Travesty

A literary form (also known as *low burlesque*) of burlesque in which a serious subject is treated in a trivial manner. Cervantes' *Don Quixote* is a well-known example of a *travesty*. (See **Burlesque, p. 211.**)

Trimeter

A line of poetry consisting of three metrical feet (see **Metrical Foot, p. 221**).

Trochee

A metrical foot consisting of an accented syllable followed by an un-accented syllable (see **Metrical Foot, p. 221**).

Understatement

As a figure of speech *understatement* (also called *meiosis*) occurs when a sentiment or idea is presented in a far less significant way than it actually deserves. Robert Burton, a man of encyclopedic learning about human knowledge and conduct, used understatement in his *Anatomy of Melancholy* when he wrote: "I did for my recreation now and then walk abroad, look into the world, and could not choose but make some little observation."

Unities

Applied to drama, the term *unities* refers to *action, time,* and *place.* The *unity of action* refers to the development of one main action or plot; the *unity of time* provides that the action transpire in twenty-four hours or less (some playwrights have narrowed the time span of a play to the exact period that it takes to be performed); the *unity of place* provides that all the action be set in one place. Ben Jonson's *The*

Alchemists is a play which scrupulously observes all three dramatic unities. Such observance has been associated with the *classic* theater, and playwrights, among them Shakespeare, have been roundly criticized by classicists for not adhering to the unities. Ultimately, the concept of the unities is traceable to Aristotle. However, Aristotle insisted only that a play have unity of action. He refers to the unity of time, but he does not set it forth as a rule to be observed by playwrights. The unity of place, he scarcely mentions. It was not until the Renaissance that the observance of the dramatic unities became a critical doctrine associated with classicism.

In recent times some novelists and short story writers have attempted to observe the dramatic unities in prose narrative. Many of J. D. Salinger's short stories, for example, observe them carefully, and Joyce has done the same in his long novel *Ulysses.*

Utopia

A word coined by Sir Thomas More from the Greek meaning "nowhere." The word has been widely applied as a genre designation to those literary works which depict an ideal society. Utopian literature is indirectly didactic (see p. 214); the ideal society described serves as a norm to which an actual society is urged to conform. Some well-known utopias are Plato's *Republic,* Bacon's *New Atlantis,* More's *Utopia,* Bellamy's *Looking Backward,* and Morris' *News from Nowhere.*

During the twentieth century a related genre has developed, the *anti-utopia.* In such works the author provides a horrifying look into the future. His teaching takes a different form; instead of providing a norm, he indirectly urges man to reform his present society by showing the consequences of continuing it unchanged. Examples of anti-utopian literature are Aldous Huxley's *Brave New World,* Zamjatin's *We,* and Orwell's *1984.*

Verisimilitude

That quality which gives a literary work the semblance of truth. The term should not be confused with *realism,* for a work may have *verisimilitude* even though its subject and setting are farfetched. Swift, for example, achieves verisimilitude in *Gulliver's Travels* through attention to minute detail, even though the work deals with highly imaginative journeys.

INDEX

Numbers in **boldface** type refer to glossary entries.
Italics designate "words as such," as well as book titles.

Trager, George L., *An Outline of English Structure* (with Henry Lee Smith), 165
Transformational grammar, 185, **192–194**
(*See also* Immediate constituents [IC's])
Transforms, 149
Transition, **194–196**
between paragraphs, 195–196
between sentences, 194–195
Transitive verb, **196**
Travesty, **233**
Trimeter, **233**
Trite expression, 118
Trochee, **233**
Try to, try and, **55–56**
TV, 56–57
Type, type of, **56**

Umlaut (*see* Mutation; Round vowel)
Underlining (*see* Italics)
Understatement, **233**
Uninterested, 20
Unique, **56**
Unities, of action, place, time, **233–234**
Unless, 60
Until, 55
Upon, 43
Usage, levels of, 150
Utopia, **234**

Velar, **196**
Velar nasal, 155
Verb, **196–197**
agreement with subject, 110
anomalous, 113
finite, 134
intransitive, 147
irregular past and past participle forms, 172–174

Verbs, linking, 151
linking (with adverb), 109
nonfinite, 134
principal parts of, 172–174
strong, 184
transitive, 196
weak, 184
Verbal, 43
Verbal, **197**
gerund, 137
infinitive, 197
participle, 162
Verb marker, 197
Verisimilitude, **234**
Verner, Karl, 197
Verner's law, 197–198
Very, 56
Video, TV, **56–57**
Vocabulary, **198–199**
degeneration, 199
elevation, 199
generalization, 198
specialization, 198
Vocative case, 117
(*See also* Direct address)
Voice, **199**
active, 199
passive, 199
Voiced, voiceless consonants, **200**
Vowel, **200**
back, 116
front, 135
lax, 200
long, 200
(*See also* Great Vowel Shift)
round, rounded, 179
short, 200
tense, 200
Vulgate English, **200–201**

Wait for, wait on, **57**
Waken, wakened, **11**
Wake, waked, woke, **11**
Want, **57**
Want in, want out, want off, **57**

Way, away, **57**
Way, ways, **57**
Weak verb, **184**
Webster's Third New International Dictionary, 3
(*See also* Grammar)
Webster III (see *Webster's Third New International Dictionary*)
Well, 28
West Saxon, 161
What all, who all, **57–58**
What-clauses, 111
What with, **58**
When, is when, **58**
Where, is where, **58**
Where, that, **58**
Whether, 30-31
Which, who, that, 177
While (conjunction), **58–59**
Who all, 57–58
Whoever, whomever, 59
Whose, of which, **59**
Who, that, which, 177
Who, whom, **59**
Will, 48–49
-wise (suffix), 109
Within, 32
Without, unless, **60**
Woke, 11
Wordiness, **201**
Word order, **201–202**
fixed, 201
free, 201
Words, abstract and concrete, 105
Word Study, 3
Would of, 18
Would rather, 28
Writing, expository, 133

Xmas, Christmas, **60**

You, one, **60**
You understood, 154

Zero form, 193, 202
Zero inflection, **202**